The Giants

of Sales

The Giants
of Sales

WHAT DALE CARNEGIE, JOHN PATTERSON,
ELMER WHEELER, AND JOE GIRARD
CAN TEACH YOU ABOUT REAL SALES SUCCESS

Tom Sant

AMACOM

American Management Association

NEW YORK • ATLANTA • BRUSSELS • CHICAGO • MEXICO CITY
SAN FRANCISCO • SHANGHAI • TOKYO • TORONTO • WASHINGTON, D.C.

Special discounts on bulk quantities of AMACOM books are available to corporations, professional associations, and other organizations. For details, contact Special Sales Department, AMACOM, a division of American Management Association, 1601 Broadway, New York, NY 10019.
Tel.: 212-903-8316 Fax: 212-903-8083
E-mail: specialsls@amanet.org
Website: www.amacombooks.org/go/specialsales
To view all AMACOM titles go to: www.amacombooks.org

This publication is designed to provide accurate and authoritative information in regard to the subject matter covered. It is sold with the understanding that the publisher is not engaged in rendering legal, accounting, or other professional service. If legal advice or other expert assistance is required, the services of a competent professional person should be sought.

Library of Congress Cataloging-in-Publication Data

Sant, Tom.
    The giants of sales : what Dale Carnegie, John Patterson, Elmer Wheeler, and Joe Girard can teach you about real sales success / Tom Sant.
      p.   cm.
    Includes index.
    ISBN-10: 0-8144-7291-5
    ISBN-13: 978-0-8144-7291-0
    1. Selling.   2. Sales management.   I. Title.

    HF5438.25.S265   2006
    658.8′ 1—dc22

                                 2005033827

Printing number

10 9 8 7 6 5 4 3 2

For Susan . . .
my partner, my wife

CONTENTS

Preface ix

I f Freud was right that our birth is our destiny, then I was destined to be in sales. Both my father and my grandfather—my mother's dad—were salesmen.

Grandpa covered a territory in Nevada for the Shupe-Williams candy company. The area he covered was broiling hot in the summer, mighty cold in the winter, and desolate all year round. I can vividly remember how Grandpa would load his sample cases into the trunk and take off in his Nash Rambler (no air conditioning, of course) to make his rounds for a week or more, stopping at small grocers, drugstores, gas stations, motels—anybody who might carry candy near the checkout counter or on the shelves. He had been covering that territory for years and years, and he would come home with wild stories of things he had seen or heard in the tiny gambling dens and ratty saloons along the way. Grandpa liked the people who were his customers, and apparently they liked him. They bought a lot of candy from him. When he finally retired, the company put a new man into his territory. He lasted about six weeks. The heat and the loneliness got to him. The next guy couldn't stop gambling. The next one got himself into a mess at a brothel. It was a wild territory with some unique challenges, and it turned out that my grandfather—quiet, calm, a little shy, friendly and yet reserved, and persistent—had been uniquely suited to it.

Dad started out with Nabisco after the end of World War II. He had been a Marine, having enlisted well before the war started. When war was declared, he was a drill instructor at Camp Pendleton. Soon he was in combat. He was wounded at Guadalcanal, patched up in Hawaii, then sent back to lead a platoon of the Second Marine Division in the invasion of Tarawa. It was even bloodier action. Most of the men around him were killed. Somehow Dad survived the invasion, but he was wounded again, this time losing the sight in one eye.

No longer medically fit to serve in the Marine Corps, he was discharged and had to find a job. He took a job driving a delivery truck and making calls on small stores for Nabisco.

The man who hired him, Lee Bickmore, was then the manager of the branch office in Salt Lake City. Eventually, though, Bickmore became the president and CEO of Nabisco. He made the statement that my father was the greatest natural salesman he had ever seen.

My father loved selling, and he was phenomenally good at it. He quickly rose from route salesman to "special salesman," handling larger accounts like chain stores. From there he was transferred to Chicago, where he sold Nabisco's line of ice cream cones over 26 states. Now, instead of selling directly to customers, he was responsible for motivating branch sales reps and resellers to do more. Flying at the dawn of commercial air travel, he racked up a million miles with TWA—in three years! (And since this was in the era before loyalty programs and frequent flyer miles, all he got was a plaque from the airline.)

Wherever he went, he set sales records. He became Nabisco's one-man landing force, hitting the beaches in branches that were underperforming with the mission to turn around the sales. And time after time, through his own personal selling efforts and by teaching and inspiring the sales team that reported to him, he did it.

As a kid, I sometimes helped him write his "sales letter." This was a monthly message that he sent out to each sales rep when he was the branch manager. Dad had barely finished high school and he was a poor speller, so my job was to edit the letter, clean it up a bit. I was about 12 or so. I suppose it was the start of my interest in how language could be used to motivate people and generate business.

As fathers and sons do, particularly during those teenage years, we drifted apart. Part of it was rebellion on my part, but, to be honest, part of it was a growing problem with alcohol on his. When he drank too much, he was a different guy, and it seemed that his drinking too much was becoming the norm instead of the exception.

I left home for college at 17, determined to become a teacher. No sales for me. No, sir. I didn't want *that* kind of life. I eventually got my doctorate in English at UCLA and became an instructor at the University of Cincinnati.

It wasn't long before I was doing some "consulting" work on the side. For the most part, that work consisted of teaching local businesspeople how to write better or, in some cases, doing the writing for them. I got the chance to teach an after-hours course at General Electric's aircraft engine plant, and from that I was asked to help one of the groups there write a couple of marketing pieces. Then I was asked to help with a small proposal. Then a bigger one. Pretty soon I was making a lot more money from my part-time consulting than I was from full-time teaching.

I found myself using both the academic knowledge of rhetoric and persuasion that I had acquired in school and the pragmatic knowledge that I had picked up from being my father's son. Apparently it was a good combination. The proposals I was writing won, even when nobody thought they had a chance. And I kept getting more and more assignments.

Soon I was also doing work for Procter & Gamble and for some local banks. And then I landed a contract with AT&T to train the company's mid-market sales force in writing effective sales letters and proposals.

But to get those contracts, I had to sell myself. People weren't just calling me up and asking for me by name. I had to go out and make the calls, qualify the prospect, develop an understanding of the prospect's needs, and develop a solution. I was selling.

Destiny had reared its head.

Eventually Dad got into recovery and was able to stop drinking. For the last 25 years of his life, he was sober, something that made me very proud of him. I told him that it was like having an old friend come back again, somebody who hadn't been around for a long time.

But he had to start over financially. And he only had one skill: He could sell.

He caught on with a small company in Los Angeles that manufactured foam rubber for furniture cushions, car seats, baby seats, and so forth. He knew nothing about foam rubber. He knew nothing about furniture. He knew almost nothing about Los Angeles. But he got in his car and he started calling on prospects and he started regaining his skills. And within a year he had sold so much foam that his employer told him to stop. The company couldn't manufacture enough of the stuff to keep up with his orders! He didn't stop, though, so the company expanded the factory, and he went on to rebuild his life and his finances by doing something that he enjoyed and that he was remarkably good at. He was selling.

A few years ago, I was the keynote speaker at an international conference for resellers being held by Microsoft. The conference was held in the Staples Center in Los Angeles, so my wife and I invited my parents to go down with us. We thought they might enjoy the trip, and, to be honest, it was a chance for me to show off a little. My parents had never seen me work.

By then Dad was nearly 80 years old. Decades of smoking when he was a young man had ravaged his lungs, leaving him with emphysema. He had arthritis in his hips, so walking was a bit uncomfortable, too. But he was up for the trip, and once he got there, he turned on the old charm and was entertaining the young men and women at the various trade show booths with his usual stream of jokes and witty comments.

Finally, it was time for my speech. We ushered my parents into seats down in the front row and I went up to the podium. About 800 people filled the room. The lights went down.

I didn't go up there with a plan. It was just one of those spontaneous moments. But before that room full of strangers—men and women who had to sell for a living, who had to sell to keep their own businesses going, who knew what a demanding and important job professional selling is—I decided to introduce the greatest natural salesman that either Lee Bickmore or I had ever known.

The crowd was loving and generous. They gave my father an ovation that made him feel like a rock star. Aching hips or not, he leaped to his feet, turned and waved to his fans.

It was just a moment, and then it was gone. I gave my speech, shared some tips, and tried to help them win more business by using language more effectively in their presentations and proposals.

A few months later Dad passed away.

I was grateful for a lot of things. That he had gotten his life back together. That he had found a way to stay sober and enjoy his grandkids. That in the profession he was so good at he had found a way to rebuild his finances and his self-esteem. And that I had a chance to show him that people understood how difficult and how important the work he had done most of his life really was.

I get angry when I hear people say derogatory things about salespeople. Usually, comments about "brochure pimps" and "sales weasels" are made by people who have never had to sell anything in their lives, who wouldn't have the guts to put their entire income on the line and risk it on their ability to make a deal happen, who think that selling is a matter of wining and dining and tickets to the big game. That's not selling, of course. Sales is knowledge work, and if you're not extremely intelligent, gutsy, persistent, and competitive, you won't make it.

Sales is a vitally important profession in a free economy. Without good salespeople, new ideas and better products don't find a market. Nimble new companies can't compete against the established mammoths. Big problems don't get solved because managers never see that the solutions are out there.

I'm proud that a big part of my career has been in sales.

But I'm not surprised.

It was destiny.

PART ONE

SELLING IN THE
TWENTY-FIRST CENTURY

CHAPTER 1

STATING THE OBVIOUS

"People who ignore the past are doomed to repeat it."
—GEORGE SANTAYANA

Professional selling is the most important American invention of the twentieth century. It's more important than the telephone, the airplane, the computer, or any other mechanical or electronic innovation of the last century.

How can I say something so preposterous?

Because it's true.

Because without knowing how to sell those other inventions effectively, the industries that were created around them would not have developed as quickly as they did. Without professional sales methods, the development of our society and our economy would have been delayed. It was professional selling skill that moved those products into the mainstream, making them a fundamental part of our infrastructure. In my view, professional selling is the engine that has powered our economy—and ultimately the economy of the world—for the past hundred years.

Our predecessors figured out how to sell effectively by figuring out what works. It didn't happen in a laboratory or a research institute. It wasn't motivated by abstract intellectual curiosity. It happened in the offices and shops and boardrooms where buying decisions were made on a daily basis. And it was motivated by the most pragmatic of issues: the need to close the deal.

John Henry Patterson, for example, developed a *process* for selling—a sequence of steps—that kept his company growing even in the midst of recessions, and that became the foundation for the methods used today by the most successful sales organizations in the world.

Dale Carnegie—yes, *that* Dale Carnegie—discovered truths about human relationships that have been used by such powerhouse business leaders as Lee Iacocca, Mary Kay Ash, and Tom Monahan to build businesses.

Elmer Wheeler developed and tested ways of delivering sales messages, boiled down to brief statements, to figure out which ways worked the best. He tested thousands of sentences on millions of people, tapping into fundamental truths about the way the brain works and how persuasion occurs.

And Joe Girard, born into abject poverty in the slums of Detroit, discovered a technique for generating qualified leads that put him in the *Guinness Book of World Records* as "the world's greatest salesman." By himself, working from a small office in a neighborhood Chevrolet dealer, selling to one buyer at a time, Girard sold more cars than 95 percent of all the dealerships in North America. In one day he sold 18 cars, in one month he sold 174, and in a 14-year career he sold more than 13,000!

The principles that these people discovered still work today, because they are rooted in fundamental human psychology. I know they work because I used them to build my own business. I've used them to help my clients. And I have seen outstanding sales performers use them to win and win again. I know that these ideas still work. And I know that by revisiting the four key ideas that revolutionized selling in the twentieth century, we will learn how to sell more effectively today.

Professional selling is truly a recent innovation. A little over a century ago, nobody knew how to approach the task of selling goods and services to another business or how to sell to a government agency. There was nothing that even approached the systematic, efficient sales methods that we take for granted today. Even retail sales from a local business to a consumer was a haphazard affair.

Modern professional selling had to be invented. It took the creative genius of certain individuals to articulate the best ways to qualify customers, develop a selling proposition, and close business.

This book presents the ideas of four figures that I think can truly be called giants because of the innovations they first developed—John Henry Patterson, Dale Carnegie, Elmer Wheeler, and Joe Girard. And yet, of those four individuals, the only familiar name today is Carnegie's, even among people who make their living in sales.

Schoolchildren recognize the names of the Wright brothers, of course, and Edison and Bell. Some people recognize the names of Turing and Shockley as key figures in the development of the modern computer.

But Patterson? Wheeler? Girard?

"Never heard of 'em!"

The fact is that in our society, selling has never been treated seriously as a core part of business operations. Marketing gets plenty of recognition, and advertising has a lot of glamour. Management? Oh, yeah, that's very important.

But sales? I don't think so.

In fact, there were a lot of business gurus running around just a few years ago predicting the end of selling as we know it. It was doomed.

SOME THINGS ARE FOREVER

It seems funny from our vantage point, but as recently as five years ago, business experts were predicting that the profession of sales would soon be obsolete. According to these gurus, traditional face-to-face selling had no future.

I'm not talking about isolated figures, either. These were some of the best and brightest stars on the business scene. There was a whole set of books that appeared during the late 1990s and on up through 2002 that argued that the rise of the Internet would inevitably mean the decline of sales.[1]

The basic message of these books and articles was always the same: We were on the threshold of a bright new world, one in which technology would bring customers and vendors into direct, close, personal contact. The results were going to be spectacular, too. Happier customers. Greater profits. Increased market share. Stronger customer loyalty. Greater efficiency. Wow! Sounds cool, as a Web developer might put it.

However, the truth is that professional selling is just as important as it has ever been. In fact, in some industries, where commoditization has generated tremendous pressure on profit margins, selling value and communicating differentiators is absolutely vital. Companies that have flirted with the idea of selling over the Internet know that the Web is a powerful tool that offers a limited set of customers the opportunity to engage in a digital form of "catalog shopping." They also know that without a strong, sales-oriented infrastructure, no business that sells products or services to consumers, to other businesses, or to the government is going to survive. No matter how hard we try to "foster community" through our web site, the reality is that people bond with people. And no matter how sophisticated our use of Internet technology may be, with mass customization creating a personalized experience and collaborative filtering targeting customers with optional products or services that they are likely to find appealing, the fact remains that in a competitive selling situation, you need professional salespeople.

No, the Internet hasn't changed everything, in spite of the predictions of the business and technology gurus of the past decade. Some things changed, sure, but professional sales remains a vitally important part of our economy. A lot of us buy books and other stuff on Amazon. A lot of people enjoy browsing around eBay, the world's biggest garage sale. Companies use their web sites to transact business, and sometimes, as in the case of Dell, for example, they do it very effectively. My own career was based largely on developing software applications to help salespeople do their jobs faster and better, so I have a heartfelt enthusiasm for the value of computer-based applications in the sales and marketing arena, particularly those that run over the Internet. But the reality is that nothing has replaced the role of a talented, motivated, properly trained salesperson. And nothing will.

DÉJÀ VU ALL OVER AGAIN

Mark Twain once learned while he was in London that papers in the United States were publishing his obituary. In the interests of accuracy, he sent the American press a telegram: "Reports of my death have been greatly exaggerated."

Salespeople might feel justified in sending a similar message. But that experience happened to Twain only once. Oddly enough, this isn't the first time so-called experts have predicted that selling would become irrelevant.

Back in 1916, a reporter for the *New York Times* asked, "Are salesmen necessary?" His theory was that advertising was so efficient, companies didn't need a sales force any longer.[2] Traditional face-to-face selling was doomed because it was too inefficient and too expensive. Advertising, based on the latest research into psychology, would eliminate the need for any salespeople at all.

Earlier, professor Walter Dill Scott of Northwestern University had argued that in the modern world ("modern" is relative—he was writing in 1904), advertising had "superseded the market-place, and is, in many cases, displacing the commercial traveler."[3] Salesmen would still be needed to go out and take orders from customers, but their role in persuading customers to buy, in articulating customers' needs and desires, was no longer important.

Sounds kind of familiar, doesn't it?

Admittedly, advertising made some amazing advances in the first couple of decades of the last century. Before then, advertising had been a rather primitive affair. Few people even had a clear idea of what it was supposed to accomplish, much less how to go about it. If pressed, advertising people at the turn of the century would say that the goal of advertising was to keep the name of your company or your product in front of the public.

A couple of things happened to change that. One was the emergence of new agencies that were more bottom-line-focused. Albert Lasker, a partner at Lord & Thomas, had great success writing ad copy for some of the agency's clients, particularly a hearing aid company. But why were his ads working? What was going on in the ads that made them effective? Even Lasker didn't know, although he knew that it had to be more than just putting the firm's name before the public.

Lasker found the answer to his question in 1904 when John E. Kennedy, a copywriter for Grape-Nuts, Postum, and Dr. Shoop's Family Medicine, sent a note up to the offices of Lord & Thomas from the saloon downstairs.

The note said in part, "I can tell you what advertising is. I know you don't know. It will mean much to me to have you know what it is and it will mean much to you." Lasker bit. He invited Kennedy up and wanted to know what Kennedy's definition was.

Kennedy's answer: "Advertising is salesmanship in print."

What Kennedy had identified was the fundamental purpose of advertising: to move products. If an ad didn't cause consumers to buy, it wasn't good advertising. Kennedy also had another concept, which he called "Reason-Why Advertising." In other words, every ad should give the reader a reason why he or she should buy the product. Lasker quickly hired Kennedy and had him train other copywriters at Lord & Thomas in his techniques. He also adopted Kennedy's ideas for testing ads and tracking results. All in all, this marked the birth of the modern advertising industry, as Lord & Thomas became the most influential agency in all of America.

For all their success, neither Lasker nor Kennedy thought that advertising could replace sales. Rather, they saw it as an adjunct to the sales operations that a company already had in place. But as advertising copy became more and more like a sales pitch, some people speculated that it might make the salesperson unnecessary. If you added in the research coming out of psychology labs in American universities, it seemed that the poor consumer would be virtually helpless against the persuasive power of a well-written ad.

If you then combined all of that with the growth of mail-order houses like Sears Roebuck and Montgomery Ward at the turn of the century, the roles of both the salesperson and the local retailer were called into question. According to historian Daniel Boorstin, the rise of mail-order business was a "triumph" of national enterprises over small, local businesses. Moreover, "it spelled the defeat of the salesman by advertising."[4]

Wait a minute—haven't we heard all of this before? As Yogi Berra said, this is déjà vu all over again.

The rise of mail-order shopping didn't spell the defeat of selling in America. It did herald the emergence of a new model for doing business, one based on rising prosperity, reliable railroad service, and universal postal delivery. But the defeat of the salesperson? No. Just take a look at the numbers: According to figures collected by the U.S. Census Bureau in 2000, out of a total working population in the United States of 130 million people, approximately 15 million men and women make their living in sales. That's almost 12 percent of the entire workforce. For a profession that is supposedly in decline, it seems to be pretty darn healthy.

"I DON'T GET NO RESPECT"

Sales continues to be the engine that makes commerce move forward. There's an old cliché: If nobody sells, nobody works. It remains as true today as it ever was.

In fact, in today's high-tech environment, sales may be more important than ever. Back in the 1990s, Gil Cargill, a former IBM sales rep and a leading sales consultant and trainer, coined the phrase "high tech with high touch" to describe what he saw as the right direction for the rapidly emerging field of sales force automation. His point was clear: As our working world becomes increasingly dehumanized by the use of computer-based tools, people value meaningful human contact more than ever. This is somewhat ironic, given the predictions of the Internet gurus. However, it seems to be true that the more dependent we become on technology, the more we crave human interaction.

But this leads to a perplexing question: Why isn't sales respected?

Schools of business in universities all across the country offer courses in marketing and advertising. In fact, many of them let students major in those fields. But almost none of them offer courses in selling.[5]

Why?

Is it too mundane? Too close to hands-on work? Is there a sense that selling is not a proper academic subject for rigorous study? I truly don't know the answer. Even in special programs where selling is either an important component—business management, for example, or programs in entrepreneurship, where the obvious career path will require an understanding of the sales organization or may even require the student to do some selling—actual courses in sales are missing. What about outside the business school? Same thing. For example, if you look at the typical course offerings in speech communication departments, the classes are filled with people who are much more likely to find careers in selling than they are in broadcasting. And yet selling is not covered.

I think a compelling argument can be made that sales is the quintessential American profession. The fact that it is largely ignored in the field of higher education is inexplicable. It's a fundamental part of contemporary culture. Everywhere around the world, one of the dominant stereotypes associated with Americans is the image of the assertive, clever salesperson.

American fiction, plays, and movies have reinforced this stereotype, often in a negative way. The best-known salesman in American literature is Willy Loman, the character in Arthur Miller's *Death of a Salesman*, whose career involved traveling "way out there in the blue, riding on a smile and a shoeshine."[6] Even though Miller's play is more about the damaged relationship between Willy and his son, it is often taken as a commentary on the dysfunctional nature of the traveling salesman in general. A more explicit portrait of sales at its worse—venal con men engaging in deceptions and distortions, lying to their customers and themselves, vulgar, lost, utterly without hope—is delivered in David Mamet's *Glengarry Glen Ross*. The corrosive scramble for leads, good leads that these salesmen can twist into closed deals, makes real estate sales look like a sure path to hell. The shady world of aluminum siding sales doesn't fare much better in *Tin Men,* and the "investments" being sold in *Boiler Room* result in federal racketeering charges. There are other unflattering portraits of the salesperson elsewhere in American literature—in Herman Melville's *The Confidence Man,* for example, in Eugene O'Neill's *The Iceman Cometh,* and in Eudora Welty's "Death of a Traveling Man."

Other professions have come in for criticism from writers, of course. Lawyers have been skewered repeatedly, and politicians are often portrayed as self-serving, greedy, or corrupt. But there are also examples of heroic or noble lawyers and politicians. Can anybody think of a salesperson who is the hero of a movie or novel? I can think of only one, the made-for-television story of Bill Porter, *Door to Door.* This movie portrays Porter, who was born disabled by cerebral palsy, as a heroic figure who allows nothing to stand in his way as he trudges the mean streets of Portland, carrying his sample bag, knocking on doors in quest of a sale. The interesting thing about *Door to Door* is that it's based on a true story and a real person. The reality could not possibly have been more contrary to the conventional stereotype of the person selling door to door.

Like Bill Porter, real people who make their living in sales are almost never anything like those stereotyped images. (And, without exception, the novelists and playwrights who have produced those images have never sold anything in their lives.) Most salespeople would say that our job is not to trick people into buying shoddy goods that they don't really want or need. Instead, it's all about understanding the customers and their needs, and then matching up a product or a service that most effectively meets those needs. It's about communicating clearly and honestly. It's about solving problems. At its core, sales is knowledge work. It requires a rare combination of skills to be successful—communication, management, analytical, and other skills that cover the full range of business acumen.

Sales is also an evolving profession, and in many crucial ways it is more difficult than ever. A hundred years ago, sales could be physically demanding: Traveling around the country by rail was difficult and dirty, and hauling giant sample cases was a challenge even for the fit. Now the challenges are more likely to be cognitive and emotional. Today's salesperson uses more technology than a commercial pilot did 20 years ago. It ranges from handheld PDAs, software for tracking account activity, inventory reporting systems, configuration tools, and Web-conferencing applications to the ordinary use of laptops, cell phones, spreadsheets, e-mail, digital documents, search engines, fax machines, and so on. But mastering the technology is nothing compared to the challenges of mastering the subject matter—understanding the products and services at an expert level, understanding the customer's business, and gaining insight into how to bring those elements together for mutual benefit.

The pressure to succeed, to achieve results quickly, to meet management expectations is as great as ever, with the added complication that rapid communications and comprehensive sales-tracking systems give the salesperson almost no room to maneuver. Failure to deliver results means quick termination in many industries. How quick? A decade ago, when I was working with MCI, the average time one of their salespeople lasted in the job was seven *months*.

One further complication comes from the fact that in industries that sell big-ticket solutions to other businesses, the salesperson often must work as part of a team, must demonstrate cross-disciplinary insights, and must coordinate a complex set of relationships within his or her own company as well as within the customer's. For some salespeople, the most difficult part of the job is getting fellow employees to collaborate promptly to meet the customers' expectations.

In its earliest days, professional sales was the province of the "commercial traveler" or "drummer," who rode out in a horse-drawn wagon loaded down with merchandise or hopped from town to town via the railroads, calling on local merchants in an effort to place his goods. Thomas Watson, who became the head of IBM and one of the most influential business leaders in the world, started his career sitting on a buggy, hauling sewing machines around the New York countryside and trying to sell them at one farmhouse after another. As the profession evolved, it became more efficient and effective, in part because a few geniuses came up with new ideas or adapted ideas from other fields to produce better results in sales. The result was that by mid-century, as the world was poised to rebuild itself after World War II, Americans had created the most powerful vehicle for fueling the economy that had ever been seen. Whether the transaction involved a business selling directly to consumers, as in a retail environment, or a business selling to other businesses, or even the increasingly important area of businesses selling to governments, the techniques and processes of professional sales that had been developed during the preceding half century or so resulted in spectacular success.

Of course, one reason for that success is that salespeople are notoriously pragmatic. If it works, they'll do it.

TAKING A CHANCE ON YOURSELF

Some years ago, a group of programmers started complaining to me about our salespeople. They were pushy, constantly calling the development team to find out when a certain feature would be released or if a potential customer could use the product in an unusual way.

"What do you want them to do?" I asked.

"Stop telling customers about all these advanced things. Don't talk about our development road map and where the products are heading. Just sell the basic stuff."

"One size fits all?" I suggested. "Take it or leave it?"

That seemed like a fine idea to the developers.

Then they started to complain about the big money salespeople were paid and the easy life they had and on and on.

It seemed pretty obvious that this band of programmers had no idea what it was like to be living on a commission with only a modest draw to cover expenses. To need to turn a lead into an opportunity. To have to qualify that opportunity quickly and begin to develop a client-centered solution. To deal with threats from competitors and indifference or hostility from within the client's organization. To cope with the pressure of making a presentation to a team of decision makers on which six months' income might be riding. So I tried to help them visualize the kind of pressure that creates.

"Here's an idea," I said. "How about we abolish salaries in the development group and pay for performance. You're on your own to write code. You can write it any way you want to. You can write any kind of code you want for any kind of application. But you only get paid if it sells. There's no guarantee. You'll get 15 percent of the gross revenues your work generates. If it generates nothing, you get nothing. Each of you will have a quota for how much revenue your work must produce. And if it fails to produce that amount of revenue after a full year, you will be terminated. But if it sells a lot, you can become very rich. What do you think? Big risk, but big reward! Sound good?"

They hated the idea, of course. It sounded horrible. A couple of them pointed out that they had families, car payments, a mortgage. Others said that working under that kind of pressure would be counterproductive. Another one argued that without a lot of information from the market—what customers were looking for and what our competitors were doing—it would be impossible to write programs that sold well.

"Exactly. But that's what a salesperson is dealing with. They all have families and mortgages and car payments, too, and they'd love to have perfect information, more information than we can possibly give them. And the pressure to perform is tremendous. They have to deliver presentations that are worth hundreds of thousands, even millions of dollars. They have to generate enough revenue to hit their quota. It's kind of a tough way to make a living."

The developers nodded. They could see that.

"But here's the good news," I said. "Fortunately for all of us, they're willing to take the chance. That takes guts. And because they're successful a lot more often than not, all of us have steady paychecks."

The programmers thought about it for a few minutes. They agreed that working the way the typical salesperson had to work was simply too risky for them. And, for a while at least, they became a lot more supportive of our sales team.

Working on the firing line forces you to become very practical very fast. You can't afford to waste time or effort. You want to know what's going to work. If something—a technique, a bit of information, a software tool, a piece of equipment—is not going to help you get the job done, you don't want to know about it.

That's why the revolutionary ideas that transformed professional selling in the first half of the twentieth century spread so fast. The world itself was changing. The traditional role of itinerant peddler or drummer was no longer adequate to the demands of a modern economy. Industrialization and urbanization were changing the economic landscape at a furious pace. In America, for example, the creation of the national railroad system and, much later, the building of the interstate highway system meant that commerce could be conducted on a national basis rather than regionally. Likewise, the creation of a single national currency after the end of the Civil War (before then, states and local banks issued their own currencies) made it possible to set stable prices and sell with confidence anywhere. The rise of chain stores changed the nature of selling, too, because sales reps no longer called on the local storekeeper. Instead, they called on buyers located at corporate headquarters. This was a different kind of selling—more complicated, worth much more money, and often taking much longer to complete. But by the end of the nineteenth century, it was obvious that chain stores were the wave of the future. The Woolworth chain had become so dominant that it built the tallest building in the world in 1913 to house its corporate offices. The A&P grocery chain exploded from 200 stores in 1900, to 400 in 1912, to more than 11,000 in 1924. Gradually transnational corporations that conducted business all over the world began to emerge, setting a new pattern for success.

In this rapidly changing business environment, salespeople and the companies that employed them were looking for answers. They were in search of excellence, to borrow a phrase that became popular in more recent times. They were in pursuit of best practices. They were, ultimately, looking for results.

One of the most influential figures in the development of best practices in selling, John Henry Patterson, had no particular interest in sales as a profession. He just wanted to figure out the best way to sell more cash registers faster. He had a purely pragmatic interest—unless his sales force was more productive, his company was going to fail, and he would be personally wiped out. By observing closely what his salespeople were doing and which methods produced the best results, he developed a sales process that he believed would raise performance across the company.

Was he right? Was he ever! When Patterson ran National Cash Register, it was arguably one of the half dozen most influential companies in the world. The sales processes he developed were copied by dozens of other companies, most notably by IBM. Although they were modified and elaborated from time to time, the basic methods Patterson developed have continued to be the foundation for high-tech sales today. In fact, if you have ever attended a sales-training course that focused on understanding the customer's needs and selling a solution to those needs, you have received instruction based on Patterson's original approach. The ideas he developed, ideas that kept his company growing even during recessions, are embodied today in such popular sales programs as Solution Selling, SPIN Selling, and Strategic Selling.

If you are a professional salesperson looking for answers on your own, the challenge is to cut through all the hype and figure out what really works. There are dozens of experts out there, and all of them seem to offer different theories and approaches. Some emphasize the importance of establishing a rapport with the customer. For others, it's a question of attitude—you have to be enthusiastic and persistent, and the sales will follow. Others say that the key to higher close ratios is all in the way you communicate—the right words and the right body language will win the customer over every time. Still others offer very tactical approaches, techniques that they claim enabled them to set records in selling automobiles or life insurance or real estate or whatever. Whom do you believe? Who's right?

If you have been in the sales profession for a few years, you have probably been trained in two or three different "methods." Which methods these were probably depended on where you were working. Sometimes, when a company hires a new sales vice president, that person wants to bring in the method that he or she knows best and have everyone trained in it. Sometimes the company has developed its own approach. Sometimes it just sends sales reps to a public training class. The point is that everybody takes the use of the "right" method very seriously and encourages the entire sales team to use it. Then, if the company gets a new sales vice president, the current method is discarded and everybody has to learn a new one. Or if you go to work for a different company, you are told that the way you were trained is not the way your new employer wants you to sell.

So what's going on here? Is there one method that's better than all the others?

The answer is that almost all of these methods work—sometimes. It depends on the situation you're in. It depends on what you're selling, where you're selling it, and whom you're selling to.

The reality is that a sales method that works beautifully in one kind of sales environment may fail miserably in another. For example, many high-end sales professionals, men and women who sell expensive, complex solutions that have an impact on the entire enterprise, have been trained in a process-oriented methodology that involves following certain specific steps in the sales process, gathering certain kinds of information, making very specific kinds of presentations at particular stages of the sales cycle, and gaining incremental commitments from the customer along the way. These approaches work extremely well in complex selling environments. But they usually fail when they are applied to government sales. In fact, they may require the salesperson to engage in activities that are expressly forbidden by Federal Acquisition Regulations! That's not to say that these approaches require the salesperson to do anything unethical. It's just that because these methods were developed in complex, business-to-business selling environments, they do not map well to the government sector.

The fact is that different methods of selling may work wonderfully in one environment and rather poorly in another. Matching the method to the situation is one of the challenges the salesperson, the sales manager, and the company all face.

By going back and looking at what the early masters of modern selling taught us, we can avoid wasting our time on fads and foolishness. More important, we can avoid damaging our customer relationships by adopting lousy advice. Most important of all, we can sell more effectively.

CHAPTER 2

FOUR WAYS TO SELL

Generally speaking, sales methods fall into four broad categories. For each kind of sales process, there are gurus and training programs and books and audio tapes to show you the way to do it. All of the gurus will assert to you that their method is the right way—the *only* way to sell.

Well . . . what did you expect? The gurus are selling you something.

Each of the four basic ways to approach selling has some real strengths and can improve results. But each also has some significant limitations.

For us, the goal is to understand the basic approaches and to recognize when and why each of them works. Then we can match the method to the particular selling environment in which we are working.

1. PROCESS-ORIENTED SALES METHODS

One type of approach treats sales as a process, a series of identifiable steps. The assumption is that when salespeople follow the steps correctly, they will be successful—provided they have a reasonably competitive product or service to offer. These process-oriented approaches have dominated the sales-training market for the past generation. Their success stems from a number of factors:

+ *They're relatively easy to teach.* Because they proceed in a step-by-step fashion, they tend to be linear and therefore easy to diagram and easy to present. In addition, each step can be treated as a unique training module with its own learning objectives. Salespeople can stay focused on a given step until they demonstrate an appropriate level of mastery.

+ *They address the needs of sales management.* Managers like process approaches because they can track the progress of each opportunity by compar-

15

ing it to the sequence of steps. If the deal has progressed to the "ROI agreement" phase or to the "proposal" stage, a sales manager has a pretty clear idea of what work has been accomplished, what interim agreements have been reached, and—most importantly for the purposes of sales forecasting—what the likelihood is of the deal closing.

♦ *They tend to be effective in complex sales.* Systematic, process-oriented sales methodologies are easier to implement by a team of salespeople. Focusing on the steps in the process helps minimize the confusion and delays that can occur when the customer's decision is in the hands of a team, or when gatekeepers must be handled before the final decision maker can be approached.

♦ *They have been adopted by highly influential corporations.* In particular, process-oriented methods have been adopted by the high-tech sector—computer manufacturers, software providers, and telecommunications vendors. These industries have been among the most influential in our economy for decades, so other companies have imitated their behavior. Also, when salespeople and sales managers have left one of these companies to take a position in a new firm, they have tended to take with them the sales process that they are used to and in which they have the most confidence. As a result, the method spreads.

2. RELATIONSHIP-DRIVEN SALES METHODS

A second approach to selling can be characterized as relationship-driven. In the view of the trainers and authors who recommend this kind of selling strategy, what matters the most in winning a sale is how strong a bond you forge with the decision maker. That bond, that individual relationship, which is based on trust and mutual respect, is the basis on which one vendor will be chosen over another. For a long time, relationship-driven approaches dominated sales training, but about 20 years ago they began to fall out of favor. However, they have a number of unique strengths that make them effective in the right situation:

♦ *People prefer to buy from people they trust.* Who wouldn't? Whether you're buying a new dress or a new tie or a CT scanner for the hospital where you work, your decision will be influenced by whether or not you trust the salesperson. You'd have to be a masochist to insist on buying from people you don't like.

♦ *Relationship-driven approaches tend to result in more repeat business.* Selling somebody the first time may depend on the product or the price, but selling that person time after time depends on the quality of the relationship.

♦ *The salesperson's value is maximized.* If selling depends on establishing a strong relationship, the role of the salesperson is paramount. Who else is there?

✦ *These methods work well in selling intangibles, such as intellectual capital or services, and in selling commodities, where there is little differentiation between one product and another.* Process approaches depend on having a clearly defined problem or need and an equally clear, well-differentiated solution. But sometimes customers don't fully understand what they need. Maybe they are vaguely aware that needs will emerge in the future, so they want to establish a relationship with a firm that can help them. Sometimes they see the service or product as being a commodity, so they choose to buy it from somebody they enjoy working with. (This is why relationship-driven approaches are successful for law firms, medical groups, accountants, banks, and consulting firms.)

3. LINGUISTIC APPROACHES

I can't count how many times I've conducted a seminar with a sales team, working on their proposals or sales presentations, in which someone has asked for the "magic words" that will produce the results the team wants. For some reason, people believe that certain words or phrases can exert tremendous power over a customer's mind. As a result, whether they are looking for some kind of subliminal message or maybe a hypnotic suggestion or perhaps just a compelling way of recommending their solution, salespeople eagerly seek insights into both verbal and body language. The mystique of advertising probably plays a role in creating these expectations. Another source of faith in "magic words" comes from tales of direct-mail pieces that produce huge volumes of business. Although fewer in number, the sales experts who advocate these methods have tremendously loyal followings. Why? There are a couple of reasons:

✦ *Scientific research backs them up.* Linguistic approaches are often tied to empirical research in cognition. Recent versions of these approaches are based on studies of how the brain processes information to make a decision. Understanding how the brain works can help a salesperson deliver his or her message more effectively so that the customer says yes sooner.

✦ *They are testable.* A salesperson can quickly determine whether or not the method is working simply by trying it in the course of a sales call. If the outcome is positive in more trials than not, the salesperson can reasonably conclude that the method works. In my own work with clients who write sales proposals, we have been able to track results based on changing the way the message is delivered. By restructuring the executive summary, for example, we have seen clients increase their win ratios dramatically—sometimes by more than 100 percent!

There are similar examples from the fields of direct-mail marketing and telemarketing where slight changes in the wording of a letter or a call resulted in dramatically increased responses.

4. TACTICAL METHODS

A final type of sales training focuses on tricks and techniques. You've seen this kind of material. Eight ways to close. Four steps to overcome call reluctance. Three ways to overcome price objections. Often this kind of training tends toward the manipulative, but there are sound techniques in selling, just as in any profession, that can make a person's job easier. There are several reasons why salespeople buy books and listen to audio tapes that contain this kind of information:

✦ *They believe that their success is limited only by a particular skill deficiency.* A salesperson may be good at most aspects of the job, but stumble when it comes to uncovering new leads or closing business or avoiding price discounts when the customer applies pressure. Specific, tactical training can be exactly what this salesperson needs. Think of a golfer whose game is sound from tee to green, but who can't putt. Lessons that reduced the number of three-putt greens would dramatically lower that golfer's scores.

✦ *Techniques are often trainable in short, focused sessions.* Looking at the entire sales process can be overwhelming. And the salesperson out in the field may have little control over how that process is defined. Similarly, gaining more ability to build a relationship or communicate more effectively may seem like too much to tackle. But applying a specific tactical approach, using a sales technique right away, sounds less daunting.

Ultimately, I would argue that all of these approaches to improving sales have merit. Which one is going to be the most productive for you depends on your own skill set, on what you sell, and on who your customers are. But it will be very much to your advantage to understand all four approaches, to know where they came from, and to see how and why they work.

On the Shoulders of Giants

A couple of years ago I had the pleasure of co-presenting with Gerhard Gschwandtner, the publisher of *Selling Power Magazine,* a Webinar titled "On the Shoulders of Sales Giants: What We Can Learn from the Masters of the Past to Sell More in the Future."

I chose that title for our presentation because it echoed the famous comment of Isaac Newton, who once said, "If I have seen further, it is by standing on the shoulders of giants." In suggesting that his accomplishments were due to the achievements of the scientists and mathematicians who had come before him, Newton was acknowledging the importance of the ideas and theories that had preceded his own articulation of the fundamental laws of the mechanical universe. It seemed to Gerhard and me that the same could be said about modern sales techniques.

Sales books tend to go in fads. Somebody comes up with a novel way of framing the challenge of selling, a clever title, or a new tool, and rapidly becomes recognized as an authority. But when you peel back the surface of most of these books, they are all variations on some simple themes. Almost all of the shelf-full of new sales books that get published each year are exploring ideas and techniques that have been around for generations. Understanding the origins of these basic approaches to selling will make a salesperson more flexible and more resourceful. Practicing them will make the salesperson more successful.

During our one-hour Webinar, we focused on sales techniques that the audience could use *immediately*. Techniques that have stood the test of time. Ideas that were first advanced in an earlier age, in a simpler economy, but that still deliver results because they are rooted in fundamental principles of human psychology.

Our goal was to help people understand the basics, connect them to the past, and help them understand how and why these techniques still work today. In just an hour, we had to skim the surface a bit, but we hoped that our attendees, all of whom were professional salespeople, would find the material helpful.

Now salespeople by nature are skeptical. Unless they see a clear and immediate benefit from what you have to offer, they're not likely to be interested. So we delivered the message and waited to see—would the reaction be favorable?

Favorable? Unbridled enthusiasm was more like it!

The feedback from that brief Webinar was tremendous. Attendees said that for the first time, they saw the big picture in sales methods. Now it all came together for them. They could take *all* the training they had received, *all* the books they had read, and integrate these pieces into a single approach that really worked for them. And later they told us how they were using the techniques to shorten the sales cycle, increase win ratios, and increase the size of the deals they were closing.

THE INVENTION OF MODERN SELLING

During the first half of the twentieth century, Americans learned how to sell more efficiently and effectively than any other nation on earth. Soon these ideas were picked up and spread around the world.

These ideas and insights improved sales results in different cultures and for a wide range of products and services because they are rooted in fundamental principles—of psychology, of linguistics, of group dynamics—that transcend national and cultural boundaries.

The four figures I focus on—John Henry Patterson, Dale Carnegie, Elmer Wheeler, and Joe Girard—each made a unique contribution to the development of modern business and professional sales. What's more, their ideas still work, even if they have been buried under the avalanche of sales books that have poured from the presses in recent years.

As I suggested earlier, you probably recognize Carnegie's name. His best-known book, *How to Win Friends and Influence People*, continues to be a best-seller to this day. The company he founded continues to offer courses in public speaking and effective selling all over the world. Business leaders from Lee Iacocca of Chrysler to Tom Monaghan, the founder of Domino's, all give the Carnegie approach credit for helping them succeed.

It's less likely that you recognize Patterson's name, unless you are a veteran salesperson or have an interest in business history. Patterson created the National Cash Register Company and was one of the most influential business leaders in the world at the dawn of the twentieth century. But compared to some of his contemporaries, like John D. Rockefeller and Andrew Carnegie, Patterson is not well remembered today. And his innovations, which led to the development of modern sales processes, are seldom noted. But Patterson was as influential in the development of modern sales processes as any single individual who ever lived. In fact, it's no exaggeration to say that he invented the modern sales process.

What about the other two? Who are they, and what did they contribute?

Joe Girard is simply the greatest salesman in the world. At least, that's what it says in the *Guinness Book of World Records,* and when you read about his accomplishments, my guess is that you'll probably agree. But even more important than his personal success is the idea he developed: the concept of nurturing leads in a closed-loop cycle that generates phenomenal amounts of repeat business and overcomes buyer resistance.

Elmer Wheeler was the person who coined the expression, "Don't sell the steak—sell the sizzle!" That phrase has become part of our contemporary folklore. But what does it really mean? And what else did Wheeler come up with? You might be surprised to learn that Elmer Wheeler's ability to craft selling sentences that work often increased his client's sales by 40, 50, or even 100 percent! And the principles he used still work today. He understood the fundamentals of psycholinguistics before there was such a discipline.

Selling is a tough job. If you're in the field, you know that. You don't need me to point it out. And it doesn't matter what kind of selling you're doing. Whether you're selling a $30 pair of jeans in a chain store in a mall, selling leases for commercial office space, selling a hundred-million-dollar contract for complex system integration products and services to a government agency, or something that falls in between, you face some very basic challenges. You have to identify potential customers. You have to understand what a specific customer needs. You have to win that customer's trust as somebody who can help her or him get it. You have to communicate your recommendation clearly and convincingly. And you have to close the deal.

To learn the best way to succeed in this difficult job, it will help you to stand on the shoulders of giants. That's the purpose of this book: to help you succeed by learning some of the most powerful ideas in the history of selling.

PART TWO

John Henry Patterson

The Process of Selling

CHAPTER 3

DESPERATE IN DAYTON

J ohn Henry Patterson had a problem: His business was on the verge of failing. In fact, if sales didn't improve dramatically, there was a good chance that he might go bankrupt. If he did, it would wipe him out financially, and it would ruin his brother, Frank, too, whom Patterson had convinced to invest in the new business.

Financial ruin was bad enough. Seeing his brother and his brother's family wiped out was horrible. But for a man as proud—some might even say as arrogant—as John Henry Patterson, there was an even worse consequence of failing: He would become the laughingstock of his community, Dayton, Ohio. For him, that would be even more painful than going broke.

For years, Patterson and his brother had been extremely successful. Starting as a toll collector along the canal routes that linked Ohio to the eastern part of the United States, Patterson had raised himself up step by step until he and Frank had owned their own coal business. Selling coal at retail to local Dayton businesses and householders, the Pattersons had become so successful that they were eventually able to buy their own coal mine so that they could guarantee a constant supply and control costs. They dominated the local market. But with domination had come boredom.

In fact, by 1884, when Patterson was 40 years old, he was nearly numb with boredom. So he and his brother sold their coal business and headed west, looking for new opportunities and adventures. After traveling through the Rockies for several months and flirting with the idea of raising beef cattle, they returned to Dayton in November and made a fateful decision: They decided to invest their fortune in high technology.

At least, they were investing in what passed for high technology in 1884.

At that time, few inventions targeted the worlds of retail or commercial business. Almost all innovation was targeted at the two big sectors of the

American economy—farming and manufacturing. But three new inventions were introduced in the final decades of the nineteenth century that had the potential for transforming office work and retailing. Speculators were excited. Scoffers laughed. What were these three inventions? The telephone, the typewriter, and the cash register.

It's hard for us to imagine today, but these were extremely risky endeavors. Each of them represented the kind of cutting-edge technology that we associate today with the Internet or with space travel or with medical discoveries. And, believe it or not, none of them was an immediate hit.

For the first decade or more, for example, Alexander Graham Bell and his business colleagues couldn't interest anyone in using the telephone and faced huge obstacles in creating the systems necessary to make telephone service feasible. Business owners in particular ridiculed the notion that they would ever need to use a telephone. Getting people to accept the telephone was amazingly difficult. In one particularly bad moment of discouragement, Bell and his partners offered to sell the patent on the telephone to Western Union for $100,000. But the president of Western Union, a man of limited vision named Orton, refused it, asking sarcastically, "What use could this company make of an electrical toy?"[1]

Similarly, the first practical typewriter faced huge obstacles to acceptance. It had been invented just a couple of years before Bell invented the telephone by a man named Christopher Latham Sholes, who sold his patent to the Remington Arms company in 1873. Unfortunately, the action of the type bars in the early models was slow, and they tended to jam frequently. Few office managers could foresee typewritten documents replacing handwritten copies for important business papers, nor could they envision a time when the ability to type would be a basic requirement for anyone seeking an entry-level position in office work. To make matters worse, office workers themselves were resolutely opposed to typewriters. They didn't want to learn this cumbersome new way of creating documents, and the poor spellers among them realized that they could no longer hide their ignorance behind illegible handwriting. (Now, of course, we rely on the spell checker in our word processing software to keep us safe from such embarrassment.) And some business owners objected to typewriters because they made correspondence appear "impersonal." As a result, business offices were slow to adopt the typewriter, although by the early 1880s very large corporate offices had started to use it.[2]

The cash register was an equally tough sell. Business owners didn't think they needed one, and clerks were absolutely opposed to them. They found the idea of installing a cash register insulting and degrading. To them, the machine implied that they were thieves and that the owner or manager didn't trust them. The fact was, of course, that a huge amount of theft was occurring, and for many years clerks all across the country found ingenious ways to sabotage or circumvent the cash register. Dishonesty was rampant, a fact that many store owners already knew. In fact, some of them overlooked a good deal of pilfering as a trade-off for the low wages that shop clerks were paid.[3] Before the cash register was widely accepted, shopkeepers and store owners simply kept their cash in a drawer underneath the counter. Sometimes the drawer had a lock on it, but for the sake of convenience, the lock was seldom used until the close of the day. Purchases were supposed to be recorded by hand in a ledger book when they happened, but there was no way to know if the record of transactions was accurate. This system was basically all anyone had used for thousands of years, and it seemed to work just fine. It had worked from the earliest days, when Babylonian merchants had inscribed transactions on soft clay tablets, and it worked now with pen and paper and cash in a drawer. Who needed some complicated, expensive contraption to store money and track sales and refunds?

Patterson's answer to that question would have been, *Everyone needs a cash register.* In fact, Patterson's decision to invest in this particular form of high technology came from a combination of local knowledge and personal experience. The local knowledge stemmed from the fact that the cash register had been invented and patented in 1879 by James Ritty, a saloon keeper in Dayton. Ritty was pretty sure that his bartenders were skimming money from the cash drawer, were probably pouring free drinks for their friends and themselves, and perhaps were making change incorrectly, all of which was cutting into his profits. His doubts about their honesty and accuracy became obvious in the nickname he gave his invention: the "Incorruptible Cashier." Ritty then founded the National Manufacturing Company in Dayton to manufacture and sell cash registers. These early cash registers were pretty primitive affairs. When a sale was made, a bell rang on the cash register and the amount was noted on a large dial on the front of the machine. Entering a sale punched holes into a paper tape, so that the shopkeeper or saloon owner could keep track of sales by adding up the holes at the end of the day.

Ritty's approach to selling them was even more primitive. His idea was to sell one to a shopkeeper, then pay that shopkeeper a commission for selling cash registers to other merchants. Whether a dressmaker or a saloon keeper or a banker would have the time, energy, or inclination to sell cash registers as a sideline was a question that Ritty never considered. As a result, the cash register business was slow going, and National Manufacturing was barely staying afloat when Patterson bought it.

He knew about Ritty's machine because he lived in Dayton and because he was one of the few people who had bought one. In fact, he had been so pleased by the results that a cash register had delivered in one of his retail outlets that he thought he could make a go of it. He truly believed that the cash register was such an obvious boon to any business owner who dealt in cash that only an idiot would not want one. After all, hadn't he proved the value of having a cash register in his own business?

He and Frank had bought a coal mine near Coalton, Ohio, a hundred miles southeast of Dayton. Like other mine owners, they also ran the local retail store in Coalton, selling all the general merchandise that the miners working in his mine needed. But the Coalton retail store consistently lost money. Patterson couldn't figure out why. Based on the volume of merchandise it was selling and the prices being charged, the store should have yielded a decent profit. Instead, the numbers were in the red at the end of each year. Since the store was so far from Dayton, neither of the Patterson brothers could be there in person to keep an eye on it. John thought that installing a cash register would at least give him a paper record of daily receipts, which might give him some insight into what was going on. Frank objected. A cash register was expensive, and it probably wouldn't work, he said.

John persisted, and his hunch paid off. Installing the register revealed where the problem was: Various miners, in collusion with certain crooks, were carrying off merchandise that was never rung up for sale. The brothers were essentially the victims of an elaborate shoplifting scheme.

Once the register had proved its value in Coalton, Patterson ordered two more for the Dayton coal offices. Again Frank objected. This time he said it was an unnecessary extravagance because they didn't suspect that anything was wrong in the Dayton offices. But his brother's reply was unanswerable: "How do we know that there isn't something wrong that we *don't* suspect?"

Once again his instincts proved correct. One of the offices experienced a consistent discrepancy between cash receipts at the end of the day and the actual cash on hand the next morning—the office was always short, and always by the same amount. After some sleuthing, they discovered that a night watchman who had been fired two years earlier had been showing up each night and helping himself to his wages out of the cash drawer. Since the police had been used to seeing him around the place at night, nobody questioned his presence. But the night watchman's thefts had cost the Pattersons around $1,200, a huge sum in 1880—roughly equivalent to $50,000 today.

These personal experiences were the basis for Patterson's personal enthusiasm. His decision to invest in the cash register business was finally cemented when he and Frank were on their trip out west, looking for a new venture. In Colorado Springs they met a vacationing businessman who was able to relax and leave his store in the hands of his senior clerk for the first time in his career, because the clerk was mailing him the paper strip from a cash register every day.

Patterson concluded that every retailer should have a cash register and that every intelligent retailer would quickly buy one. And so, for $6,500, he bought the rights to Ritty's patent and the operation known at the National Manufacturing Company.

The machine he now had the rights to manufacture and sell was a crude apparatus that worked by punching holes in appropriate columns on a strip of paper. It was a device "which virtually nobody understood or cared to understand, and for which there was no demand whatever."[4]

Patterson was what Geoffrey Moore has called an "early adopter"—a visionary who sees beyond the machine or the technology to understand its potential as a business tool. But as Moore pointed out in *Crossing the Chasm,* early adopters are few and far between. To make a technology company a success, you have to convince the mainstream of potential customers that there is value in your innovation. You have to move the product from a curiosity to a necessity. And that was something that James Ritty had been unable to do. In fact, nobody at that time had figured out how to do it on a consistent basis.

When Patterson took over, the company had one sales rep. It was still following Ritty's original sales plan of encouraging retailers who bought a cash register to sell them. In the five years before Patterson bought it, the company had sold a total of about a hundred machines. Two years after Patterson took over, it was selling 12 machines a month. This was a big improvement, but it wasn't enough. Patterson and his brother were facing bankruptcy. Something had to be done.

Many of Dayton's business leaders had ridiculed the brothers for being so foolish. The Pattersons were throwing their money away on this ridiculous investment, they said. What on earth had gotten into the hard-headed coal merchant John Henry Patterson? Had he gone insane?

In fact, Patterson himself quickly doubted the sanity of his decision. In a classic example of buyer's remorse, he actually tried to get out of the deal shortly after he entered into it. He had offered to give Ritty his patent and his company back plus a bonus of $2,000 for voiding the contract, but Ritty wouldn't do it.

What would have happened if Patterson had managed to get out of the deal? Well, eventually somebody else would have developed a successful cash register business. Others were already working on similar concepts when Patterson got into the business. But the real consequences if Patterson had walked away extend far beyond the question of whether or not retailers would start using cash registers.

In simple terms, it would have been a disaster for the American economy. It would have stunted the growth of high technology in the United States. It would have had a negative impact on the rise of the computer hardware and software industries. Why? Because in the process of figuring out how to sell cash registers, Patterson figured out how to sell any complex product. He invented the fundamentals of modern selling as a definable and repeatable process. Eventually, somebody might have discovered the value of a structured approach. Maybe that person would have promoted it zealously. Maybe people who were trained in that method would have gone on to lead dozens of other companies and thus spread the sales method throughout the economy. But with that many "maybes" in the equation, it seems likely that without Patterson, the development of professional sales would have been delayed by a generation or more.

Patterson took over the business, which he renamed The National Cash Register Company, at the dawn of the great age of invention—besides typewriters and telephones, Burroughs had developed the concept of the adding machine in 1888, and Edison had developed the first light bulb just three years before Patterson's investment. The problem was that none of these early innovators had developed an effective way to promote and sell their technology.

Patterson faced the classic dilemma faced by many contemporary entrepreneurs: He was producing a product so innovative that there was no market for it, a product in which the world had no interest, a product so complex that its largest group of potential users couldn't understand it. As Patterson quickly learned, running a factory without any established demand for the product it produces is an extremely expensive and risky way to do business. He had to find a way to sell his complicated, innovative product to skeptical consumers.

The answers he found have had repercussions throughout American business for more than a hundred years. Some of the most powerful and influential leaders in American industry worked for Patterson and took his methods to their next assignments. As a result, the Patterson philosophy on selling spread everywhere. Some of the men who worked for Patterson (and the jobs they went on to hold) include the following:

A. J. Lauver	General Manager	Burroughs Adding Machine Company
Alvan Macauley	President	Packard Motor Car Company
William Benton	Founder	Benton and Bowles Advertising; later U.S. senator
C. E. Steffey	General Sales Manager	Addressograph-Multigraph Company
Charles Kettering	Vice President	General Motors Corporation

E. A. Deeds	Chairman of the Board	National Cash Register
Edward Jordan	Founder	Jordan Automobile Company
Henry Theobald	Founder	Toledo Scale Company
J. E. Rogers	President	Addressograph-Multigraph Company
Jacob Oswald	President	Roto-Speed Company
R. H. Grant	Vice President	General Motors Corporation

However, by far the most influential of all the men who worked for Patterson was his vice president of sales, Thomas Watson. Watson led the National Cash Register sales force for years and not only followed Patterson's methods himself, but inculcated them into hundreds of the company's sales reps. Eventually, Watson angered Patterson, as almost all of his senior managers did. (Patterson was notoriously cantankerous and difficult to work for.) Patterson fired Watson, apparently because the young man had become too "popular" with the sales force. At that point, Watson cast about for something to do and finally took the helm of a struggling little company in New York called the Computing-Tabulating-Recording Company. One of Watson's first moves was to rename the company, calling it—drum roll, please—International Business Machines. That's right: IBM.

Three initials, just like NCR. And a sales method that was an exact copy of what Watson had learned from Patterson. In fact, Watson even stole Patterson's slogan, "Think," and had it posted around the offices and factories of IBM.

By the middle of the twentieth century, IBM had became the world's most influential technology company, of course, and was the model for effective technology sales. Later, when Xerox's patents ran out and it suddenly had to start selling in a competitive marketplace, it adopted the IBM sales model, which means that it, too, was using Patterson's approach. And from the Xerox professional sales methods, either directly or by inspiration, have arisen many of the most successful sales approaches used in our own time—Professional Selling Skills, Strategic Selling, Solution Selling, SPIN Selling, and many others.

It's no exaggeration to say that Patterson's ideas about how to sell a complex product to a large, national market were the foundation for selling high technology in our own time. His ideas continue to work today.

Except that he got the most important one from his brother-in-law.

THE BROTHER-IN-LAW WHO SAVED HIGH TECH

Patterson himself had no prior experience in selling, other than selling a commodity, coal. But taking orders for a commodity required no innovative thinking. You didn't have to convince the customers that they needed coal. When the snow began falling and the firewood ran out, customers figured out pretty quickly that they had to buy coal from somebody.

Even for companies that manufactured a product, selling had not advanced very far from the days of the peddler and the drummer. A manufacturer's rep traveled by cart or train, maintaining regular contact with the trade, building up good will, and taking orders. There were virtually no systematic sales practices. In fact, hardly anyone had even thought about selling as a distinct function within a business, a professional discipline that could be studied and perfected, like accounting or engineering. A sales rep's most important asset was his circle of contacts, but these contacts were typically limited to a certain kind of buyer. A shoe salesman, for example, sold to merchants who carried shoes in their stores. Even if the sales rep changed companies and started to represent a different shoe manufacturer, he would go back to the same customers he had been seeing all along.

Selling was seen as transactional. A salesperson engaged with a customer or prospect, showed the product that was being offered, and either did or did not close a sale. The actual sale was seen as an event. It was something that either happened or didn't. Some people were better at getting it to happen than others, but no one knew why. Some sales professionals were thought to be more "dynamic," to have more "magnetism" or more "pep." Successful selling was a matter of "personality."

Vague nonanswers never appealed to Patterson. By 1886 he had abandoned the notion of having customers sell the machines to other merchants in their area and had hired five sales agents. Quickly he saw that one or two of his agents were outselling the others. Why? How?

To get the answers, Patterson organized the first sales convention in 1886. By now the company was managing to sell 12 cash registers a month, but Patterson had a bolder vision than that: He wanted to sell 5 a day! To get there, he had to make sure that each of his sales agents was producing as much business as possible. He had all five of his sales agents come to Dayton, where they received training on some new features of the cash registers and how these features increased value for the customer. But he also had his top-producing sales rep, a man named Harry Blood, who was based in Chicago, explain how he consistently managed to sell a cash register for each bartender who worked in a saloon. At first, when Patterson asked him, "How do you sell?" Blood insisted that there was nothing special in his methods, but Patterson persisted. Blood finally admitted that he was careful to establish a personal relationship with every man who might use the cash register, not just the owner of the business, before bringing up the question of a sale at all. This was useful, and Patterson made sure that Blood shared his tip with the other reps. Then the other men shared some tips and techniques that worked for them.

In this first sales conference, Patterson had come up with two of many innovations in modern selling: holding a regular sales meeting, and having sales reps trained not just in product features but in sales techniques as well. The meeting was so effective that Patterson decided to have a sales meeting once a year.

Patterson had also invited his brother-in-law, Joseph Crane, to attend the sales conference as an observer. Crane himself was a successful businessman in Dayton, and he had previously been successful in selling wallpaper. Crane sat in on the meetings and listened to the various conversations among the salesmen. Eventually Patterson asked him what he thought of the way they were pricing the cash registers.

"The price is all right," Crane said, "and you have a good product. But you don't know how to sell it."

"What do you mean?" Patterson snapped.

"You're making the mistake," Crane explained, "of trying to sell the prospect in his store, where he can't give you the right sort of attention."

Crane went on to explain the importance of getting the retailer to go to a separate location—a display room in a hotel or at the NCR offices. Many manufacturers' reps used this method of selling, but it was new to the NCR team. Some of them resisted, of course—it would be too expensive, too difficult; it would require a pretty powerful demonstration to make it worthwhile for the retailer. No doubt there was also some resentment at having an outsider tell them how to sell their own product more effectively. However, Patterson thought Crane's advice made a lot of sense.

Later in 1886, Patterson convinced Crane to join NCR as a sales agent. Apparently, Crane wasn't too adept at the mechanical or technical side of the business. He spent a whole day at the factory trying to take one of the cash registers apart, so that he would understand how it worked. The next day he tried to put it together again. He failed at both tasks. However, in spite of his mechanical ineptitude, he still felt himself "fully equipped to go out and explain them."[5]

This is an interesting insight that Crane and later Patterson himself shared. A sales rep does not need to be a technical expert. The salesperson needs to understand the product, and needs to know where and how to get answers to technical questions that are beyond his or her expertise. But a good sales rep really needs to bridge the gap between the company and the customer, linking the product (or service) and its functions to the client's particular business environment and needs. That seldom takes detailed technical knowledge. Instead, it takes business savvy and an ability to listen closely to the customer and make connections between the issues she cares about and the capabilities of the product or service. Crane recognized that his inability to assemble or repair a cash register meant nothing. His ability to show how the cash register could increase profits for the store owner meant everything.

Crane was a brilliant salesman, but even he stumbled a bit at first. On his first sales trip, he went to the small town of Findlay, Ohio, and after a rough start—there were no hotel rooms available, so he slept in a barber's chair the first night—he got demos scheduled with 16 merchants. But after 16 demos, he didn't have a single sale. He wondered why. The merchants seemed to like the machine, but they weren't buying. What was wrong? Why wasn't he closing the deals?

Crane reviewed his first presentation and made a note of a point or a feature that he had forgotten to mention, one that in retrospect he thought that customer would have been interested to hear. He wrote that point on a slip of paper. He did the same with the second presentation, and made another note. He went through all 16 presentations and realized that in each there were things he had forgotten. Crane concluded that his lack of fluency in presenting the machines thoroughly and pointing out the key features that solved a particular merchant's problems might have been the reason he had not closed any of his deals. He hadn't sold because he hadn't presented effectively enough with a clear, persuasive message tailored to the customer.

Once he had reviewed his performance and focused on delivering the message more persuasively, Crane finally made his first sale, to a restaurant owner. The next day, he closed three more deals. Crane continued to use his slip of paper with all the points on it as a crib sheet, but he also realized that getting an order wasn't simply a matter of going through every feature the machine had to offer. That would exhaust and bore most merchants. Instead, he needed to uncover the customer's biggest worry or problem or fear, show which features addressed that issue, and then demonstrate the value of buying the machine to the merchant in a systematic way so that the prospective purchaser fully understood it.

Eventually, through repetition, Crane reached a point where he didn't have to refer to his crib sheet at all, so he tore it up. Now he could identify the customer's concerns, then explain all the appropriate points in the right order, usually in the exact same words. In fact, by the end of his first 90 days, he noticed that he was saying virtually the same thing to every prospect and that he had an extremely high success rate.

What Crane had discovered was that for a sophisticated solution like the cash register, there were a limited number of reasons that people needed it. It might be worry about theft, it might be concern about sloppiness in keeping the books, or it might be fears that carelessness in making change was eating into profits. There weren't too many other problems that the cash register solved. By quickly focusing on the particular set of problems that a given customer worried about, Crane was able to position the cash register as a solution, not merely as a piece of equipment. He was selling value, not technology, a problem that many salespeople in high tech, software, IT services, and related fields still have today. By focusing on impact and value, rather than technical features or operational details, Crane was selling a lot of cash registers.

John Henry Patterson, always one to measure and track performance, noticed how successful his brother-in-law had become. Curious about how he was achieving such outstanding results, Patterson summoned Crane to his office and demanded to know how he sold cash registers. Crane admitted somewhat sheepishly that he said basically the same thing, word for word, at every demonstration. Patterson found that hard to believe—it flew in the face of the accepted wisdom of the time. Sales was about "magnetism," about "personality," about connecting with the customer. Crane assured him that he was serious—he was saying the same basic words in the same order, time after time.

"Doesn't giving the exact same presentation over and over become monotonous?" Patterson asked.

Crane said that it didn't because he was giving it to different people each time. Their reactions and their particular circumstances—the kind of business they were in, the number of employees they had, the specific problems they faced, the worries they expressed about profits—put the presentation in a different light each time. The initial positioning of his presentation offered some opportunity for variation. After that, it was a matter of connecting the dots.

To prove his point, Crane then had Patterson do a little role playing. "You forget everything you know about a cash register and imagine that you are a grocer in a country town. Pretend you've never heard of a cash register, and I will explain it to you," he said.

Crane went through his pitch, exactly as he had dozens of times before. When he was through, Patterson admitted that after hearing Crane's presentation, he would have bought a cash register from him on the spot. Patterson then had his brother, Frank, come in, and Crane did the whole thing over again. Frank admitted that he would have bought one, too.

Patterson realized what he had in Crane's method: a way of systematizing the sales force to maximize its results. Once more he had Crane give the presentation, this time with a secretary writing it down verbatim as dictation. Patterson had it typed up and sent it out to the other salesmen with a note:

"Crane sells more machines than any of you fellows, and he sells them this way. I suggest you all learn this."

Naturally, almost all of them ignored Patterson's advice. They each had their own way of selling, and they saw no reason to adopt Crane's. They sold on personality, on charisma, on relationships. This speech that Patterson had sent them had way too much "Joe Crane" in it. Where was the room for their personalities? For their style? For their own pizzazz?

Acknowledging that they might have a point, Patterson revised the text, making it a bit more flexible, and issued it again, this time as the *NCR Primer*. He presented it at the sales conference in 1887 and told the men that they had to learn it. This time it was more than a suggestion. It was an order.

Again he was met with obstinate refusal. Perhaps it was jealousy at Crane's success. Perhaps it was fear that they wouldn't be able to succeed with this new method of selling. For whatever reason, the sales force, which now numbered 12 men, defied their boss.

The matter finally exploded in 1893, when Patterson forced the issue. The company—like the rest of the country—was mired in an economic recession, and sales were slipping fast. He made knowledge of the *Primer* compulsory. Learn it and use it, or get fired!

The move was criticized widely, both within the company and outside it. Most of the criticism was directed against the notion of a set way of selling being applied uniformly across industry segments, markets, and geographies. It wouldn't work; it was foolish; it was a waste of time.

But the reality was that in spite of extremely adverse economic conditions, NCR actually grew during the recession years, much faster than any other manufacturing company. Patterson's insistence on his sales agents following the process outlined in the *Primer* had made the difference. The proof was easy to see: The method worked.

CHAPTER 4

A PRIMER ON PROCESS

A fter Patterson insisted that every sales agent in the field use the sales method that Crane had developed, the company's sales began to soar.

What made Crane's approach so powerful? It focused entirely on the customer's needs rather than on the company's product.

At first, Patterson had made the mistake of thinking that it was the specific words that Crane used and the order in which he said them that was the key to success. As his other sales reps finally showed him, that wasn't where the power of Crane's approach resided. Rather, it was in the way the sales cycle was systematically organized.

Once Patterson grasped that fact, he became resolute in training the NCR sales reps to think like businesspeople. They weren't making pitches, they were solving problems. They weren't there to demo a cash register, they were there to understand a merchant's business and to suggest ways to make it better. Although Patterson didn't use the term, what he was developing was the first sales force to use a *consultative* approach.

Crane's presentation proceeded in four steps—steps that are just as effective today as they were a hundred years ago. These four steps allow the decision maker to move gradually from awareness that he or she might have a problem that is affecting profitability, to a sense that there might be an answer, to conviction that the NCR cash register not only was an answer but was an answer that offered superior value and would pay for itself quickly. The four steps of Crane's process are:

> *First, the approach—identify the customer's problems.* Where are customers losing money? What goals are they failing to achieve? What gaps in their current capabilities are keeping them from being suc-

cessful? Patterson constantly told the sales agent, "Never talk cash register when you first meet customers. Talk about their problems. There is nothing in which customers are so interested as their own business." That's still great advice.

Second, the proposition—develop a specific value proposition. Identify the specific areas where losses are occurring, and quantify them. Summarize the losses and show the potential for increased profitability in concrete dollars and cents. The more you know about the customer's business in detail, the more convincing your value proposition will be.

Third, the demonstration—show how the solution fits. Summarize the customer's problems and the potential for increasing profits. Then show how the solution works, not in terms of its technical functions, but in terms of its business impact. Functions and features are relevant only in terms of the value they deliver. Technology for its own sake is not part of the selling message.

Fourth, the close—ask for the order. Assume that an intelligent businessperson will want to buy. If the customer has objections, answer them and close again.

And that's it!

What made it so revolutionary? Well, for one thing, for the first time in history, a selling argument was consistently developed from the customer's point of view rather than from the company's desire to make a sale.

It was also the first time that selling was seen as a process, something that could be repeated over and over, rather than as a transactional event. This concept flew in the face of customary sales practice, as we have seen, and it provoked tremendous resistance. But it was Patterson's most important contribution to modern selling. Defining sales as a process, a sequence of specific steps that can be identified, tracked, and measured, means that sales can be taught, it can be measured, and it can be improved.

With his single-minded focus on this concept, Patterson was applying to sales the same kind of thinking that Frederick Taylor had applied to running a steel mill. Taylor is remembered today as the "father of scientific management," a precursor to modern quality control theory and the patron saint of efficiency studies. While he is often symbolized as a tight-lipped analyst with a clipboard and a stopwatch, Taylor was actually much more flexible in his view of business processes. However, he did believe that inefficiency and waste were something that no business could tolerate. Taylor initially applied his methods in steel mills, but they soon extended far beyond any particular industry or sector of activity. The first sentence of his major work, *The Principles of Scientific Management*, states, "The principal object of management should be to secure maximum prosperity for the employer, coupled with maximum prosperity for the employee."[1] By identifying and applying consistent processes, and then carefully measuring the results of those processes, a manager could steadily improve productivity, thus bringing about greater prosperity. Taylor believed that the key was to find the most economical way to perform a given task. By breaking down that task into specific steps, then figuring out the best way to perform each step, you gain maximum efficiency and repeatability. His basic principles have become the foundation of modern management:

- ✦ Develop a systematic way of performing every job, including the sequence of actions to be performed, the set of standardized tools to be used, and the proper working conditions.
- ✦ Select workers with the right characteristics and abilities to do the job.
- ✦ Train the workers to do the job the right way, following the right process and using the standard tools, and establish incentives that motivate them to comply with the process.
- ✦ Support these workers by planning their work and by smoothing the way as they go about their jobs.

For Taylor, methods were more important than people: "In the past," he wrote, "the man has been first; in the future, the system must be first." However, he also claimed that following methodical processes was ultimately a means of unleashing workers' creativity: "In tomorrow's enterprise," he wrote rather prophetically, "the knowledge worker will be freed to release creative energy that will result in an era of enormous innovation and discovery, fulfilling the potential and promise of the mind." However, in its basic form, Taylorism maintained that workers were theoretically interchangeable. In this light, it's pretty easy to see why salespeople, who believed that their success was due to their personality, their smile, and their gift of gab, might resist a more methodical, process-oriented approach.

Patterson believed that the operation of a sales organization could be as orderly and systematic as that of a factory or administrative operation. He recognized that there were no rules or formulas that would make someone who lacked the basic qualities of good judgment, intelligence, tact, and drive into a successful sales agent. He was also well aware that no two selling situations were exactly alike. But, he claimed, it was still true "that all prospects were alike to a far greater extent than they differed from one another, and to this extent the selling process could certainly be standardized and systematized."[2]

Almost 20 years ago, I was hired by a client, Cincinnati Milacron, to improve its win rates on its proposals for complex machine tools and integrated manufacturing cells. In working with the company, I learned a lot about its business. I learned that it had seven basic lines of equipment, and that each line had a certain set of options for tooling, control, measurements, and so forth. It sold its machines into specific industries—automotive, aerospace, heavy equipment manufacturers, and a few others. Having the benefit of being an outsider, and therefore being unaware of any of the past history that had resulted in these product lines, market segments, or optional features, I suggested creating a simple database of content. Describe the requirements that were common in each industry. Describe how the different types of machines were used functionally in those industries. Write up the machines' operating parameters. Write up the options. Then, when the sales engineers had to write a proposal, they could just select the paragraphs or chunks of text they needed and assemble them into a draft document.

A few of the engineers with whom I was working became very excited by the idea, but in general it was greeted with a lot of resistance. Every deal is different, they said. This would produce boilerplate proposals that would offend the customer. Our customers are all technical experts, and they don't want to hear this general, business-oriented stuff. And so on.

Eventually the engineers began to use the idea, and I introduced the same basic idea to other clients. Within a few years, it became obvious that it worked. Proposals, like the overall sales process in general, contain elements that recur frequently. Not every proposal contains the same elements, but in a variation on the Pareto principle, 80 percent of proposals are based on the same 20 percent of content. By focusing on that core set of content, you can easily automate the creation of proposal drafts for the vast majority of opportunities. Now, more than a thousand companies around the world automate their proposal process based on this simple concept.

It's the same concept that lies at the heart of the NCR sales approach. I'd love to claim that I was the first person to recognize it, but I wasn't. Patterson and his brother-in-law beat me to it by a mere eight decades!

Patterson recognized that the details will vary from one sales call to another, and that getting the details of a customer's business situation right is an important part of the process. However, in general, every customer will be interested in the same basic content, presented in the same basic order. By teaching his sales reps how to use that order of presentation, he was improving results by standardizing performance and leveraging the commonalities inherent in every deal.

Clearly, the four steps outlined in the NCR *Primer*—the *approach*, the *proposition*, the *demonstration*, and the *close*—constitute a process in Taylor's sense: a set of steps that must be performed in exactly the right order, using the right tools (words, graphics, and demonstration equipment), and in the right conditions (away from the prospect's place of business, with no clocks, calendars, or other distractions on the walls, and in an environment that was businesslike).

BUT WHY DID IT WORK?

Interestingly, recent research into the psychology of decision making has revealed that these four steps correspond to the way people think when they are making a decision. In other words, Crane had stumbled onto a technique that was efficient and effective because it matched the way decision makers are likely to consider the information at hand when they are trying to make up their minds. First, they want to know if what you are talking about is relevant to them. If you start by focusing on their situation and the problems they are experiencing, the question of relevance is answered immediately.

Next, they want to know if you will be framing your conversation in terms of the criteria that matter to them. For Patterson's sales agents, the presentation was always couched in terms of improving profitability. For many businesses, this remains a sound approach, although in today's somewhat more complicated economy, it's possible that a decision maker will be more concerned about eliminating hurdles or gaps in the technical infrastructure, or overcoming noncompliance with regulatory standards, or rapidly penetrating a new market, or any of a hundred other areas of impact that may matter as much as profits.

Third, because the customer now recognizes that the salesperson is addressing an issue of relevance with the potential to deliver a payoff in an area that matters, that customer becomes interested in hearing the solution and evaluating it. That's the demonstration part of the sales process, and it's vital that every feature of the cash register—or whatever we are selling—is linked to the customer's business concerns and potential payback. Then, if the solution shows strong potential for solving the problem and delivering the right results, the customer is ready to say yes. That's when the sales agent moves to the final stage of the process, the close.

Patterson wasn't interested in the psychology of decision making, of course. He was interested in selling cash registers. And he knew that Crane's method worked, so he wanted all of his sales reps to use it.

However, because it's based on fundamental principles that govern the way people process information when they are making business decisions, the method embodied in the *Primer* still works today.

RESISTANCE FROM THE SALES FORCE

In this era of process-oriented approaches to selling—methods like Strategic Selling, Solution Selling, SPIN Selling, and others—it's hard for us to believe that Patterson's sales agents objected to this method so strenuously. But they did. They attacked it as a soul destroyer, a sales method that eliminated initiative and resourcefulness, an approach that prevented salespeople from using their intelligence. They saw it as a way of dumbing down the job, of de-skilling the sales force, a way to reduce sales to the lowest common denominator. They complained that the sales agent who was equipped with nothing but a "canned," systematic presentation would be helpless when dealing with a sharp, aggressive prospect, one who demanded quick thinking and creativity. How could the robotic sales rep ever handle the unexpected, the novel? Plus, it made the job routine. Repeating the same presentation over and over gave the sales rep no opportunity to use personal creativity.

To Patterson, none of those criticisms added up. What he knew was that the sales reps who used the method sold the most cash registers. He was so confident that the sales process would produce results if it was applied properly that he actually experimented with hiring men who had no previous sales experience. He felt that they would be less likely to fight him on using the method, and since the method was so effective, it would give them the tools to perform at a high level. Interestingly, this is almost the same argument that many of the process-oriented sales methodologies use today in trying to convince sales managers to implement them. Teach your people this method, they say, and it will raise the average, it will help your turkeys soar like eagles, it will turn your ordinary performers into superstars.

For a while, Patterson actually found that it was difficult to hire experienced sales reps who would use the NCR method. Turning to people who had no prior experience in sales became a matter of expediency. And the success of these inexperienced reps simply strengthened Patterson's faith in the process. For example, at one point he hired a young man, Bill Lockwood, who had been working as a cement finisher, laying sidewalks around Dayton! Lockwood was trained in the method of the *Primer*, given a sample cash register to use in demos, and sent to Indianapolis, one of NCR's most valuable markets. Although he got off to a slow start, selling nothing for the first two weeks, Lockwood eventually sold 14 cash registers by the end of his first full month in Indianapolis and had opportunities for that many more in his pipeline.

Many of the other sales reps still resisted. On one occasion, one of Patterson's top performers grew indignant when the boss criticized him for not following the *Primer* approach. "I sold a hundred and eighty registers last year," he declared to Patterson. "That's darn good, and you know it! How many registers did you ever sell in a year?" Patterson replied, "If you can sell a hundred and eighty registers a year demonstrating the way you do, you can sell four hundred using the right way."[3]

Another agent told him in 1893, "I'll give it to you straight right at the start, Mr. Patterson. I'm no parrot. Selling is all personality. Memorized selling talks may be all very well for the greenhorns, but I've been at this business too long to change my methods."

"That's fine," Patterson replied. "We're always looking for better methods."

The agent then showed Patterson how he preferred to demonstrate the register, going through the sales pitch the way he liked to do it, while Patterson watched without comment.

When it was over, Patterson walked over to the register with an air of bewilderment. "That was certainly fine," he said. "There's only one question. Just where do you put the money in this thing?"[4]

The rep had made the same mistake so many salespeople make, particularly when they have become totally familiar with the product or service they're selling: He forgot to present from the customer's point of view. How often have you seen a presentation that was so loaded with in-house jargon, or read an executive summary that was based on so many unexplained assumptions, that the customer never had a chance of understanding it?

Patterson wasn't looking for blind obedience. He was just trying to find the best way to sell cash registers. To the extent that the *Primer* worked, he wanted his sales force to use it. And he never said anything to suggest that he thought the memorized presentation could substitute for good judgment or intelligence. But he did believe that using the method made good salespeople into better ones, and he had the numbers to prove that agents who used the method sold more machines than those who did not.

As a result, Patterson continually tested the agents on their ability to repeat the literal text, and he could be savage in criticizing them when they failed or when they regurgitated the text like a schoolboy reciting a memorized poem. Flat, lifeless, detached presentations were no better than presentations that deviated from the text. He wanted them to learn to sound spontaneous and natural.

THE IMPORTANCE OF MASTERY

Patterson believed fervently in the power of the process to produce sales. As resistance continued, he became fed up with excuses and sometimes used venomous sarcasm to communicate his anger. However, he eventually resorted to something even more frightening than sarcasm: personal inspections.

In 1893, Patterson visited the sales offices in all of the major cities, reviewing all of the agents in turn, their selling methods, their closing methods, and their mastery of the process. To make sure the sales agents were doing it correctly, he made them deliver the presentation to him, as Crane had done that very first time in his office. If they made a mistake—if they stumbled on the words, or waved a finger in the supposed customer's face, or chewed gum, or committed any of hundreds of other "sins" in their delivery—Patterson would erupt.

Patterson played the role of a drugstore owner and had each man present to him. It quickly became obvious which men were following the sales methods presented in the *Primer* and which were not. The experience was grueling. Some of the agents froze up completely and could not perform. Agents who could not demonstrate the cash register to Patterson's satisfaction were drilled until they could, or else they dropped out. Many quit at this point. But it was the start of a practice that continued for years. And it communicated Patterson's resolve—no more half measures.

Over the years, Patterson became obsessed with having the sales agents follow the sales process to the letter. In fact, NCR lore is filled with stories of his blowing up when one of them failed to do it correctly. Some of his more notorious antics include:

✦ Attacking a cash register during a sales meeting with a sledge hammer and reducing it to a pile of shapeless junk.

✦ Intentionally bumping into a pitcher of ice water with his elbow while he was speaking, knocking it to the stage, where it smashed.

✦ Kicking furniture to make a point. On one occasion, Patterson had the Denver rep give a sales demonstration. The Denver agent had a bad habit of shaking his finger at the customer when he got excited, and, sure enough, he got going and began shaking his finger. After he had done it four or five times, Patterson suddenly jumped up, walked over to the agent's desk, and kicked the side panel out of it. Then he turned to the agent and said when he overcame his habit of shaking his finger at prospects, he could buy a new desk. Until he cured himself of it, he could sit at this desk with the side panel smashed in. (Supposedly, the agent never shook his finger at a prospect again for the rest of his life.)

There's no question but that Patterson was what in today's jargon we would call a control freak. Eventually the *Primer* grew to be over 200 pages long (!) and contained detailed instructions on every aspect of selling, from what to wear to how to sit. Reasons why sales reps failed were identified: lack of knowledge, lack of dignity, poor health, uncouth manners, sloppy appearance, and so on. The sales agent was given directions on what kind of suit to wear, what kind of collar and tie, and much more. (This particular set of instructions was the origin of the famous IBM dress code. Watson brought it over wholesale from his experience at NCR.)

At one point, Patterson even had the *Primer* thumb tabbed, like scripture, for ready reference. This was probably no coincidence—for Patterson, the *Primer* was like a Bible. He also had the *Primer* profusely illustrated, showing the sales agent exactly how to hold his hand while demonstrating a particular feature of the cash register. At one point, the manual contained detailed instructions on manners and conduct. One page contained a list of 50 "don'ts"—including:

Don't fail to seat the prospect properly.
Don't point your finger or pencil at him.
Don't sit awkwardly on your chair.
Don't put your feet on his chair.
Don't slap him on the knee.
Don't smoke.
Don't chew gum or tobacco.
Don't tell funny stories.

The fact that injunctions like these were necessary suggests the kind of behavior that was common among salespeople at that time. But it also suggests how controlling Patterson could become. In spite of the gradual upgrade in the sales force and the change of environment (from selling in saloons to dealing with more mainstream businesses), the list of "don'ts" didn't disappear until 1912.[5]

Aside from his being such a controlling personality, was there any reason for Patterson's insisting on his sales reps memorizing and mastering the NCR presentation so completely?

In fact, there was. He was attempting to develop in them an ability to do something difficult with a high degree of excellence. Although he acted as though the only standard he would accept was perfection, in reality his goal was to force the sales reps to develop fluency and mastery through knowledge and repetition. He knew that some of his sales agents had an aptitude for selling. They were gregarious, clever, ambitious, and competitive. Those were wonderful qualities. But unless they also developed the ability to explain a complex piece of technology in language that the customer could easily understand and in terms that made the product's value clear, they would not succeed. They were engaging in a different kind of selling. They were the first sales force to master the techniques necessary for making what Neil Rackham called "the major sale"[6]—the complex sale of significant value that affects the way the customer's business operates, how the employees do their jobs, or how valuable assets are managed. Such sales often take longer to complete, involve an ongoing relationship with the customer, and carry heavy penalties if either the salesperson or the customer makes a mistake, including wasted money, wasted time, or damaged careers.

Even with all the aptitude in the world, skills must be learned. Becoming a skilled piano player will require, according to some estimates, more than

10,000 hours of focused practice. Many of those hours are spent simply learning the scales and repeating exercises. But it is mastery of the basics that enables the pianist to inject his or her own personality and creativity into a performance. Mastery also implies that a person can perform successfully even when the task varies. Golfers who can score well only on their home golf course have not truly mastered the game. True mastery of the game would mean that they would be able to post a competitive score even on a course they've never seen before.[7]

Patterson was trying to prepare his sales agents to perform at the top of their game, no matter what situation they were in. He also knew that will-power alone was not enough. Simply *wanting* to be successful in sales wouldn't guarantee that an individual actually would be successful. Sales agents needed total mastery of the material and the skills associated with delivering that material, both combined with the focus necessary to keep moving toward their goal.

Today we might refer to this experience of total mastery as "being in the zone" or "being on your game." One researcher has called this sense of optimal experience "flow," stating that it is characterized by information emerging into conscious awareness effortlessly, at the exact instant it is needed, and in congruence with the individual's goals. This sense of "effort-less effort" is the hallmark of mastery. The tennis player, the pianist, the salesperson making a presentation does not have to think about what to do next. The thought and the action are one. The process simply flows.[8]

Patterson knew that all kinds of distractions would come up to disturb the sales reps. They would be rejected, sometimes with rudeness. Customers would throw all kinds of oddball objections at them. Sales presentations might be cut unexpectedly short when a prospect had something more im-portant come up. Competitors might try to sabotage their sales efforts with rumors, innuendos, or outright lies. With all of these distractions and dis-couragements in their path, an effective salesperson had to stay on task and on message. Behavior is a function of individuals interacting with their envi-ronment. Even Patterson, control freak that he was, knew that you couldn't control very much of the environment; however, through training and repe-tition, you could prepare the individual. Sales skills, he believed, were based on knowledge—somebody had to teach the agent what to do and how to do it. Then those skills had to be developed through practice—rehearsing and rehearsing until they became automatic. Not surprisingly, this is the exact pattern recognized by cognitive psychologists as the foundation for develop-ing skills.[9]

Selling always occurs in a human context. You have to interact with people to make a sale. You may not have to go belly to belly with the cus-tomer. In fact, you may be able to do your selling over the phone, or even, as the gurus in the 1990s predicted, via the Web. But the more complicated the sale, the more likely it is that you will need to interact extensively with the customer on a personal level. These interactions can be divided into two components: the events that come before a specific selling behavior, which are called *antecedents* in the jargon of psychology, and the *consequences,* the events that come after the selling behavior has been executed. Antecedents set the stage for your behavior. Consequences determine what you will do next.

Suppose you were one of Patterson's agents, calling on a particular saloonkeeper (the vast majority of NCR's customers for the first decade or more were saloonkeepers) for the first time. Your goal is to generate interest in the cash register. But how? Are there certain ways of introducing yourself, for example, that will lead to a conversation about the saloonkeeper's business? The *Primer* would teach you to use the following introduction and to expect the following consequences:

The Approach:

Sales Rep: I am from the National Cash Register Company and I have called to interest you in a way to increase your profits.

The prospect usually responds that he is not interested in buying any cash registers.

Sales Rep: But you are interested in increasing profits, aren't you? There are only two ways: One is by increasing sales. The other is by decreasing expense. My business has to do with decreasing the indirect expenses that are taking a part of your profit out of your pocket all the time.

Prospect: What are indirect expenses?

And with that, the presentation is off and running. The customer is engaged. Notice that the presentation didn't start with an overview of the company and its capabilities. Crane had learned that the consequences of an opening that focused on NCR would consistently be negative: He would never get the prospect's interest. Instead, the approach tried to engage the prospect by focusing on a problem of vital concern: increasing profits. It was a safe bet back then that a retailer working in a competitive field would be interested in maximizing profit. It's still a safe bet. If we are selling to a division of a huge corporation or to a government agency, the decision maker's attention may not be attracted by profit. The division or the agency may have other goals that are more important. But even today, more than a hundred years after Patterson and Crane laid down the first rudimentary approach, financial measures of performance are the most common and the most important ones that business managers look to improve. On Wall

Street and on Main Street, it's all about earnings and profits before anything else.

All right, so the *Primer* told the sales rep to start out by focusing on some aspect of prospective customers' businesses that they were worried about, like increasing profits. You may regard this approach as somewhat crude. Fair enough. Perhaps it was innovative 125 years ago, but it's fairly standard today, isn't it?

Well, actually, no. It isn't.

All too often, salespeople start their sales calls by focusing on their own company or their product. They don't bother to address what the customer probably cares about the most: his or her own business problems! We did a survey a couple of years ago to find out how most sales presentations start. Nearly 40 percent begin the same way: with the history of the sales rep's company!

For example, think about the way the typical bank's business development manager, or BDM (that's "salesperson" to you and me), starts an initial sales call. Suppose the BDM is going to see a restaurant owner in hopes of landing the restaurant's payroll and treasury services, and maybe even placing a business loan for expansion. So how does the typical banking sales call start? Probably very much like this:

BDM: Thank you for meeting with me and my colleagues this morning. As you may know, our bank has been serving the local market since 1911. We were actually founded in 1868, and for 15 straight years we have been voted the best bank in the tristate area. We have been profitable every year since our inception, and today we are proud to claim a capital ratio greater than 18 percent. We have an experienced team of banking experts, including Pat Smith, who has 15 years of experience as a relationship manager in this market, Terry Knight, who has nearly 10 years of experience in treasury management, and Chris Kendall, with 20 years of lending experience. If you examine the yield curve of the loan facilities we typically put in place, you can see that . . .

It's boring!
It's irrelevant!
It's self-centered!
And it's all too typical.

If Patterson and his brother-in-law were in charge of this sales force, they wouldn't let people drone on this way. Patterson would probably smash a few water pitchers along the way, but he would almost certainly insist that the BDM focus on the customer's business first:

BDM: It's a pleasure to meet you. I've read some terrific reviews of your restaurant, and I've enjoyed a lot of great meals here myself. Now, I understand that you're planning an expansion? And that you might build another restaurant in the north county?

The difference is pretty obvious, isn't it? Of course, starting out in a customer-focused way actually requires doing some homework. But that was part of what the *Primer* taught, too. The NCR sales manual encouraged the sales agent to gather information before the first visit. Learn the prospect's name and something about her or his characteristics and peculiarities, aims, and achievements. Know the names of the other owners of the business. Learn who has the authority to buy. Learn about the store, and learn what aspects of it are of particular interest or concern to the merchant. When you enter the store, look around and make observations. Observe how the clerks wait on customers, how they handle transactions, the sales ability of the clerks. As the *Primer* said, "Knowledge is power and you will be in a position to secure the merchant's attention by showing him you understand his business."[10]

And what of today's equivalent of the high-tech sales team at NCR? Do you think it would do any better than our hypothetical bank? The answer, from my observation of dozens of high-tech companies, is *no*. For example, I recently had the opportunity to watch a sales team from a provider of enterprise resource planning software start out a sales call with a prospect. I was there because my own company had developed a very strong relationship with the prospect, so strong that the senior executive asked for our opinion on choosing a software vendor. Other than getting the order, almost nothing gladdens the heart of a salesperson more than having the customer ask for advice. It shows that the customer really trusts you and respects your business insight. So we knocked ourselves out to consider the options and make the best recommendation.

The software firm we thought was the best fit was invited in to present. We were also invited to attend because we were essentially filling the role of consultants for this project. Naturally, we were a little nervous about the presentation. We wanted the firm's representatives to do a good job, to confirm our customer's opinion of us, and, more importantly, to identify the right solution for the customer's business.

So how did it go, you ask? Did the sales rep address the customer's issues in managing the manufacturing plant? No. Did he focus on the need for projecting inventory levels to minimize cost overruns? No. Did he discuss the customer's recent entry into a manufacturing arrangement in China? Of course not.

Instead, the salesperson hooked up his laptop computer to an LCD projector, flipped that baby open, and displayed a screen with about 20 different icons on it. And he then proceeded to click on each and every icon, showing the function it represented, going through all of the screen forms that came up, and droning on about technical details of the system architecture: ". . . and so to complete a forecasting module, the user selects from a dropdown list of options, indicating here the database format, and then selecting the configuration option for output, including, as you can see here, an option of web display or print format . . ."

It was painful. And embarrassing.

When the sales rep was done, he turned around with a big smile of relief. He'd made it! He'd clicked on every icon in less than an hour!

"So, are there any questions I can answer for you?" he asked.

Well, the customer had a few questions, all right, but none of them were for him. Instead, after the rep had gone, the senior executive turned to me and barked, "What were you thinking!? That was the worst sales presentation I've ever seen!"

I had to admit it was up there in the top ten. And I felt bad about it. I was sorry that my customer's time had been wasted. And I was very sorry that a good solution, one that probably would have delivered some outstanding business results, had been passed over because of an inept sales process. To this day, I believe that the software was an excellent choice. But because the sales message was presented so poorly, we'll never know.

That's the kind of disastrous mistake Patterson was trying to armor his sales team against. Everybody tends to do what feels right and easy when under pressure. By drilling the structure and language of the NCR sales call into his sales agents' heads, Patterson had helped to guarantee that when they were under pressure, they wouldn't revert to an "old" way of selling—talking about the company or jumping straight into a product demo. As one of Patterson's sales reps wrote, "The Demonstration evolved from a standardized program into a practically instinctive technique. Gradually it developed from a routine presentation based upon the mechanical features of the register into a selective procedure based upon the specific needs of the individual prospect."[11]

Eventually, Patterson realized that salespeople were not likely to master the new method of selling on their own. They needed coaching, reinforcement, and the pressure of being in a group activity. He saw the value of formal, group instruction clearly demonstrated when National Cash Register sponsored a display at the Chicago World's Fair in 1893. A group of young men was hired specifically to staff the display, but Patterson found to his horror that they knew almost nothing about cash registers. He pulled them all into a hotel room, where he created a short, focused presentation based on the *Primer.* He also listed the most common questions that the crowd was likely to ask, along with the best answers. Patterson then drilled the young men in small groups until they were all perfect.

Patterson decided that he could do the same thing with his sales reps. This was the origin of the first training schools, which were held in Dayton in 1894. However, like so many of his innovations, the sales school, which came to be known as "Sugar Camp," was not widely accepted at first. The sales agents found their weeks at Sugar Camp anything but sweet. According to Patterson,

> Nothing we have ever started in connection with our organization was subjected to so much ridicule as the starting of a school to teach our men. It was considered beneath their dignity to a good many people, as treating them too much like children, and for this reason we lost a good many agents. For years there was hardly any person connected with our institution who believed in it, or had any faith in it. They looked upon it as a fad of the most foolish kind.[12]

At that time, everybody knew that "salesmanship was a Gift." You couldn't make a great sales rep, you couldn't train one—you had to find men and women who had an innate talent for it, like a musical genius born with perfect pitch. The notion of the "born sales rep" was widely accepted. Experienced sales professionals resented the idea that training could work because it seemed to bring selling down to the level of a trade, something that could be taught from a textbook. But Patterson did not yield.

The first sales training school was held on April 4, 1894. It was attended by 37 men. The company paid all expenses. The training was held in a cottage under the elm tree on the lawn of the old Patterson farmhouse in Dayton, with the men sleeping in tents like Army recruits. Crane was in charge of the instruction, and the men were drilled on the *Primer* and the newly developed *Book of Arguments,* a handy guide to overcoming objections. Several dropped out after a day or two, but most of them passed the course and were installed in new territories or returned to the field. After the close of the first session, Patterson announced that every agent and salesperson must go through the school—there would be no exceptions. After two years, every sales rep who had remained with the company had completed the training, but many of the old-timers and the self-proclaimed "born salesmen" chose to quit rather than undergo four or five weeks of intensive training.

As usual, Patterson kept records of everything. By tracking performance, he was soon able to see that sales veterans who went through the training doubled their sales afterward. New men did better from the start than old-timers who insisted on sticking to their old "personality" selling.

One unexpected benefit of the sales school was that it made true sales management possible for the first time. Patterson's sales managers developed strategies, forecast results, coached to improve weaknesses, and organized effort. Managing a staff of "born salesmen" made that kind of centralized control impossible, because everybody was doing something different. With no consistent approach to the market, for example, there was no way to forecast the pipeline. It was impossible to determine how likely any given opportunity was to close, what stage of the sales process it might be at, or whether all of the necessary steps in the process had been completed.

Ultimately, of course, Patterson's judgment was vindicated. Other companies quickly imitated the sales training school, mainly because NCR continued to rack up sales success, increasing revenues year over year. It was particularly influential among companies that sold products to other businesses, and it became part of the IBM way of operating when Watson took over there.

If we were to summarize the key conclusions to be drawn from Patterson's insistence on training and absolute mastery of the sales process, they would be that the sales professionals cannot be fully successful unless they are fully prepared. Salespeople must know the key points of the message so completely and totally that nothing, no matter how unexpected, can rattle them. And the message must always, *always* be based on the customer's self-interest.

CHAPTER 5

PATTERSON'S LEGACY

Patterson spent a large portion of his time and energy and money in "the effort to develop and teach the Primer technique, and he succeeded in teaching it, not merely to the NCR organization but pretty much to American business as a whole." In fact, some 50 years after he first bought NCR, it could be said that "there are very few selling organizations in the country today that do not derive their operating technique, in part at least, from Patterson's *Primer.* . . . It was, in fact, the first practical and complete demonstration of what we know as modern . . . salesmanship."[1]

One contemporary sales guru has stated that Patterson was "arguably the best salesman of all time . . . due to his ability to blend the emotion that makes the sale with the logic that figures out the reasoning behind it."[2] But his contributions were actually a lot more concrete than that. Here is a partial list of some of Patterson's innovations just in the sales area:

+ Formal sales training
+ A detailed sales manual
+ Direct-mail advertising in support of targeted sales campaigns
+ Annual and quarterly sales quotas
+ Guaranteed territories
+ The 100 Point Club—special recognition for the top achievers
+ Special celebrations ("President's Club") for top producers
+ Sales campaigns drawn up annually to give everyone a fresh start

Every one of these was an innovation introduced by Patterson—a remarkable list of "firsts" for anyone. But there's even more in his record. Besides his creative thinking in sales, he also introduced innovative ideas in factory management, employee relations, hiring practices, health and welfare policies, and much more.

Patterson was actually one of the very first business owners to introduce physical fitness and health programs as part of the regular workday. He believed that regular breaks for exercise helped workers stay mentally alert and physically strong. Some of these ideas came from other figures that Patterson was following, including Henry Bowditch, a Harvard physiologist; John Kellogg, the patron of whole-grain foods and the founder of Kellogg's cereals; and the strongman and exercise advocate Eugene Sandow. All of them were invited to NCR headquarters in Dayton, where they were feted as honored guests and invited to give lectures and programs for the workforce. Their ideas and advice were also published in NCR's various employee publications.[3]

But perhaps the most serious of Patterson's personality quirks was his unquenchable, ruthless drive to succeed. He would do anything to drive a competitor out of business, so that by 1902 NCR was estimated to have a 95 percent market share. In this regard, he was a man of his times. Many business leaders at the dawn of the twentieth century tried to create monopolies. Rockefeller was doing it with Standard Oil. Carnegie sought to corner the market in steel. Even the Wright brothers spent huge amounts of time and money fighting patent infringements so that they could monopolize the development of the airplane. But Patterson went further than most. He was so ruthless in trying to dominate his industry that he makes today's tough competitors, like Bill Gates or Jack Welch, seem downright beatific by comparison. Patterson and Watson were actually charged with engaging in aggressive business practices that crossed the line, although the charges did not hold.

Largely because of Patterson's ruthless drive, NCR achieved a huge reputation and influence, far in excess of its actual size as a business. Its revenues were much smaller than contemporary concerns in steel, oil, copper, sugar, harvesting machinery, or tobacco. It was not in a basic industry. It did not sell direct to the consumer. At that time it had a narrow range of products—it was a niche specialty. But it had tremendous prestige. One of the most important sources of influence for the company was the fact that Patterson hired outstanding people, trained them thoroughly, and then fired them hastily. As a result, they went on to become senior executives at other companies, implementing and adapting Patterson's ideas.[4] Almost without exception, those executives took the best of Patterson's ideas with them and used them in their new businesses. Chief among those ideas was his whole approach to selling: treating it as a definable process, training salespeople until they achieved mastery of their material, using a customer-centered approach, tying the product to achieving the customer's goals, and more. At one time it was confidently claimed that there was not a selling force in the country consisting of 25 or more persons that did not include at least one man who had been trained by NCR.

Eventually other companies, particularly Watson's IBM, surpassed NCR in prestige and influence. From being a high-tech innovation, the cash register became a commodity product, part of the accepted infrastructure of doing business. Meanwhile, IBM was developing new concepts and new products, including some of the earliest commercially viable computers. In promoting these products and the services associated with them, IBM continued to use a sales method based closely on the Patterson process. Other companies copied IBM's methods and hired away IBM's sales executives and managers. Out of this tangled web of cross-pollination and inbreeding, a number of popular sales methodologies have emerged.

PROFESSIONAL SELLING SKILLS

Another major branch from the original NCR trunk was developed at Xerox, which created a sales course internally called Professional Selling Skills. Designed to train Xerox sales reps how to sell complex products against tough competition, it proved tremendously successful. It was a bit ironic that Xerox should develop one of the most influential variations on process-orientated sales methods, because for years the company didn't need to do any selling at all. Its patent on the xerographic procedure gave it exclusivity in a product that had tremendous value to businesses. Only when competitors emerged did Xerox learn that many of its customers thought that the company was high-handed or even arrogant, and were eager for an alternative. As a result, Xerox invested heavily in developing an effective selling process.

As was Xerox's habit with so many of its successful ideas—such as the mouse, the graphical user interface, distributed computer processing, and quite a few others—it decided to spin the sales program off as a separate company. That led to the creation of Learning International and one of the first consultative selling skills courses, known as Professional Selling Skills or PSS. Again, the method emphasized steps, breaking down a sale into component phases and training the salesperson how to execute each step the way a top-performing salesperson does. In fact, the whole method was supposedly based on research into the techniques used by top performers, with the underlying assumption that these techniques are repeatable by anyone who understands and practices them.

The most recent iteration of Professional Selling Skills is now offered through Achieve Global, a training company that acquired the assets of Learning International and two other training companies, Zenger Miller and Kaset International.

The essence of the PSS approach is recognizing that almost nobody wants to be sold anything. However, people do want to make informed decisions. By structuring the sales process as a means of facilitating the decision process, a salesperson overcomes some of the resistance that a prospective customer may have and builds a stronger working relationship. The PSS course tends to focus on the steps of a typical sales cycle, which may occur in a single call or may extend over several months:

1. Planning the call
2. Introducing yourself and starting the call
3. Asking questions and probing for insight into the customer's business
4. Proposing or presenting a solution
5. Handling objections and negotiating terms
6. Closing the deal
7. Following up after the sale has been made

The number of steps in the cycle is somewhat arbitrary, but one of the strengths of the PSS approach is that it focuses on discrete tasks within the sales process at a more granular level than Patterson's four-step method did. The *Primer* strongly recommended learning as much as possible about a prospect before the first visit, but it didn't make that an explicit step in the sales cycle. PSS recommends doing the necessary research on the customer, the company, its customers, and its key competitors so that you can speak intelligently about the company's business when you start.

Don Hammalian, one of the original coauthors of the PSS sales-training program at Xerox, pointed out to me that PSS was one of the first attempts to use "programmed instruction" for professional training. This put the course at the forefront of innovative teaching methods, particularly in the attempt to train salespeople behaviorally.

The actual course was built on research into "what we now call 'best practices' based on field observations," Hammalian recalls. "We were trying to take a more scientifically valid approach that could be statistically validated in terms of results."

Because of the course's design and its use of a process approach to break down the task of selling into incremental steps, PSS proved to be an excellent foundation course for people who were new to sales. Over the years, the course evolved quite a bit, but from the start it had a strong core on which people could build their own style.

Hammalian is rather amused to look back at the original course, compared to what it became and what is taught in other process-oriented courses today. "The first PSS model," he recalls, "was a highly manipulative, product-focused model that no one would advocate today. But it evolved into a 'need satisfaction' model with much more emphasis on understanding the customer and building a strong relationship."[5]

The roots of the "need satisfaction" model are present in Patterson's original *Primer*, although the need tended to be restricted to just one thing—increasing profits. Later, the definition of customer needs became more sophisticated in PSS and in many of the other process-oriented approaches.

SOLUTION SELLING

Others from Xerox also began developing sales training based on the "new" consultative methodology for handling complex sales. Mike Bosworth began his career in 1972 with Xerox Computer Services (XCS), and claims on his web site that from 1976 through 1982 he was "the primary architect and deliverer of XCS sales training." In 1983, Bosworth founded Solution Selling, a sales-training organization. In 1993 he published *Solution Selling: Creating Buyers in Difficult Selling Markets*.[6] Like PSS, the Solution Selling method moves through a number of distinct phases:

1. Precall planning and research
2. Stimulating interest
3. Establishing the critical business issues
4. Establishing the "buying vision"—the understanding of value and reasons to move forward
5. Mapping the organization
6. Negotiating access to the most senior decision maker
7. Managing the product evaluation plan
8. Negotiating
9. Closing

If you look at the pattern, you can see that, while using different names and having a different segmentation of the phases, the Solution Selling approach touches on the same basic elements that the *Primer* taught. The approach is handled in phases 1 and 2, the proposition in phases 3 and 4, the demonstration of the solution in phase 7, and, obviously, the close in phase 9.

As in the "blue sheet" approach used in Strategic Selling, discussed later in this chapter, the student of Solution Selling is expected to master a process for establishing strategic alignment between the salesperson and the buyer by going through a "Nine-Block Vision Processing Model." Some salespeople find this whole process a bit overwhelming and confusing, since it involves a combination of three different kinds of questions—open, closed (or "control" questions, in Solution Selling jargon), and confirming—and three different kinds of information—reasons for the need, the impact of the need on the business, and the dimensions or "vision" of the solution. However, for someone who is relatively new to managing a complex sale, going through the process can be a revelation. The original version of *Solution Selling* has been updated by Keith Eades, while Mike Bosworth has written a new book, *CustomerCentric Selling*, which is his own take on a sales methodology appropriate to our times.

Solution Selling has been successful in quickly providing salespeople who are relatively new to the job with a rather sophisticated set of skills. One of the most useful techniques that Solution Selling teaches, for example, is a method for arousing a potential customer's interest during an initial phone call or even in a voicemail message. Rather than blurting out, "Hi, this is Sally Finley of Oakmont Chemical Supply, and I wanted to talk to you about whether you need any hydrochloric acid," students in the course are taught to approach a prospect by focusing on examples. Mention something outstanding you helped a client who is very similar to this prospect to accomplish. Using that method, Sally might say, "Mr. Plunkett, this is Sally Finley of Oakmont Chemical Supply. We recently helped Jack Brown at Amalgamated Acid Wash lower his cost of operations by more than 10 percent by setting up a just-in-time chemical supply system for him. Is that something you would be interesting in hearing more about?"

The trick is to focus on results delivered to a company similar to your prospective client, bought by a manager who is similar in title or role to the person you're trying to reach. It's a good idea to have three or four of these mini-case studies (Bosworth called them "reference stories"), just in case the prospect says that he doesn't have the same kind of problem or goal that your reference account did. It's a good technique, and it helps overcome the awkwardness of making the initial call. You have given yourself permission to make the call because you have something concrete and relevant to share.

STRATEGIC SELLING

Strategic Selling was originally written by Robert Miller, an executive at Kepner-Tregoe, a consulting firm that specializes in developing systematic processes for decision making, and Stephen Heiman, who had nearly two decades as a successful salesperson at IBM before he also joined Kepner-Tregoe. Their book was extremely popular, providing a blueprint for sales process management that was adopted by hundreds of companies. They identified six factors, or "key elements," that contribute to success: buying influences, red flags, response modes, win-results, the sales funnel, and the ideal customer profile.[7]

One of the most useful concepts presented in *Strategic Selling* and the workshops that teach it is the notion of "buying influences." What Miller and Heiman point out is that in a complex sale, one in which several people must say yes before the deal is consummated, it's important to understand who those various people are and where their interests lie. They point out that in every complex sale there are at least four roles:

+ The *economic buyer*, who is the person who can give final approval to buy and who usually looks at your recommendation in terms of its potential to deliver a big impact or a compelling return on investment
+ The *user buyer*, who looks at your solution in terms of its impact on how he or she works, usually judging it based on its likely ability to make life inside the cubicle better or worse
+ The *technical buyer,* who looks at your solution through a narrow filter of specific technical requirements—which might be related to software design, system architecture, engineering approach, or even legal or contractual terms
+ The *coach,* who believes in your solution and provides you with insight into the organization, power structure, unspoken decision criteria, and other useful information to help you navigate the dangerous waters successfully

This level of insight into buying behavior within a large organization was fresh and helpful when *Strategic Selling* first appeared, and it continues to be useful. Others have modified, amended, and extended the concept, but without dramatically improving it. If you are dealing with decision teams rather than purchasing agents, you probably recognize these roles from your own experience and recognize that the sales process requires addressing all of the buyer types and showing them that they will get the kind of solution they seek.

Over the years, some salespeople have complained that the method is overly complicated. First, they have to gather all the information about the six key elements. Then they have to record the information on a special form, called a "blue sheet." Filling out the notorious blue sheet can be so time-consuming that the salesperson may have to put off seeing the customer until tomorrow. The four-quadrant Win/Win Matrix definitely has the whiff of Kepner-Tregoe consulting about it. This may be a liability that is inherent in process-oriented approaches to selling. After all, the NCR *Primer* became longer and more detailed as time went on until it became unwieldy and was cut back from a lengthy tome to a booklet.

On the positive side, *Strategic Selling* has showed salespeople, particularly those with a complex, expensive, technical solution, how to penetrate a large organization effectively. Getting to the decision maker is far more difficult for today's salesperson than it was in Patterson's day, when the sales agent walked into a store and was probably talking to the owner immediately. As a method, Strategic Selling is systematic, it is process-oriented, and it helps salespeople—particularly those who are new in the role—succeed in selling complex products and services. Indirectly, Patterson's methods continued to spread.

SPIN SELLING

One other influential figure merits some discussion as a descendant of John Henry Patterson: Neil Rackham, the author of *SPIN Selling*. From a background as a research biologist investigating the way the human brain processes the sense of smell, Rackham somehow migrated into research into sales methods. Like some of the others who fall into the sales-as-process camp, Rackham offers best practices that work in selling a large deal. These best practices, which emerged from Rackham's research, have little to do with the sales skills that are traditionally taught in Sales Boot Camp 101: handling objections, learning closing techniques, and asking open-ended questions. Using a high-pressure close, for example, on a major sale is most likely to ruin the deal. Using tricky language to deflect an objection or asking only open-ended questions is likewise not appropriate when the salesperson is trying to sell a product or service or a combination of the two that can have a major impact on the way a business operates. Instead, according to the research he and his colleagues conducted (Rackham reports that the research involved over 35,000 sales calls, 40 researchers, and 12 years of effort in 23 countries—a "mammoth project," as he himself describes it), every sales call, from the simplest to the most sophisticated, goes through four distinct phases: preliminaries, investigation, demonstration of capability, and obtaining commitment. Within these phases, moreover, the best salespeople use a particular kind of questioning—the SPIN approach—to uncover the customer's needs and build credibility and trust.

"The simplest finding, valid in all 23 countries where we studied it," Rackham says, "was that it's not what you *tell* that makes a call successful, it's what you *ask*. That was a revolutionary finding at the time, when many people believed that nothing was as important as a good sales pitch."[8]

What Rackham and his colleagues discovered, though, was that a truly effective presentation must be built on an understanding of customer needs, and you get that understanding by asking questions.

"The practical advice at the heart of SPIN is that when you sell, focus on questions first and foremost," Rackham says. "This means making questions the basis of your call planning. When we studied how top performers planned in Xerox and IBM, we found that most of them just jotted down half a dozen key questions. That's all it takes. By contrast, less successful salespeople planned what they wanted to tell, not what they wanted to ask."

The kinds of questions that need to asked are embodied in the acronym

SPIN, which stands for Situation, Problem, Implication, and Need-payoff. (The last term is a bit of a kluge, designed, one suspects, to make the acronym sound better than it would have if he had used "Payoff." After all, SPIP Selling just doesn't have the same ring to it.) Situation questions focus on the company, its background, and the customer's current operations, processes, competitive situation, and so forth. Because a good salesperson finds out as much of this information in advance of the sales call as possible (something that Patterson advocated in the *Primer*), these questions are used sparingly, more for confirming that the salesperson's understanding of the situation is correct. Problem questions focus on the customer's problems, needs, issues, gaps in capability, or pains. From these, the salesperson moves to implication questions, which probe into the consequences of not solving the problem compared to the value achieved by eliminating it. Finally, need-payoff questions address the value or positive impact that the customer expects to see from a good solution. From there, the sales process moves to a demonstration of the vendor's capability (what the *Primer* also called the demonstration, emphasizing that it must constantly link back to the customer's specific needs and desired outcomes), and then to the close.

SPIN Selling has been hugely popular. It offered an intelligent, research-based approach to the sales process, and it emphasized the value of focusing on the customer's situation and interests at the outset. In a later book, *Rethinking the Sales Force*, Rackham identified the importance of starting with the customer's situation: because "the purpose of the sales force is value creation, not value communication."[9]

Another useful tip that comes from the research that Rackham and his colleagues performed is that too often a salesperson stops selling once the order is in. That's a mistake, he says:

> Research shows that it's vitally important to reinforce the rightness of the customer's decision. As a result, top salespeople will often "resell" the product or service once the decision has been made to make sure that the customer feels the decision was a good one. That's excellent psychology. After an order has been signed, the salesperson has nothing immediate to gain from talking with the customer. So the seller is seen as neutral, rather than self-interested. Salespeople who build good long-term customer revenue streams do a lot of this "reselling."

Rackham strongly recommends the approach as a basic step that all salespeople should include in their process.

THE COMMON CORE

The similarity between all of these popular sales methodologies and what Patterson advanced is obvious. I'm not trying to suggest that these more recent approaches don't add anything new. Obviously they do, and I've pointed out a few of the unique ideas or techniques that each of them offers.

That said, each of these methods views the fundamental structure of the sales process, particularly in selling a complex or technical solution to a nontechnical buyer, in very much the same way as Patterson saw it. In fact, some of the tips that appeared in the *Primer* a hundred years ago would fit right in with these more recent books. Here are some of the recommendations, slightly updated into contemporary language, that NCR sales reps received.

Focus on the Customer's Problems

+ After making the approach and establishing the proposition and before doing the demo, prepare a detailed "weakness sheet" that documents where losses could occur in the customer's current system.
+ If appropriate, make a second call to discuss the various details of the "weakness sheet" with the customer to gain buy-in.
+ Never start to demonstrate the product until you have gone over the ground covered in the approach (that is, the customer's problems and goals) with specific details relevant to the customer's business.
+ Using the summary of weaknesses, demonstrate the product, showing how it eliminates those particular weaknesses. Key points to cover during the demonstration phase:
  1. First, remind the decision maker of areas that pose the possibility for loss.
  2. Second, show the actual operation of the machine, and if possible, have the prospect do it, so that she or he can see how that kind of loss becomes impossible.
  3. Third, compare the existing process or system with what you are recommending, reinforcing the comparison with a chart or diagram.
  4. Link each function you demonstrate to solving the merchant's problems.

Customize Your Message

+ Adapt the content of your presentation and your own style in delivering it to suit the prospect.
+ Use visual aids to summarize the arguments made during the approach. For example, illustrate each step in the demo with a chart or diagram, preferably customized to the merchant's business.
+ Make the demonstration environment as much like the merchant's

store as possible. (Patterson even provided his sales reps with curtains that could be hung on the walls of the hotel room where they were giving the demo. The curtains were painted to look like the interior of a drugstore, a grocery store, a saloon, and so on, so that the sales rep could create the right atmosphere by hanging the right curtain.)

✦ Match the demo to the kind of business the merchant typically engages in—single-item cash sales, multiple-item cash sales, charge sales, deliveries, and so forth.

Keep It Simple and Nontechnical

✦ Demo only the functions that have definite application to the prospect's business.

✦ Use simple words. Make your statements short and to the point.

✦ Illustrate your points with simple sketches and diagrams. Words convey different meanings, but pictures convey and impress ideas in the simplest and most convincing way. (Patterson liked to use flip charts himself, but he no doubt would have endorsed slides and computer-generated graphics enthusiastically.)

Stay Focused on the Goal—Making the Sale

✦ Always have a clear purpose or goal that you want to accomplish on each call.

✦ Put yourself in the merchant's place from the very start. Let her know that you don't want to force yourself or your product on her, but are interested in seeing if you can be of help to her.

✦ Give the prospect plenty of opportunity to talk, to tell you what's on his mind. Talking is only a part of salesmanship. Listening and thinking are even more important. Ask questions, acting as if you want to learn from the prospect. Get the customer's story first before you go into yours.

✦ Read the customer's expressions to see if there are questions or concerns that she has not voiced.

✦ Avoid directly disagreeing if the customer raises an objection, but do not put off replying or say that you'll get to it later. Deal with the objection at the time it is raised, but avoid disagreeing outright.

This list of tips is paraphrased from the *Primer,* but you can see how relevant it is today. If any of these tips appeared in classroom materials used to teach PSS, Strategic Selling, Solution Selling, SPIN Selling, or any other process-oriented approach, no one would blink twice. They fit right in.

One final word on the various sales methods that can trace their DNA back to Patterson: In almost every case, the author starts out by ranting about "traditional" sales methods and how they don't work any more. Rackham cites the typical sales training program that focuses on feature/benefit presentations right out of E. K. Strong's 1925 book, *The Psychology of Selling,* plus a lot of tactical training on closing techniques, overcoming objections, and asking open-ended questions. That kind of sales training is "fine for low-value sales [but] the traditional selling methods people were using ceased to work as the sales grew larger."[10] Miller and Heiman write about "future shock selling," and claim as their first premise, "Whatever got you where you are today is no longer sufficient to keep you there."[11] And Bosworth argues that Solution Selling is a new approach, something that transforms selling from what it has been. Even in his recent book, *CustomerCentric Selling,* he compares the method he is advocating with the "traditional" approach of making presentations, focusing on features, talking mainly to users, and just plain talking too much.

The question is, who teaches this so-called traditional method? Where would someone find an advocate of it? Since more than a million salespeople have been trained in just these three methods over the past 20 years, we might suspect that the authors are simply setting up a straw man so that they can knock it down.

Even more to the point, for all their rhetoric, they're still offering a process-based approach to selling, just as John Henry Patterson did more than a century ago. And although they've developed new terms and new tools, in reality they haven't moved all that far beyond what he advocated: Ask questions about the customer's business situation. Address the customer's business problems and tie every aspect of the solution to the customer's business. Demonstrate measurable value.

In the depths of the Great Depression, two of Patterson's disciples looked back on the sales method that NCR had developed under his leadership and saw that it was the most important innovation for encouraging business of the past half century. In fact, they claimed, the ability to create public acceptance and stimulate demand for products that were previously unwanted and unknown "is the one really new and significant development" from that period.

And in that development, the most significant individual influence and personality was unquestionably John H. Patterson's.

> Most of what we recognize as sound, constructive sales promotion stems from Patterson, either directly or through the men whom Patterson trained in fundamentals. In many instances they carried the theory and the practice . . . farther than he did, and modified his methods under specific conditions that he was not obliged to meet. But the basis of all modern selling is to be found in the system . . . that Patterson originated and was the first to apply.[12]

CHAPTER 6

THE PROS AND CONS OF
SALES AS A PROCESS

Process-oriented sales approaches have obviously become pervasive in our society. Companies large and small have invested millions of dollars in training their salespeople in one of the various process-oriented approaches. For companies that are selling a high-tech product or service, for start-ups that are trying to move past the early adopters into the mainstream, and for firms that must involve an entire team in the selling process, the process-based approaches work very well.

We have already mentioned many of their strengths, and there are a lot of them. The most important one is that they work. They produce a lot of closed business. Salespeople who use these methods tend to win more than people who do not, particularly if their company and their solution match the profile just outlined. I want to emphasize this point, because now I'm going to point out some serious weaknesses of relying blindly on a process-oriented methodology.

THE CONS

There are some serious pitfalls in using a structured sales methodology. That doesn't mean you shouldn't do it. But you need to have your eyes wide open. You need to be conscious of what you're doing. Any sales method that runs on autopilot will degenerate pretty quickly into a robotic pantomime of the real thing. In spite of Patterson's dismissing of their complaints, in some cases his salespeople were right. Individuality matters. In sales, it's not just the method. Sometimes it's the man. Or the woman. We'll take a much closer look at the role of personality—rapport, credibility, and trust—in the next section, but no one who has any extensive experience in sales would deny the importance of the personal element. In fact, even the e-commerce web sites that were supposed to replace selling as we know it have found that they are more effective if they create the appearance of personalization.

Here are some other potential weaknesses of the process approach to sales.

They Can Be Too Rigid, Too Dogmatic

One author of a popular process-oriented sales methodology claimed at a conference that if salespeople followed his process correctly, they would never have to write a proposal again. That struck me as a ridiculous claim, and I told him so.

"No, no," he said. "All you have to do is bundle up the letters that finish each stage of the process and hand them to the buyer. They'll give the customer everything he needs to make the decision. You don't need to write a formal proposal or respond to an RFP or any of that nonsense."

"That won't work," I said. "In the first place, an RFP often asks for specific commitments to technical or other requirements that aren't covered in your letters. In the second place, if you don't actually answer the questions in the RFP, you will be tossed out of the bidding process as noncompliant. And in the third place, . . ."

"No, no, not if you do it my way," he insisted. "Salespeople have to write these proposals because they don't sell properly. If they follow my method . . ."

Well, this conversation degenerated pretty quickly, and neither one of us convinced the other, as you might have guessed.

Besides the odd claim that you could ignore one of the buyer's major requirements—responding to an RFP—I thought this particular guru was demonstrating an irrational, dogmatic faith in his own brand of sales religion. If you win, it's because you followed his methods. If you lose, it's because you didn't follow his methods carefully enough.

Similarly, there are times when you can short-circuit the formal process because the customer is ready to buy. Why go through all five or nine or twelve steps of the cycle if the customer says yes after step 3? But oddly enough, people sometimes insist on doing the entire dance. While consulting with AT&T some years ago, I learned that many of the senior account teams were documenting meetings with their customers that had never occurred. Why? Because the sales process being used at that time required a specific sequence of meetings. When salespeople were able to close the business quickly, without going through all the meetings and interim decision points, they found that their sale wouldn't "count" toward their accreditation. So they were fudging the evidence. That's taking a process approach to a ridiculous extreme.

They're Not Universally Applicable

The third point I was going to make in that argument with the sales guru was that federal, state, and local buying guidelines will prohibit the purchase of any goods or services from any vendor if the department or agency involved hasn't gone through the required buying process. Usually, that process is very tightly controlled to assure its fairness and transparency. That means that the kinds of meetings and side agreements and interim decisions that are usually part of one of these sales process approaches simply don't work. They can't. Given the constraints of the Federal Acquisition Requirements, which is the set of regulations that controls how departments and agencies of the U.S. government buy things, if a government employee allowed a salesperson to sell using one of the process-oriented approaches, there's a good chance that one or both of them would end up in jail.

There are other environments in which these approaches don't seem to work very well. For example, high-end consulting, the kind delivered by Accenture, Deloitte, PricewaterhouseCoopers, Bearing Point, and similar firms, is often sold based on relationships established at the top levels of both firms. A similar phenomenon occurs in pharmaceutical sales. And in sales of ongoing professional services, such as accounting, legal representation, corporate banking, HR consulting, and so on, the deal is often based on relationships and a general "feeling" of competence and credibility rather than on defining a specific problem or need. Finally, anyone who sells directly to consumers, even for extremely expensive purchases such as luxury automobiles or real estate, is not likely to find a process-oriented approach very useful.

They Can Get Too Complicated and Overly Analytical

Some years ago, I was working with a committee at one of the world's leading engineering and construction companies. This committee had been commissioned to redesign the sales process for the company. On the committee were a number of engineers and project managers, and, yes, even a couple of salespeople. This was a company that had an international reputation for handling complex construction projects, such as huge oil tanks, pressure vessels, nuclear reactor vessels, distribution terminals for petroleum and liquid natural gas, and so forth.

When I walked into the room for our first meeting, I saw that one wall, about 30 feet long and 10 feet high, was almost completely covered with words, arrows, dotted lines, diamonds, and other symbology. It looked kind of like a computer program, kind of like a mad scientist's formula for converting coal into gold. What it was, unfortunately, was the committee's analysis of the company's sales process. It was so complex, so detailed, so full of options and variations, that I doubted that the committee would ever finish defining it, much less implementing it. Moreover, since my role affected only a tiny portion of the overall plan—which, if I remember correctly, was symbolized by a couple of feedback loops in the lower right-hand corner of the wall—I also suspected that I would never see any actual work from this project. The committee had buried itself in minutiae. It would never be able to finish its task. Explaining the process had become an end in itself.

Sadly, my hunches proved true. I never got the chance to work with these people, they never finished their task, and their company didn't survive. It was suddenly acquired by another firm, broken up, spun off, reconfigured, renamed, and all the other things that happen when companies lose their way.

The process approaches were heavily adopted by high-tech companies during the past decade. One reason is that they work. The other reason, though, is that they offer the appealing opportunity to get lost in the details, something that a highly analytical personality enjoys. For a sales team with a strong technical or analytical bent, it's probably much more fun to fill out forms and draw up maps and flowcharts than it is to go out and actually engage with customers.

There's a real temptation with these process-oriented approaches to sales to keep making them more and more specific. Even Patterson fell prey to this temptation, as I mentioned. By 1904 his beloved *Primer* had ballooned to more than 200 pages total length! But, to his credit, he realized that it had gotten out of control. From Crane's brief, focused presentation to this densely worded tome—it was not the path he wanted the NCR sales process to follow. After 1904, the *Primer* was consistently cut back until by 1910 it was a mere booklet of 56 pages.[1]

Even the most popular and widely accepted sales processes contain elements that are pretty complicated. Target Account Selling was one of the fastest-growing sales-training programs of the past decade.[2] It outlines a seven-step process for sales: Assess the opportunity, set the strategy, identify the key players, align yourself with supporters and decision makers, plan the best way to establish value to the customer, review the plan, and then carry it out. That sounds pretty straightforward and reasonable. But when you get into the details, it tends to get a mite complicated. For example, take just the first three steps:

1. *Assess the opportunity.* This requires answering "four key questions," each of which leads to second-level questions that must be answered. For example, the first question, "Is there an opportunity?" leads to four additional areas of focus, each of which has four questions to answer, for a total of sixteen. Then we move on to the second of the key questions and answer

five more secondary questions. This continues until, just to assess the opportunity, we have answered more than eighty questions about ourselves and a similar number of questions about our major competitors and have filled out a spreadsheet with dozens of cells on it.

2. *Set the competitive strategy.* This involves completing a goals analysis for both ourselves and the prospective customer, then choosing from among five different strategies, each of which has several variations. Oh, yes, and there's another spreadsheet, plus a flow diagram summarizing the strategy portion that identifies a dozen decision points.

3. *Identify the key players.* This is not merely a matter of figuring out names and roles. No, we're now entering the murky waters of politics and power. If you thought assessing the opportunity was tricky, you ain't seen nothing yet. At the end of this stage, you end up with an "influence map" that looks like an aerial view of Tokyo at rush hour.

And so on. Even if you spread this out over several days, the typical salesperson very quickly goes into overload. There's just too much to think about, too much stuff to enter into too many boxes. It's a great system. It's smart, and it's thorough. But how many sales teams actually fill out every form and complete every step of a process this complex? How many have enough information or time to do it, even if they think it's worth the effort? But, of course, that's the other big problem: Is it worth it?

I fully expect to get nasty letters from various sales gurus telling me the error of my ways. But having participated in numerous sales campaigns in hundreds of companies, I can only tell you what I've seen. People just don't do this stuff. Salespeople have a very pragmatic approach to their profession: If something gets them closer to closing the deal, they'll do it. Otherwise, they blow it off.

For example, I interviewed one woman, vice president of sales for a major software firm, who had taught her sales force the process of filling out the Blue Sheet required as part of the Miller-Heiman Strategic Selling process. But even as she demonstrated how to do it, she knew that her sales team would never use it. And she knew that she wouldn't require them to. It was too time-consuming, too complicated, and, in her opinion, it didn't offer enough of a payback to the salesperson who put all the time and energy necessary into it. So why did she bother? Because (1) the company had invested a lot of money in training everybody in the methodology, (2) it was an opportunity to remind the salespeople of some of the issues and players they might encounter in a complex sale, and (3) she was completing a personal MBO worth a few thousand dollars. Good enough reasons, I suppose, even if the practical impact of learning how to fill out the Blue Sheet was negligible.

Seeing sales as a process makes perfect sense. So does keeping it simple.

They're Reductive

Every sales problem must be a nail, because our method is a hammer. If you lose, it must be the salesperson's fault. Somehow you didn't do the process right. You didn't ask the right questions during the investigation phase. No, wait, that was the old method. I guess you didn't build the customer's vision-in-process in a way that forced him to agree.

Patterson himself took the same angle, telling his sales agents:

> It is your fault if you fail to close the sale after explaining the register. Don't say "What is the matter with our register?" or "What is the matter with the merchant?" Find out what is the matter with you. Recall what you said and consider what you ought to have said. Did you antagonize him at the start by contradicting him? Did you give him a chance to tell his story first? Did you fail to answer questions fairly and clearly? Did you talk too much? Did you prove conclusively the claims you made in your approach?[3]

Considering how much resistance within his sales force Paterson had to battle, we can perhaps understand his truculence here. Stop complaining about the products, the customers, or the sales methods, he was saying. Start looking honestly at yourself. Fair enough. But sometimes even the best system doesn't produce great results if the salesperson is not well matched to the customer base. A brash, abrasive personality might work just fine with some accounts, but turn off many others, even though the sales system is being followed word for word. And I hate to mention it, but sometimes a company doesn't offer a competitive product or service, which means that it's darn hard to sell, even with the greatest of approaches.

They're Rigid

Sales is knowledge work. Successful salespeople know a lot and are able to use what they know in practical ways. Oh, they might not do very well on *Jeopardy*, and their SAT scores might not stand out. But they have a kind of fluid intelligence that enables them to grasp what really matters in a particular business situation, link that up with what they have to offer, and articulate it in ways that make sense to the customer.

Peter Drucker has pointed out the big difference between knowledge workers and the manual workers who were the object of Taylor's management philosophy: The knowledge worker almost never has a completely repeatable or prefigured work routine. Knowledge workers are constantly making it up as they go along, figuring out how to handle what circumstances and fate happen to throw their way. Most of the time, a knowledge worker—and this is particularly true for the salesperson—has to configure a response to a given situation. As a result, Drucker claims, knowledge workers can't be supervised or controlled, at least not in the conventional sense that Taylor had in mind. And they are ultimately the only ones who can make their work more productive.

The more detailed and rigid a work system becomes, when applied to true knowledge work, the more likely it is to produce conflict, exceptions, and even deception. To get the job done, to be productive, the salesperson will deviate from a process that isn't working at this particular moment in this particular set of circumstances. In fact, failing to do so would probably jeopardize the deal.

At some level, Patterson may have recognized that. He drilled his sales agents over and over, forcing them to memorize the words in the *Primer* and to deliver them word for word. But he seemed to believe that he was preparing them to function flexibly within the boundaries of an effective message. Like jazz musicians who have spent years practicing the scales, his sales agents were able to improvise successfully around the basic chord structure of the NCR sales message when they needed to. Patterson saw the NCR system of selling as fundamentally a system of thinking, one that was "as old as Aristotle," but that depended for its success on adherence to specific rules of presentation. As he commented once, "Remember, it is not what you say that sells him; it is how you say it and what he understands and believes." Achieving a sufficient level of understanding and belief might, at times, require some flexibility on the part of the salesperson.

Unfortunately, in some companies that have adopted process methodologies, the focus is on compliance. One reason for that is clear: The books and courses that teach the methods are based on "empirical" observation of "master performers"—superstar salespeople, "Eagles," high flyers, whatever you call them. These are today's equivalents of Joseph Crane. But in today's work environment, simply enforcing compliance with the patterns that supposedly represent the master performer is not likely to produce the most effective sales force. When faced with a new question, a new kind of opportunity, a new form of competition, salespeople who simply comply with the pattern may lack the creativity and flexibility to modify the way they sell in order to achieve the ultimate goal: winning the business.

They Lead to a Checklist Mentality

Sometimes the process approaches undervalue the qualitative components in selling—especially the value of strong, personal relationships. People who are involved in a highly structured sales process—both the customer and the salesperson—may feel used, rushed, or herded. The methods tend to focus on completing steps, rather than on confirming understanding and agreement. As a result, the salesperson may acquire a "checklist mentality": First, did you ask the 12 needs analysis questions? Check! Then, did you demonstrate capability? Check! Next, did you define value and payback parameters? Check! Did you submit the proposal? Check!

We all know that merely going through the motions, even the motions of a really excellent process, will eventually backfire on you. In my own experience, the worst sales proposals I have ever seen were produced by sales forces that were trained in one of the process approaches. Why? Because they saw the proposal as just one more element in the sequence of events. What it said and how it said it didn't matter. All that mattered was that it was submitted. Move on to the next step in the process.

Of course, what happened when a salesperson submitted that generic, error-ridden proposal was that the whole process came to a skidding halt. The customer would look up from going through the document and ask a fatal question: "Do we really want to work with people who put out something that looks like this?"

They Treat Customers as Clones

Most of the sales process approaches assume that all buyers are alike in at least one important respect: They're all value buyers. If the sales process is followed so that the account executive is able to demonstrate superior value or a quicker payback or a larger return on investment, the customer will buy.

However, the fact is that some customers don't buy value. They buy price. Research done by Dr. Reed Holden has identified four kinds of buyers in business settings.[4] The first, which constitutes a disturbingly large group, will buy strictly on price. No matter what you say, buyers in this group regard you and your competitors as being all the same. You cannot differentiate yourself on value, because there are no differences, according to these buyers. As a result, what you are offering—whether it be a product or a service—is a commodity, in their view. And they just want to get it as cheaply as they can.

A second group of buyers does think about total value. People in this group recognize that acquisition cost is only one element in the formula of total cost. Transition and replacement costs, maintenance and support, and all kinds of other factors, including potential impact on the business, may tilt the value equation in one direction or another.

A third group of buyers actually wants your advice. These buyers seek to do business with you not only because they need the goods and services you can provide, but also because they want your insight, your experience, your guidance. For these buyers, the buying decision is based on which vendor is most likely to work with them long-term as a strategic partner.

Buyers in the fourth group, according to Holden, really want superior value or even a strategic relationship, but they act like they want only price. He calls them "poker players" and suggests that they keep their true motives hidden because they worry that showing them may be seen as a sign of weakness, resulting in higher prices than they otherwise would get.

This taxonomy of buying behavior makes a lot of sense. It also suggests that some of the single-minded focus you see on uncovering the customer's problem and then quantifying the value of your solution may, in fact, be missing the point. That's not a reason to abandon a process-oriented approach to selling, but it does suggest that we may need more flexibility in our processes—different processes to suit different kinds of buyers.

THE PROS

Well, we've just covered a lot of weaknesses that are inherent in process-oriented sales methods. But lest you get the notion that they're not worth learning or using, let me reiterate the most important positive fact about them.

They work.

Patterson proved it, and hundreds of companies since then have proved it, too. The weaknesses I've described are real enough, but they undercut the effectiveness of a process approach only if sales management loses its focus on the ultimate goal. Running the perfect process is not what matters. Winning business is.

Besides the fact that they produce good results, there are at least half a dozen other advantages to learning and using a process-oriented sales methodology.

They Provide Consistency

By putting a specific sales process in place, teaching it to the sales force, and enforcing its use through management reviews, tools, and group pressure, a company gains consistency. This was one of the goals that Patterson had in mind from the start. He wanted each NCR sales agent to represent the company and its products in a consistently professional manner. He wanted each one to be well-spoken, neatly groomed, polite, and informed. Repetition of the same sales messages, stated in the same way, would add to the effects of advertising and trade shows in creating an impression of NCR and its products throughout the market.

Beyond that, however, he wanted all the sales agents to be as successful as they could be, and using the process was a way to achieve higher performance across the field. In other words, the theory was that the standard bell curve of performance, from superstars on the right to duds on the left, would shift a couple of notches to the right. The great would become even better, but, perhaps more importantly, the poor would become competent—and the general level of success for the entire organization would go up.

Well, that's a good theory, but is it true? Does consistency matter to win ratios? According to every sales-training organization out there, if you turn your sales force over to that organization's care and feeding, wonderful things will happen. Unfortunately, objective evidence supporting these claims is a bit thin, and we're probably not being too cynical if we look at them skeptically.

The closest thing I've found to objective verification of the impact on win ratios of applying a consistent methodology to the sales process comes from a subcategory of that process—writing the sales proposal. The Association of Proposal Management Professionals, a professional organization, undertook a survey of companies that had standardized on a consistent way of developing the sales proposal, drawn from the leading consulting firms in the field. (In the interests of full reporting, I should mention that the methodology that my company recommends and that is outlined in my book *Persuasive Business Proposals* was one of them, along with approaches recommended by Shipley Associates and SM&A, among others.)

What did they find? They found that win ratios went up in every company that implemented a standard methodology—*regardless of the methodology*. In other words, consistency for its own sake has a beneficial impact on results. Although it may be dangerous to extrapolate from this bit of evidence to the entire process of selling, the data is suggestive. Our common sense tells us that if an organization is unified around a standard way of working and shares a vocabulary to describe, manage, and measure that work, the organization is likely to work more efficiently. That alone can have a small but positive impact on success, since it has eliminated some of the waste that comes from miscommunication. But in the "major sales," as Rackham describes them, or the "complex sales," to use Miller and Heiman's term, where several people must collaborate on moving the deal forward, a consistent methodology brings unity to the team, keeps it focused on shared goals, and provides both tactics and strategies to keep the deal on target.

They Provide Repeatability

Any system that standardizes work processes is inherently repeatable. What has produced success in one context can be repeated in another. Sales managers like repeatability, because it reduces the range of disparate behavior and information that they need to watch. Salespeople like repeatability because it helps them gain mastery of their jobs faster.

Repeatability pays off for the salesperson who is facing a new opportunity. By looking at the mass of information gathered about the client, the decision maker, the situation, and so on, the sales rep can make sense out of it by fitting it into the template established by the sales method being used. Recognizing patterns helps the salesperson discern what matters and what doesn't in a deal. Practice in handling certain kinds of situations—asking questions of a senior executive that probe for needs or problems, for example—makes it easier to actually execute when that situation comes up.

If you follow golf, you are probably well aware that Tiger Woods has rebuilt his golf swing, not once but twice. Why would the greatest golfer in the world go through the trouble and frustration of changing the way he swings the club? Because, as he explained, he wanted his swing to be "repeatable." Under the pressure of a major tournament, he needed a process that he could rely on no matter what. The same kind of value comes from having a clearly defined, repeatable sales process. When the pressure is on, the sales team will perform.

There Is Less Wasted Effort

Have you ever worked for days or weeks or months on a sales opportunity, only to learn late in the game that the prospect doesn't have the budget approved? Most of us have. What a waste! Have you ever spent hours preparing a presentation for a prospect, only to receive a call canceling the meeting because another department had suddenly gone ahead and made the acquisition with a different vendor? Another waste! What about going all the way through the sales cycle, submitting a proposal, and then learning that you lost the deal because the proposal addressed the wrong criteria?

These types of wasted effort can be reduced if the sales process is broken down into specific steps, each of which has a gate. Early in the cycle, qualifying the opportunity should include determining whether budgetary funds are available to pay for your recommendation. If that fact is not reliably confirmed, the salesperson should stop the process to avoid wasting hours of effort with a client who can't actually buy. By the same token, gaining access to all interested parties and negotiating for the opportunity to present your recommendations to them is an important step in most of the modern sales processes—a way of minimizing the chance of getting blindsided when some other part of the client's organization rears its head and takes control.

Breaking down a complex task into steps is only part of managing sales as a process. The other part is to prepare a checklist of those steps and determine what bits of information or behavior constitute a go/no-go decision at that point. By putting "gates" in place that require the salesperson and sales manager to decide whether or not it makes sense to continue pursuing a given opportunity, an organization can eliminate a lot of the wasted time and resources that come from overly optimistic assessments of the chances of winning, vague expressions of interest and commitment from prospects that really don't mean anything, or self-deluding behavior that sometimes occurs under the pressure of making the numbers.

They Allow More Accurate Forecasting

The use of "decision gates" also applies to forecasting. One of the most frustrating tasks any sales rep or sales manager has to complete is predicting which deals are likely to close and when. And since sales forecasts are used in making important business decisions, including those involving production, hiring, and revenue projections, it's vitally important to the organization to get them right.

Patterson found to his cost that salespeople tend to inflate the numbers when they are allowed to forecast their own pipeline. At first, he simply asked each sales agent how many registers he expected to sell in the coming year. Their estimates were always rosy, and in 1888 that system finally blew up on him when the sales force projected that it would sell 30 registers a day. To meet that level of demand, Patterson expanded factory capacity and hired new carpenters and machinists to handle the volume. Unfortunately, the sales force managed to sell only about 17 a day. Patterson had to close part of the factory and lay off workers, but NCR still had excess inventory, so the company had to slash prices to move the product out. Patterson learned a bitter lesson about sales forecasts from this experience. Afterwards he took a more expedient approach. Rather than asking the sales force how many they would sell, he told them. He set a quota. And then he measured their progress weekly, monthly, and quarterly toward achieving that quota.

One of the tools that process approaches frequently use to define the pipeline is the "sales funnel." A huge volume of leads enters the top of the funnel. These are winnowed down to a smaller set of opportunities, and these opportunities are further reduced as they pass through each gate of the sales process, until at the end a number of closed deals drip from the nozzle of the funnel. By tracking all deals that move through the funnel, an organization can determine the probability that a deal at each stage will actually result in closed business. For example, by tracking activity and results over several quarters, a sales manager may know that of all the leads the company generates from trade shows, cold calling, the web site, direct mail, and so on, 7 percent result in closed business. Of the leads that move through the sales process to reach the point of a product demo, 30 percent result in a sale. What this produces is a more accurate and defensible approach to forecasting.

That also helps me as an individual sales rep. If I know that my average deal size is $75,000, and my quota is $1.5 million, simple arithmetic tells me that I have to close 20 average-sized deals this year. Calculating backward, I then know how many proposals I have to write, how many demos I have to give, how many first presentations I need to schedule, and so on, in order to make my goal.

They Are Easier to Learn

Any complex activity is easier to learn if you can break it down into a sequence of steps. Learning to sell can be a daunting challenge for someone with no prior experience in the field. By showing new salespeople how to sell, one step at a time, and giving them a safe environment in which to practice the skills associated with that step, an organization prepares the sales team to be effective. This was Taylor's point about the factory: Break a process down into its component steps, define the requirements for each of the steps, then train the workers how to perform those steps.

Process-oriented approaches to sales have another advantage when it comes to training the sales force. Typically, the description of the process includes all three of the components necessary for learning a new skill: antecedents, behaviors, and consequences. In the process approach, we identify specific events or actions or commitments that must occur—the antecedents, as they are called in psychology—that tell us that it's time to perform a particular kind of behavior or action. And we also know with a high degree of probability what the likely consequences are of performing that action.

For example, we may know that once the prospect has signed our nondisclosure agreement and arranged for the vice president of finance to attend a meeting with us, our next step is to prepare detailed pricing. The consequence of this action will be approval of our solution design and preliminary pricing or a request to modify it. Or we may know that if we have never met face to face with a prospect, we should not bother responding to a formal request for proposal, because the necessary antecedents to scoring well on the proposal review are not in place. The consequence should be that we decide to "no bid" the opportunity.

They Are Easier to Manage

Sales processes, by definition, are outcome-oriented. They involve clearly defined steps. Each step is supposed to yield a specific bit of information, an interim decision by the customer, or access to an important member of the decision team. For a sales manager, it's fairly easy to tell whether the steps are being completed, based on whether or not the information, decisions, or access are forthcoming. And it's pretty obvious when salespeople are spinning their wheels, because they are not moving to the next stage of the process.

CHAPTER 7

MAKING IT WORK FOR YOU

The important point to remember is that in spite of those negative things I said about process-oriented approaches to selling, they work. So how can you make them work for you?

If you're an individual salesperson, how can you incorporate the principles that underlie the process approach into your own activities to make those activities more consistent, more efficient, and more effective?

If you're a sales manager, how can you make sure that your company's investment in a particular sales methodology actually pays off? What parts of the process approach are most important to your team's success? How can you reinforce those elements?

First, you need to establish your own process steps. It's possible, if you're a sales rep, that your company has already defined them. Patterson had four steps; PSS has seven. Going a bit further, we can say that typical steps in the sales process include:

1. Prospecting
2. Research and preparation
3. Qualifying
4. Initial presentation (what Patterson called the approach)
5. Analysis of value and payback, key performance indicators, or other buying criteria
6. Solution definition
7. Negotiation
8. Closing
9. Follow-up

The process you follow may not include all of these steps, naturally. And some of the steps may be further refined—perhaps the solution definition requires several steps in your environment. But these are fairly typical of the various phases of the process approach. Let's take a look at a few ways you can improve your own performance in a couple of these areas.

QUALIFYING LEADS

For your own sanity and efficiency, you need to screen out the nonstarters quickly to avoid wasting time. Poor qualification leads to more wasted effort in sales than almost any other problem. Here are a few questions to ask your prospective buyer. You should customize these questions to your business or product, and put them on a laminated card in your wallet.

Before you do any qualifying, do your homework. Know your client. Review their web site, read their annual reports, read their product brochures and company history before you talk to anyone in the company. Before asking your qualifying questions, draw on your preparation and research to talk about the client's business. Have three prepared questions based on what you learned from their brochures and web site. For example:

> *"I see you are focusing on selling large business shredders this year. Is that your primary sales focus?"*
> *"Do you typically compete against the large-scale document storage companies, or are they going after a different market?"*
> *"Has the growth of digital documents affected the volume of paper that needs to be shredded?"*

Ask Your Qualifying Questions

+ Who in the prospect's organization is experiencing a problem that could be solved by using your product or service? Is this problem significant to these people? Besides the people who are directly dealing with the problem, who will gain from eliminating that problem or meeting that need? In what ways?

+ What are the consequences if the organization doesn't solve the problem, close the gap in capabilities, or meet the need?

+ How is the organization handling this issue or problem now? (To build rapport and credibility, you can share a success story of a client who had similar concerns and overcame them through the use of your product or service.)

+ What is the biggest complaint or concern about the product or service the organization is using now?

+ How does the organization calculate ROI on an investment? How does it recognize and publicize a good decision? Who determines what a good investment is?

+ What does management want to gain from improving a process or from buying your product?

- Ask for the operating numbers or statistics. How many? How often? At what cost? In which locations? Numerical results? Statistical findings? You're looking for information indicating what kind of baseline the organization has now (so that you can prove that your solution has improved the situation) and what the key performance indicators are (so that you know where to focus your value proposition).
- What alternatives is the organization considering? Has anyone in the organization seen a competitor's demonstration or product?
- Are any other employees or departments affected by this decision?
- How does the organization make decisions? What criteria are used? What are the steps? Approvals? Time frame?
- Where is the money for the purchase coming from? Whose budget? When will the money be available? Who approves the purchase, and who signs the check?
- Explain your sales cycle so that the person you are talking to knows what to expect. For example:

> *"Here at CCS we have a pre-meeting to understand your problems, then we set up a first presentation and ask that your decision maker be present, then if we are in agreement, we prepare a proposal . . ."*

- Ask for any information you couldn't find on the organization's web site so that you can review it prior to your presentation.

YOUR APPROACH

Now that you have thoroughly qualified your client, have gained an understanding of their business, and have helped the client understand your sales process, it is time to match up what you have with what your client needs. There are a few simple approaches to get you closer to a mutual agreement to proceed.

- Review what you learned about the client and their business. Make comments and ask questions that demonstrate your understanding of their business. Your goals are to build credibility and ferret out concerns. For example:

> *"I see you have increased sales in the document storage division. My client in Oregon is seeing the same type of increase. Do you think that is related to the Sarbanes-Oxley legislation?"*
> *"According to your 10-K, you are experiencing lower than usual sales in your high-tech division. I have some ideas on how my product or service will help you regain those sales and increase profits."*

+ Validate that you have the client's concerns or issues correct. At the beginning of your meeting, list the problems that the client is trying to solve on a white board or flip chart. During your presentation, whenever your product or service solves one of those problems, point to it and jot it next to the problem. At the end of your presentation, summarize by reviewing the client's concerns and the specific ways in which your solution fits.

+ Use case studies and testimonials during your interaction with the client. Be accurate with the names, places, and statistics. If someone cannot be used as a reference, don't tell the story.

> *"Blue Inc. experienced a similar rapid decline in sales during the summer months. They used our cold calling service to increase sales during June, July, and August by 21 percent over the previous year. What is your goal?"*

+ Demonstrate the potential for a significant return on investment or payback. Ask how the client will measure the impact. What are the key goals or objectives a solution must deliver? Does the client have data on current performance? Whenever possible, ask why a given metric is significant. For example:

> *"You indicated that the key goal is to improve data processing speeds to 1.5 million items a month. What will that mean for the company? Does that translate into increased profit, or does it enable you to go after larger clients? Why is that number significant?"*

+ Always take control of the next step. At the end of the meeting you might say,

> *"We at CMS usually prepare a formal proposal with pricing and long-term benefits. Are you ready to proceed with your decision and take a look at our proposal? In our experience, we have found that having a 30-minute summary meeting before generating the proposal ensures that you get what you want. When can we schedule that meeting?"*

+ Never ask, "So how do we proceed from here?" Instead, offer a next step that gets the client closer to a decision. The client will tell you if they have a specific way of doing things, and you can adjust your sales cycle to follow those rules.

CLOSING

In spite of a lot of nonsense that has been written over the years, there is actually only one closing technique: *Ask for the order.* Everything else is manipulation. If you're trying to sell in a consultative and ethical way, manipulation is ugly and unnecessary. The prospect will appreciate your directness in asking for the order if you have satisfied his needs during the sales cycle.

When getting ready to ask for the business, remind yourself of this fact: *"The prospect has a problem, and we have a solution. The prospect has some money, and we would like to get it. This is a marriage of equals, one where we both get something of value."*

Check for buying signs throughout the sales cycle, but don't ignore the fact that you *must* ask for the business. As Patterson said, it's your own fault if you don't close the sale. And you won't close it if you don't ask for it.

Are you looking for some creative or comfortable ways to ask? Try these:

"Mary, do you see any reason not to proceed with CMS?"
"Bill, can we count on your support to take our proposal through the approval process?"
"Kathy, have we satisfied your requirements, and if so, can we go forward with the contract?"
"With your permission, may I contact the procurement office/attorney and proceed with the order?"
"Jane, will you recommend CMS to the buying committee?"
"Beth, you said the next step is to take this to the monthly board meeting for approval. May I help you to write the recommendation?"

In summary, take an objective look at your sales process. If it's not explicitly defined, go ahead and identify the typical steps that must occur for you to close business. Once you have a firm grasp of the steps of the process, whether there are three or seven or nine or some other number, identify what you must accomplish in each step in order to move to the next one. How do you know when this step has been completed? What do you have to do or say or prove to get there? Are there any of the steps where you feel particularly weak—for example, doing a product demo or writing the executive summary for a proposal? Identify training or resources that can help you improve your execution in those steps.

For some people, thinking about sales as a project to be managed or a process to be executed is not a natural way to view the job. That was true for many of Patterson's sales reps, and it's no different today. But if you have that feeling of resistance, it's worth overcoming. Knowing your process and following it will make your job as a sales professional easier and will enable you to work more efficiently and effectively. You'll close more deals faster if you know what it takes to get to a close.

Learn your process, use it, and respect it. In return, the process will make you more successful than you could ever be without it.

PART THREE

DALE CARNEGIE

THE APOSTLE OF INFLUENCE

CHAPTER 8

THE YOUNG MAN FROM MISSOURI

For somebody who has had such tremendous influence on the history of selling, Dale Carnegie wasn't much of a salesman.

Originally the name was Carnagey, not Carnegie. Dale changed it many years later, when he had a small office in Carnegie Hall. Changing his name was an example of something that he struggled with all his life—trying to be "good enough," to be recognized.

Dale Carnegie was born in 1888 in a small farmhouse in Missouri and was raised on hog farms in rural Missouri. His father struggled to make a go of it as a farmer, suffering from a combination of bad luck—his hogs got cholera and the herd was wiped out; the farm was flooded more than once—and poor judgment. In spite of the family's financial troubles, however, young Dale did have the opportunity to go to college. In 1904, his family moved to a farm near Warrensburg, Missouri, so that he could attend the state teachers college nearby. Too poor to live on campus, Carnegie rode a horse to school each day after doing his chores around the farm. Dressed in shabby, ill-fitting clothing, with pants that were too short and a coat that swallowed him up, beset by insecurities and worries, Dale felt that the other students looked down on him. So he sought recognition by becoming a champion debater.

In those days, being a successful debater was right up there with being a varsity athlete. It was a way to distinguish yourself, to burnish your résumé, maybe even to attract girls. Carnegie saw that the winners "were regarded as the intellectual leaders in college."[1] The public speaking contests and debate competitions drew crowds from the town as well as the college community. This, Carnegie thought, was his opportunity.

Becoming a collegiate debate champion was not easy, of course. First you had to join the debate club and win the internal contests. Then you became eligible to compete for the college.

His first year at Missouri State Teachers College, Dale Carnegie entered a dozen competitions. He lost every time.

Twelve straight losses would take it out of most people. They might start eyeing the chess club or the Future Farmers group as a way to fit in. Carnegie himself later admitted that he felt beaten and depressed. Yet he was stubborn enough to try again. So he practiced every night, over and over, reciting passages from Abraham Lincoln and Richard Harding Davis, a popular journalist who had been a war correspondent and later became the managing editor of *Harper's Weekly*. Whether it was the choice of authors or the constant practice, Carnegie's performances improved, and a year later he won the schoolwide public speaking contest by delivering Davis's "The Boy Orator of Zapata" and Lincoln's "Gettysburg Address."

But there was more. Carnegie also won the debating contest, securing a rare double victory.

He had made himself into a big man on campus. Other students—including a lot of girls—sought him out to coach them in public speaking. During his last year in school, he won the debating contest again, a boy he had tutored won the public speaking contest, and a girl he had trained won the declamatory contest.

Dale Carnegie sure could talk!

But what could he do for a living?

He had absolutely no intention of being a hardscrabble farmer like his dad. He had no interest in being a schoolteacher. And he wasn't able to go on to higher education, because he flunked Latin his senior year and never got his college degree. So what could he do?

He decided to become a salesman.

One of his friends at school, a young man named Frank Self, had spent his summer selling courses for the International Correspondence Schools, making a whopping $20 a week plus expenses. Although it doesn't sound like much to us, $20 was more than Carnegie's father made from a whole month's work on the farm.[2]

It was 1908, the economy was booming, and everybody in America was seized with the gospel of self-improvement. What could be easier than selling correspondence courses to a willing and eager public?

Unfortunately for young Dale, a lot of things would have been easier. Carnegie applied for a job at the International Correspondence Schools' branch office in Denver, where he was hired immediately. But it turned out that Carnegie just wasn't cut out for the kind of selling he had to do for the company. He knocked on the doors, he made the stops, he traveled by train and buggy all over his territory, which consisted of rural Nebraska, but he couldn't get anyone to buy a course. The only sale he made was to a telephone lineman who was up a pole, stringing wire. Carnegie stood at the bottom of the pole and harangued the poor man until he finally agreed to sign up for a course in electrical engineering.[3]

It wasn't enough, and Carnegie couldn't live on his expense checks. He needed to make a change. From a veteran sales rep for the National Biscuit Company, Carnegie got a piece of decent advice: Sell something that people always need. The veteran sold crackers and cookies. People always needed food, so there was a steady demand for his products, even when times were tough. Plus, he was selling to store owners, who understood the value of what he offered. They were his friends; they looked forward to seeing him each week when he made his rounds. It was a comfortable, gentle way to sell. He walked into their stores, shared a cup of coffee, looked at the shelves and the inventory to see what they needed, wrote up the order, and swapped some gossip.

This sounded good to Carnegie. It certainly sounded more promising than trying to find another lineman up a pole to badger into signing up for a correspondence course. Since he had grown up on a hog farm, and since his father had occasionally tried to raise beef cattle, Carnegie knew just where to apply. He headed for Armour and Company in Omaha.

Armour hired him immediately and put him through a month-long training program. His sales territory was the Dakotas, and Armour paid him $17.31 a week—a sum so large that his father wondered how Armour and Company could possibly keep it up![4] Carnegie was optimistic, though. He felt much more confident about selling tinned meat than canned curriculum to the residents of the Dakota Territory.

The Dakotas were still the Wild West, and you had to be ready to wheel and deal to make a go of it there. Carnegie thrived in his new job and soon fell into the routine of traveling through his territory by train, stagecoach, and horseback, stopping at the local dry goods store, talking to the owner about crops and weather and local doings. Carnegie was good at the small talk, and he was skilled at making a pitch for Armour's line of fresh meats, cured bacon, canned meats, lard, and soap. He could relate to these rural people. He understood the hardships and risks of farming. He had slopped hogs for most of his life. Dale Carnegie was the real deal, and the merchants knew it. They trusted him. Sometimes, when they didn't have the cash to pay for his merchandise, they would barter with him, giving him merchandise that he would then turn around and sell somewhere else in order to make the money to cover what his customer owed to Armour.

Carnegie did well as a sales rep for Armour. He eventually became the top salesman in his territory, and his managers approached him about a promotion.

To their surprise, he said no. He didn't want a promotion. In fact, Carnegie quit.

THE BRIGHT LIGHTS OF BROADWAY

Carnegie had gotten the notion into his head that what he was really destined for was greatness in New York as an actor. Taking the money he had made selling for Armour, he quit his job, headed east, and enrolled in the American Academy of Dramatic Arts.

This was no seedy, back-alley operation. It was the most prestigious school of acting in the country. And getting in wasn't easy. Carnegie had to audition and be accepted by the school's faculty. Some of the students who were already enrolled when he arrived went on to become famous actors on Broadway and in films. Perhaps the best known was Edward G. Robinson, and later graduates include such luminaries as Robert Redford, Lauren Bacall, Jason Robards, Kirk Douglas, and dozens more. Graduates of the AADA have been nominated for more than 70 Oscars and 200 Emmys, so clearly this is the big leagues of acting.

Dale was admitted, and he loved the classes. He worked hard to learn the craft of acting. He dove into the challenge of learning to act in a spontaneous, natural way. The credo at the Academy was that actors should be believable—they should perform in such a convincing, natural way that the audience would believe not that they were playing a role, not that they were feigning an emotion, but that they *were* the character on the stage and that they really felt the emotion being portrayed. Gone were the mannerisms and gestures of old-fashioned acting, the stentorian speechifying, the exaggerated facial expressions. At the AADA, actors were expected to create a convincing image of reality, to achieve a "truth" in performance that touched the audience emotionally.

After graduation, Carnegie managed to get hired for the road company of a goofy musical about life in a circus. He had bit parts as a clown, a carnie barker, and a doctor. It wasn't Shakespeare, but it was a start. Like the rest of the actors, he made next to nothing, lived in crummy boarding houses, had to help strike the sets and haul the props around, and traveled all night in cheap, hard seats on dirty trains from one town to another. For a young man in his early twenties, it was probably a blast, but it wasn't easy. And it wasn't as glamorous as Carnegie had thought it would be.

What was worse, it didn't last. After the tour ended, Carnegie couldn't find work as an actor anywhere. So . . . he went back to selling.

Carnegie wanted to stay in New York, so he took a job as a car salesman for the Packard automobile company. Packards were luxury automobiles, which meant that Carnegie was selling to the high end of the market. He found that he hated it. He wasn't the least bit interested in the cars, and he knew virtually nothing about them. Standing around a showroom all day was boring, and it made his feet ache. He was living in a cheap tenement room, sharing his cramped quarters with a bumper crop of cockroaches. He was eating poorly, he had no friends, and once again he was failing. He became so despondent that he actually considered suicide.

Somehow he got it into his mind that he could achieve his dreams of success and fame by becoming a novelist. But he needed the time to write. His job selling Packards—or, more accurately, going through the motions of selling Packards—was too time-consuming and tiring to allow him to write. By the time he got home from the dealership each night, he was exhausted. What he needed was a decent-paying job that he could do in the evening, leaving his days free for writing the Great American Novel.

What Carnegie decided to do was to return to his moment of greatest glory: public speaking. He would offer to teach an evening class in public speaking for Columbia University or NYU, which would make him enough to live comfortably while he worked on his novel. It was perfect! He was a champion debater and public speaker, a trained professional actor, an experienced salesman. Who could be better qualified? Impulsive as ever, Carnegie quit his job at Packard and applied for a job teaching a night school course at Columbia.

Unfortunately, Columbia wasn't interested.

Fine. Columbia wasn't the only university in Manhattan. He'd take his offer elsewhere. Carnegie marched over to New York University and made the same application. No deal.

Why weren't they willing to hire him? Well, first of all, he sounded like a hick with his thick Missouri accent. He had never finished college. Acting? You must be kidding! And as for his experience as a salesperson—well, that was just one more reason to look down their collective academic noses at him, wasn't it?

Now what?

Just up the road from the Columbia University campus was the 125th Street YMCA in Harlem. It offered a few courses in an evening school that it ran, primarily designed to help working-class men and women get ahead. Of course, its little night school didn't have the prestige of Columbia. In fact, it didn't even have the prestige of the Missouri State Teachers College in Warrensburg. But it did have a program. And it might be willing to give him a chance.

The director of the YMCA program demanded that Carnegie audition for him to prove that he had enough public speaking skill himself to teach others. Carnegie leapt over that hurdle with ease.

The next obstacle was a little trickier, though. Carnegie wanted the standard salary for a night school instructor—$2 a class. The director shook his head. He wasn't sure that anybody would sign up for a class in public speaking. The YMCA had never done a course like that before.

"So I said," Carnegie later remembered, "'I will work on a profit-sharing basis.'"

Carnegie had let his self-confidence and impulsiveness get ahead of his better judgment. But now that he had made the offer, he couldn't take it back. The director agreed—they would share the profits.

Some three years later, Carnegie was making $30 a night in commissions. His class had become a huge success. He was on his way.

CHAPTER 9

THE CARNEGIE PRINCIPLES

*"Have complete course on 'How to Become a
Success,' will swap for room rent."*
—Classified ad in the *Cincinnati Enquirer,* 1933

When Dale Carnegie faced his first class at the Harlem YMCA, he experienced a brief moment of panic. These were not college students sitting in front of him. They were hard-headed, battle-weary businesspeople. They were clerks and shopkeepers from Manhattan and Brooklyn. They were blue-collar workers who wanted to get ahead. They were sales reps who needed to do better in their jobs, or else they were going to be fired.

All of a sudden, Carnegie's original plan to teach them the principles of elocution and declamation seemed pretty inadequate to their needs.

He began to talk, giving them an overview of public speaking and the skills necessary to be successful at it. They began to squirm in their seats. Pretty soon Carnegie ran out of prepared remarks. The faces before him looked blank.

"All right," he said after a moment of uncomfortable silence. He nodded to a man in the back row. "Give us a brief talk."

The man was startled. A talk!? About what? How?

Carnegie's advice was: Just stand up and talk. Talk about something you care about. Talk about yourself. Tell us something about your life, your career.

Almost out of desperation, Carnegie had reinvented the way public speaking was taught. Instead of lectures to demonstrate principles, he believed in action. Get up and talk. Overcome your fear. If you don't try it, you can't improve it.

Even though many of his students found this intimidating, they also found that it worked. In fact, they loved it. And it sent their self-confidence zooming.

Over the next quarter of a century, Carnegie taught his course, refined his methods, and learned from his students. Because he had a profit-sharing arrangement with the Y, he had to succeed. He had unwittingly made himself into an entrepreneur, and it was in his own best interests to make the course better and better, to increase enrollments, to get students to spread the word about how successful it was.

He came to believe that there were some fundamental issues that he needed to address in his class, and none of them had to do with enunciation or gesturing. First, he needed to provide a safe environment where people could overcome their fear. Everybody wanted to be admired. Nobody wanted to embarrass himself in front of a roomful of his peers. But if Carnegie could create a supportive place where people could take a chance, even fail, without being criticized or blamed or ridiculed, they would gradually become braver and take even more risks. They would beat back their fears.

Second, he believed that many of the basic flaws in public speaking arose when people tried to deliver a talk on a subject they knew nothing about and didn't have any interest in. People were more convincing and effective when they spoke from the heart.

Third, he strongly advocated removing criticism from personal relationships and from the teaching environment. He believed that positive reinforcement was the only way to build confidence. So he focused on what each student did well, realizing that his students were fully aware of most of the things they had done poorly.

ACT *AS IF* . . .

One of Carnegie's fundamental principles was that people could change their attitudes by changing their behavior. If you were scared and worried, you could overcome those feelings by acting *as if* you felt confident and serene. Carnegie often quoted the work of Harvard psychologist William James, who wrote:

> Action seems to follow feeling, but really action and feeling go together; and by regulating the action, which is under the more direct control of the will, we can indirectly regulate the feeling, which is not.[1]

Some readers may recognize in James's observation a principle often advocated in Alcoholics Anonymous meetings: *Fake it 'til you make it.*

For some critics, the emphasis on optimism and enthusiasm in Carnegie's teaching is hard to take. The idea that someone can develop a positive mood by pretending to have one seems equally ridiculous. But is it? Research into the development of a healthy personality indicates that one of the vital early steps a child must take is to learn how to engage in imitative learning. One form of imitative play is feigning, pretending, shamming. The child pretends to be scared in part to get a reaction from her parents and in part to "try out" the feeling of being scared. As one researcher has written, "Shamming mood states and social interactions is the self-practice that the infant and child rehearse in acquiring social competence."[2] In plain English, that means that the child learns to recognize moods and emotions in others from their nonverbal behavior and soon (usually by the age of three) can mimic both the external behaviors and the internal feelings associated with them. As Piaget and others have demonstrated, engaging in these "hoaxing" and "self-hoaxing" games is an indispensable step in the child's general progress toward acquiring social competence, since human communication requires that people express their feelings. "To be socially competent . . . means to have the capacity to call up mood states, or signs of them, as occasion re-quires." In fact, one of the characteristics of autism and mental illness is an impaired ability in this area.

So what? Well, this simply suggests that what Carnegie is urging us to do in acting "as if" is to draw upon the wellsprings of social competence that a healthy personality possesses.

One of the mood states that Carnegie thought was particularly important was enthusiasm. Too often, he saw the life drained out of promising presen-tations by a lack of enthusiasm on the part of the speaker. In one class he held in Philadelphia, a young insurance salesman named Frank Bettger was mumbling his way through an impromptu talk. Carnegie interrupted him.

"Mr. Bettger," he said. "Just a moment . . . just a moment. Are you interested in what you are saying?"

"Yes . . . of course I am," Bettger replied.

"Well, then," Carnegie asked him, "why don't you talk with a little enthusiasm? How do you expect your audience to be interested if you don't put some life and animation into what you say?"

Carnegie then proceeded to give the class a rousing talk on the power of enthusiasm. In fact, he got so excited that he threw a chair against the wall and broke one of its legs off.[3]

Carnegie's demonstration of the power of enthusiasm electrified Frank Bettger. It enabled him to crash through the barriers that had been holding him back from success. Eventually, he became one of the most successful sales agents in the life insurance industry, but he always maintained that enthusiasm was the vitally important element. Years later he wrote:

> During my thirty-two years of selling, I have seen enthusiasm double and treble the income of dozens of salesmen, and I have seen the lack of it cause hundreds of salesmen to fail.
>
> I firmly believe enthusiasm is by far the biggest single factor in success-ful selling. . . .

Can you acquire enthusiasm—or must you be born with it? Certainly you can acquire it! . . . How? Just by forcing [yourself] to *act* enthusiastic.[4]

Carnegie firmly believed in that principle. He started class sessions by having the students give themselves pep talks. He wrote a book about overcoming worry and depression that basically told readers that they would be all right if they (1) stopped worrying about things they couldn't change and (2) forced themselves to stay busy and act as if everything was going to be all right. This may sound simplistic, but for Carnegie it worked. He himself was subject to depression and had actually been suicidal a couple of times, but by rousing himself out of his stupor and forcing himself to do something, acting as if he were looking forward to the future, he was able to battle through.

Did acting "as if" work for others? Lee Iacocca, the man who salvaged Chrysler from bankruptcy, said, "I'm a great believer in the Dale Carnegie Institute. . . . I've sent dozens of introverted guys to Dale Carnegie at the company's expense." By acting as if they were confident, they became confident. Similarly, Tom Peters's *In Search of Excellence* argued that one of the ways in which the most successful companies were alike was in their commitment to fostering cultures of Carnegie-like enthusiasm among employees. One of those organizations is Domino's Pizza, whose founder, Tom Monaghan, is a graduate of the Carnegie course himself. He sought to keep Domino's at the forefront of a highly competitive industry by promoting enthusiasm among every employee. And John Emery, the founder of Emery Air Freight, took the course in 1948 and adopted the principle of enthusiasm as one that he would live by and use to manage his business. Emery employees have been attending the Carnegie course ever since, because of John Emery's experience there:

Dale Carnegie taught me the power of enthusiasm, and if you can be enthusiastic about what you're doing, no matter what it is, whether you're selling a product, selling a service, or selling yourself, that enthusiasm is contagious, and that's really what part of my job here at Emery is—I'm the head cheerleader.[5]

And then there's the case of Chris Gorman, a 33-year-old Englishman worth £40 million. He was born into a train wreck of a family in a housing project where unemployment was running over 25 percent. He started working as a supermarket trainee and felt lucky to have that job. In 2000 he was named U.K. Business Entrepreneur of the Year by Ernst and Young, and when he was asked how he had managed to drag himself up from his rough, deprived background, he said he owed it to reading and practicing the ideas in Dale Carnegie's *How to Win Friends and Influence People.* According to Gorman, "What he said was true in his day and it still is, even in the new economy. He made me realize that anything was possible, no matter what background you come from." And Carnegie's notion that you should treat your colleagues and customers the way you would treat your friends led Gorman to make an important decision. When he sold his high-tech firm, he made five of his colleagues millionaires—at a personal cost to himself of £10 million—because he had verbally promised them that he would. Gorman is proudest, though, of the fact that he achieved success "without stabbing anyone in the back, or ripping anyone off."[6] In spite of his rough origins, he acted as if he could be a success, and he was.

MAKE THE OTHER PERSON FEEL IMPORTANT

One of the fundamental Carnegie principles was that you can win friends and wield more influence if you can force yourself to pack your own ego away and focus on making the other person feel important. Everybody was a hero in his or her own mind, Carnegie felt, and would welcome any external evidence that supported that belief.

Carnegie maintained that the desire to feel important is one of the characteristics that makes human beings human. Animals don't have that kind of pride. But even the humblest peasant does. It was this quest for a feeling of importance that had led an "uneducated, poverty-stricken grocery clerk" to pluck a few law books from the bottom of a barrel of abandoned household goods and try to use them to make something of himself. "You have probably heard of this grocery clerk," Carnegie says. "His name was Lincoln."

For Carnegie, an even more vivid example came from his own childhood. He recalled how his father, miserable failure at farming that he was in general, nevertheless took tremendous pride in the "fine Duroc-Jersey hogs and pedigreed white-faced cattle" that he raised. When friends or visitors stopped by the farmhouse, Carnegie's father would take out a large sheet of white muslin on which he had pinned the scores of first-prize ribbons his animals had received. "The hogs didn't care about the ribbons they had won. But Father did. These prizes gave him a feeling of importance."[7]

Charles Schwab (an executive who ran steel mills for Andrew Carnegie, not the Schwab who has the brokerage firm) is quoted four times in *How to Win Friends and Influence People,* saying the exact same words: "I am hearty in my approbation and lavish in my praise." That was the way Schwab ran U.S. Steel. "Shouldn't we be able to run our own homes and offices that way?" Carnegie asked.

Carnegie went on to recommend some simple, no-nonsense ways to make the other person feel important. These were his original "six ways to make people like you":[8]

RULE 1: Become genuinely interested in other people.
RULE 2: Smile.
RULE 3: Remember that a man's name is to him the sweetest and most important sound in any language.
RULE 4: Be a good listener. Encourage others to talk about themselves.
RULE 5: Talk in terms of the other man's interest.
RULE 6: Make the other person feel important—and do it sincerely.

Carnegie had absolutely no doubt that following these six rules would guarantee a person, especially anyone in sales, great success in life. "Believe you will succeed, and you will," he promised.

However, probably no part of the Carnegie message has been the object of more criticism than his advice to show interest in the other person. It has been described as cynical and manipulative. The Nobel Prize–winning novelist Sinclair Lewis denounced Carnegie and his advice as nothing more than "yessing the Boss," saying that Carnegie wanted people to "smile and bob and pretend to be interested in other people's hobbies precisely so that you may screw things out of them."

But Carnegie denied any ill motives: "If we are so contemptibly selfish that we can't . . . pass on a bit of honest appreciation without trying to get something out of the other person . . . we shall meet with the failure we so richly deserve," he said. He insisted that the principle works only if you take a *sincere* interest in the other person. If you are faking it, you will be found out. "If we merely try to impress people and get people interested in us, we will never have many true, sincere friends. Friends, real friends, are not made that way," was his counsel.[9] You have to put yourself out to do something for other people—something that requires time, energy, unselfishness, and thoughtfulness. He gave as an example his own habit of making a note of his friends' birthdays and sending them a greeting. "What a hit it makes! I am frequently the only person on earth who remembers." He then goes on to give examples of how this philosophy works in business to help his graduates close sales, penetrate tough accounts, and make more money.

So is it cynical? Is it manipulative?

That depends on the person who applies the principles, doesn't it? If your only purpose in taking an interest in another is to lead that person to buy from you quickly, I'd say you're acting cynically and manipulatively. On the other hand, if you make it a habit to look for something special about other people and to express admiration for that unique quality, you are probably just doing something that reduces tension between people. And you are perhaps putting yourself in a more positive frame of mind.

In fact, my wife introduced me to a technique that's helpful when I'm about to deal with somebody I find particularly difficult. It doesn't have to be a business situation. It might be a family gathering where I'm anticipating that a particularly obnoxious uncle is going to ruin the event. It might be a community council meeting where one member is consistently obstreperous and rude. The technique is to identify something about that person that I genuinely respect or admire. There are times when it's darn hard to find anything. At first it might be something with an edge, like, "Uncle Ralph sure can hold his booze." But with a bit of effort, we eventually manage to come up with something more meaningful and sincere. "Uncle Ralph managed to put all three of his kids through college, even though he never finished high school himself." "Uncle Ralph has strong opinions that he genuinely believes in." "Uncle Ralph keeps himself well groomed." You get the point.

What happens? Instead of entering that family gathering and immediately getting a sour, sick feeling in my stomach when I see Uncle Ralph, I can greet him with an honest feeling of respect. And that's a much better place to be than where I was before making the effort to find something positive about him.

Now suppose I wanted to convert Uncle Ralph into a friend. Wouldn't it make sense for me to share with him the things that I admire and respect about him? Wouldn't he feel good to know that I admire the way he put his kids through college? That I think it's great that he has strong opinions, even though I don't agree with most of them?

Probably. After all, as Carnegie told us, most people like to be appreciated.

Is that manipulative and cynical? I don't think so. It's pretty obvious that I'm not going to change Uncle Ralph, and confrontation isn't much fun. So why not try something positive?

Social psychologists have proven experimentally that our actions influence our attitudes, and that they can transform other people's opinions and behavior, too. One explanation for this can be found in what is known as the theory of cognitive dissonance. The unpleasant sense of cognitive dissonance—a mental tension that we find uncomfortable—arises when we perceive discrepancies between our behavior and our attitudes. Suppose, for the sake of example, that a certain business owner is at heart a chauvinist. Although he works with women and hires them, he isn't happy about it. When one of his key suppliers puts a new sales rep in the territory that includes his store, and that sales rep happens to be a woman, he will experience cognitive dissonance and may actually request that the supplier assign a male sales rep to handle his account. (This may seem like a far-fetched example today, and I hope that's true, but I saw exactly this happen to a young female account executive for Procter & Gamble. To its everlasting credit, P&G told the account, no, she is your account manager, and we will not be making a change. The customer had to figure out some other way to resolve his cognitive dissonance.)

Leon Festinger, the social psychologist who first observed and researched the phenomenon of cognitive dissonance, argued that people will usually change their behavior rather than change their attitudes in order to manage the dissonance that they experience. They will avoid the situation or person who produces the feeling in them, or they will seek information and opinions that justify or reinforce their attitudes. Carnegie maintained that it's pointless to argue with people, trying to change them, because we will never be able to get them to change their fundamental attitudes and beliefs. Twenty years later, Festinger's research, along with numerous subsequent studies done by others in the field, proved that Carnegie was right.[10]

Carnegie's other point—that making an effort to show that we accept and like the other person is the best way to gain that person's trust and friendship—is also validated by psychological research. We experience less cognitive dissonance when we are dealing with people who are similar to ourselves, and still less when we are dealing with people who seem to accept and like us. If we behave in a way that explicitly communicates our acceptance of and respect for the other person, that person will become more comfortable with us. That causes trust to go up and increases the likelihood that the person will accept our suggestions.

INSTILL AN "EAGER WANT"

A third Carnegie principle is one that salespeople have applied in their work for generations. Carnegie found it expressed in *Influencing Human Behavior,* a book written by Harry Overstreet, a professor of psychology at the College of the City of New York. To quote Overstreet's words:

> Action springs out of what we fundamentally desire . . . and the best piece of advice which can be given to would-be persuaders, whether in business, in the home, in the school, in politics, is: first, arouse in the other person an eager want. He who can do this has the world with him. He who cannot walks a lonely way.[11]

Carnegie was convinced that this principle worked. If we wanted to persuade someone else to do something, we had to make him want to do it. It was an absolutely vital principle for sales. So, with a speaker's instinct for the power of the succinct phrase, Carnegie repeated Overstreet's principle: *Arouse in the other person an eager want.*[12]

Today, most of the process methods of selling start with the goal of identifying the customer's needs. Sometimes the salesperson is expected to bring a latent need to the surface, or to help the customer articulate the need in terms that are broadly organizational in nature. But this approach was not as common in Carnegie's day. It was being used in Dayton, obviously, but most salespeople were trained to deliver a canned pitch that was product-focused. One of the problems with this approach, then and now, is that it fails to address the questions that most customers silently ask themselves: "So what? " "Yeah, but what's in it for me?" And if you need to go back and sell the same product time after time, as Carnegie did when he was representing Armour or as the Nabisco sales rep did when he went back to the grocers week after week, a product pitch just won't work. You need to position yourself as a friend, as somebody trustworthy, and as somebody who can help the customer satisfy her needs.

What do people need, anyway? According to Overstreet, everyone has a basic set of "wants" or needs in common:

- ✦ Comfort
- ✦ Affectionate devotion
- ✦ Play
- ✦ Security
- ✦ To own something
- ✦ To be efficient
- ✦ Social esteem
- ✦ Pride in appearance
- ✦ Cleanliness

Most advertising, at least since Lord & Thomas yanked it into the twentieth century, has focused on appealing to these needs. If you look at each word or phrase in that list, you can probably come up with at least one product for which the key advertising message focuses on the product's ability to satisfy that need. Comfort? If I turn on the Golf Channel and wait a few minutes, I'll see an ad for golf shoes that emphasizes how comfortable they are to wear. Affectionate devotion? Nearly every ad for assisted living focuses on an adult child's desire to have her or his parents taken care of in their old age in a way that proves that the child really cares. The salespeople who were following the NCR *Primer* were addressing the need or "want" for more profit.

But to Carnegie, the most fundamental "want" of all was to be valued, to feel important. The idea of making other people feel good about themselves was the key to Carnegie's whole method of winning friends and influencing others. In that regard, Carnegie's understanding of human needs as motivators is closer to the hierarchy of needs articulated by social psychologist Abraham Maslow. In research with primates, Maslow noticed that some needs take precedence over others. If you deprive an animal of both food and water, the animal will try to find water first, because an organism can survive for only a couple of days without water but can last for days or even weeks without food. Eventually, Maslow categorized needs into a hierarchical pyramid (see Figure 9-1), with the most basic needs, the ones that drive us to ignore other needs until they are satisfied, at the bottom. The most basic are the physiological needs—air in your lungs, water and food in your belly. Just above those are needs for safety—shelter, warmth, physical security. The reality is, of course, that our society is blessed in being able to provide for the physiological and safety needs of the vast majority of its citizens. In spite of the problems of poverty, homelessness, crime, and terrorism, for most people the physiological and safety needs are being met. And, as Maslow's research showed, if a basic need is being met, we ignore it. (That's why he called these "deficit needs"—they impinge on our awareness only when they are not being met. If they are being met, we don't think about them.) When one category of needs is met, we instinctively move on to the next level in the hierarchy. For example, if we feel safe and secure in our community, we naturally seek to satisfy our need to belong. In this case, we are also moving from needs that are less dependent on society's functioning efficiently and more dependent on our personal interactions with others: the "belonging needs" and the "esteem needs," Maslow called them. Every-

Figure 9-1

Being Needs

Self-Actualization

Esteem Needs

Belonging Needs

Safety Needs

Physiological Needs

Deficit Needs

one wants to fit in, to be accepted by family and friends, to be part of a group. And everyone seeks validation and self-esteem.

Maslow believed that there were two different kinds of esteem needs: the need for respect from others and the need for self-respect. The first kind of respect, which comes from recognition, positive attention, praise, appreciation, and other expressions of approval from other people, is the essence of what Carnegie tells us to give other people in order to get along with them better. Although Maslow's major work, *Motivation and Personality,* appeared more than two decades after Carnegie published *How to Win Friends and Influence People,* both authors recognized that in modern society, most people have little problem getting their physiological and safety needs met, and thus they don't think about those needs much. Likewise, most people are involved in a marriage or other committed relationship, have parents or children who love them, belong to a church or club, and have a job that also provides a ready-made social environment and satisfies their need to belong to a group. What we often miss is the feeling of being accepted and valued. By giving people sincere appreciation and respect, as Carnegie recommended, we are helping them to fulfill one of their basic needs.

When we feel stressed, we may regress to a lower need level. For example, a sales rep may have difficulty focusing on hitting her sales target (which is related primarily to esteem needs) if she has run up huge debts and is in danger of losing her house (safety needs). These issues also come up in a limited sense during our normal business interactions. For example, dealing with potential customers or, conversely, dealing with a sales rep can feel stressful, particularly in the early stages of the business relationship. As a result, all of the people engaged in a sales call, fearing that they may make a mistake or be rejected, may revert to behavior that comes across as self-centered: talking about themselves and about their company, not listening to the other person, focusing on facts and details that can't be challenged. This is exactly the kind of behavior that Carnegie warns us against. We need to stay conscious of our own feelings of insecurity and resist the temptation to engage in behaviors that might temporarily make us feel safer or bolster our self-esteem at the expense of others.

DRAMATIZE!

As a trained actor and a champion debater, Carnegie knew the value of making a vivid impression on the audience. In his public speaking classes, he encouraged students to make their messages vivid.

"This is the day of the dramatization," he wrote. "Merely stating a truth isn't enough. The truth has to be made vivid, interesting, dramatic. You have to use showmanship. The movies do it. Radio does it. And you will have to do it if you want attention."[13]

Carnegie's preferred method of dramatizing was with an anecdote. In fact, one of the reasons his books remain popular and readable today is the fact that he tells so many good stories in them. They aren't long stories. Most of them are just half a page, maybe a couple of pages at most, but they're vivid and interesting and always relevant to the point he's making.

When you first pick up *How to Win Friends and Influence People,* you may be put off a bit by these stories at first, because they are dated. Who are these people he's writing about? Who the heck is James B. Boynton? Lord Chesterfield? Stefansson, the arctic explorer? "Two Gun" Crowley? Even the names we recognize seem old-fashioned to a contemporary reader. Carnegie tells stories about Woodrow Wilson, Queen Victoria, Disraeli, Teddy Roosevelt, Henry Ford, John D. Rockefeller.

But he was writing about people who were for the most part fresh in the memory of his readers. Seen in this context, what he did is no different from a writer today sharing anecdotes about Ronald Reagan, John F. Kennedy, Margaret Thatcher, Tony Blair, Martha Stewart, or Donald Trump. Instead of Stefansson, today he might quote Buzz Aldrin. Instead of Feodor Chaliapin, it might be Pavarotti.

Once we get past the unfamiliar names, we start to realize that the stories are pretty good. Sometimes they're funny; sometimes they're inspiring. But they always manage to dramatize his point.

From years of teaching experience, Carnegie had decided to have his public speaking students deliver a two-minute talk. He knew that two minutes was enough time to say something meaningful, but not so much that a speaker would utterly break down. It gave everybody a chance to speak at least once in every class. It was manageable as an impromptu assignment.

But what was the best way to use that two minutes?

Eventually he came up with what he considered the ideal format for a brief talk—something he called the Magic Formula. It was a pattern that dramatized quickly, that communicated clearly, and that was easy to remember.

According to Carnegie's Magic Formula, a speaker should start with an *example*, followed by a clearly stated *point*. The example might be a startling statistic or a brief anecdote or a headline from the newspaper, but it needs to crash through the "ho-hum barrier" and get the audience's attention immediately. Then, the point has to be made obvious. The example gets people's attention, but the point gets them intellectually engaged in the talk. Finally, the talk has to conclude with a *benefit*. What reward will someone gain from acting on the point being made? The benefit makes the whole talk important and motivates the audience toward action. What Carnegie was recommending was a presentation technique designed to appeal to the largest number of people in the briefest amount of time: Begin dramatically, tell a good story, make a point, and deliver a benefit.

If you read his major book, *How to Win Friends and Influence People,* you'll see immediately that each brief chapter follows this format. For example, the very first one, which has the folksy title "If You Want to Gather Honey, Don't Kick Over the Beehive," starts out with an *example*: New York police, after weeks of searching, had cornered the vicious killer "Two Gun" Crowley in his girlfriend's apartment. When Crowley refused to throw down his weapons and give up, they launched an assault by more than 150 officers armed with rifles and machine guns. Bullets poured into the apartment building, but Crowley kept firing back. Finally, Crowley ran out of ammunition, and the police captured him, dragging him away in handcuffs. And what did this vicious killer have to say? "Under my coat is a weary heart, but a kind one—one that would do nobody any harm."

Now that's a good story! It doesn't matter if you've never heard of old "Two Gun"; you can picture him firing out the windows of his girlfriend's apartment, hiding behind the sofa as the machine gun bullets rip through the walls, only to justify himself as though he were Albert Schweitzer or Mother Teresa.

With his dramatic, vivid example, Carnegie gets his chapter and his whole book going with a bang.

Then he makes his *point*. And he makes it as explicitly as he can: "The point of the story," he tells us, "is this: 'Two Gun' Crowley didn't blame himself for anything." And that's because most people just don't see themselves as being at fault. As a result, "Criticism is futile because it puts a man on the defensive, and usually makes him strive to justify himself. Criticism is dangerous, because it wounds a man's precious pride, hurts his sense of importance, and arouses his resentment."

Well, that point is pretty clear. If it appeared in a psychology textbook without the previous anecdote regarding the "cop killer" Crowley, we might nod and move on. But the way Carnegie has set it up, we are eager to agree.

Carnegie goes on and gives us examples of famous figures who understood this principle and used it to get the best efforts from those around them—Abraham Lincoln, Teddy Roosevelt, Benjamin Franklin. Talk about the pantheon of American history! Carnegie really knows how to get us to buy in, doesn't he?

Then, at the end of the chapter, he states the benefit: *If we refrain from criticizing others, we will get along with them better.* "Any fool can criticize, condemn, and complain—and most fools do," Carnegie tells us. "But it takes character and self-control to be understanding and forgiving."

There's the Magic Formula in action. It's a good chapter. Repeated use of the Magic Formula makes for an entertaining, interesting book, one that has been a best-seller for 70 years.

Of course, it's a book Carnegie never intended to write.

CHAPTER 10

THE 25-YEAR OVERNIGHT SUCCESS

As I was preparing this material on Dale Carnegie, I became curious about his most famous book, *How to Win Friends and Influence People*. I knew it was still in print. At least, I assumed it was. But did people still buy it?

I went to Amazon.com to check.

Well, not only is it in print, but there are several different editions you can choose from.

And as for sales? The day I checked, it was ranked 66. That's 66 out of all of the millions of books that Amazon carries! It was behind a couple of Harry Potter titles, of course, but it was way ahead of recent big sellers like *The South Beach Diet* and *Who Moved My Cheese?* Not bad for a septuagenarian.

Carnegie never planned to write the book, though. He was sailing along, no doubt making friends and influencing people at his own pace, but mainly running his public speaking workshops. They had become extremely popular, and he was making a lot of money—which, in the middle of the Great Depression, was no trivial feat.

For nearly 25 years, he had delivered the same basic course. He changed it a bit from time to time. He got rid of the elocution exercises right away. He added more group activities. Eventually he got people to talk about their biggest fears and worries and to use the class almost like a support group. But it was all intended as a way of helping to instill confidence in his students so that they could speak up in meetings and deliver talks before customers and bosses successfully.

He had written a textbook, *Public Speaking: A Practical Course for Business Men,* which was published by the YMCA's press in 1926, so that he could use it in his classes. He issued a new edition of it in 1931 because he had revised the classes a bit more and wanted the book to match what he was teaching. In 1932 he wrote a book about Abraham Lincoln, *Lincoln the Unknown,* because he truly loved Lincoln and had gathered some fascinating stories about the man. When he sent it out to the big New York publishers, though, nobody was interested. He finally got it published by a tiny house called Greenberg, and it sold very few copies. A couple of years later, the same small publisher brought out a collection of interviews that Carnegie had conducted with famous people called *Little Known Facts About Well Known People.* It was basically a bit of fluff, and it didn't sell very well, either.

As Carnegie saw it, his career was tied up in his classes. Writing was more of a hobby than anything else. After quitting his Packard sales job, he devoted himself to writing a novel, a Western, but it was so bad that nobody would publish it. Crushed, he had given up his dreams of becoming a famous author.

But one evening he gave a promotional lecture for a public speaking course he planned to hold near Larchmont, a wealthy suburb some 20 miles outside of New York. Attending the promotional lecture was Leon Shimkin, who worked for Simon & Schuster. Shimkin was so impressed by Carnegie, and by the testimonials of the former students who joined him on the stage to talk about the course's effectiveness, that he signed up. He loved the course and was fascinated by the way Carnegie got the wealthy Westchester County class members—attorneys, executives, financial kingpins—to overcome their inhibitions and speak with enthusiasm.

The lesson that galvanized Shimkin, though, occurred in the eleventh week. In that lesson, Carnegie showed how to deal with an adversary who completely disagreed with you by finding something in the other person's position that you could accept and using that as a starting point for reconciliation and collaboration. Shimkin was impressed by Carnegie's notion that by looking for the good and the positive, you could create an atmosphere in which the other person became more willing to concede a point or two in return.

Shimkin approached the editors at Simon & Schuster and proposed a book to be written by Carnegie on the art of getting along with people. He also talked to the other members of the class the following week, asking them if they had tried Carnegie's technique. They had, and they all agreed that it worked. Hearing that, Shimkin was convinced that he had a book idea that would work, too.

There was just one little problem: Carnegie refused to write the book. He had submitted his Lincoln book to Simon & Schuster, and they had turned it down. Simon & Schuster had also turned down his book of interviews with famous people. He didn't intend to give the company another chance.

It took Shimkin some time, and he probably had to make good use of the persuasive techniques for influencing recalcitrant clients that he had learned from Carnegie's class, but eventually he got him to agree. Two years later, in 1936, the first edition of *How to Win Friends and Influence People* appeared in bookstores. Shimkin promoted the book to hundreds of graduates of the Carnegie course as a way of refreshing the principles they had learned in class, and he suggested that they might want to buy some extra copies to share with their own friends and colleagues. Within weeks, more than 5,000 copies had been sold. A full-page ad in the *New York Times* helped, too. Sales continued to build quickly until the book was selling almost 5,000 copies a week. The book went through 17 printings in five months. In the first year, Carnegie made $150,000 in royalties, based on 25 cents a copy.

Overnight, Dale Carnegie was famous, wealthy, and eagerly sought after by business leaders, politicians, and celebrities.

Overnight, that is, if you don't count the first quarter of a century of work he had put in to get himself ready for that success.[1]

WHY DOES IT WORK?

At the heart of Carnegie's philosophy is a simple idea: Influence is linked to trust. Gaining influence means building trust, and trust is fundamentally a relationship. As Robert Cialdini writes in *Influence: The Psychology of Persuasion*, "Few people would be surprised to learn that, as a rule, we most prefer to say yes to the requests of someone we know and like."[2]

When we begin to trust people, we typically do it because of a combination of factors. First, we have some emotional rapport with them. They seem like decent people. They seem to like us, too. They show up on time; they return our phone calls; they don't try to B.S. us. Maybe, like Dale Carnegie, they even remember our birthday.

But rapport is only a starting point. It's vital—if there's no rapport, there will never be any trust—but next we need to establish some credibility. In a business setting, that usually means demonstrating competence, intelligence, insight, and creativity. We have a command of our own discipline, and we can call up facts quickly and accurately. But we also understand the other person's business and can comprehend what that person is saying.

Finally, trusting someone involves a calculation of risk. What if I'm wrong? What if this person is a flake? A liar? A kook? What am I risking? The more we have at stake—in terms of money, time, reputation, or opportunity—the more wary we will be of trusting the other person. As Jagdish Sheth and Andrew Sobel point out in *Clients for Life: How Great Professionals Develop Breakthrough Relationships,* one of the methods people use to decide quickly how much risk there is in trusting someone is to calculate the degree of self-interest that we observe in that person's behavior. The more self-centered people are, the less we trust them.[3]

Carnegie's methods of winning friends and gaining influence address all of these factors to some degree, but they put most of the emphasis on rapport. He correctly surmised that unless you get the other person to like you, you're not going to get very far in your efforts to persuade him or her. It's the emotional connection between people that will get you started on the road to trust. The second most important element, he thought, was displaying interest in the other person—in other words, minimizing the appearance of self-interest.

Research studies into buyer/seller relationships have indicated that these are exactly the variables that are most likely to produce a successful relationship. One study by Jamie Comstock and Gary Higgins found that all types of buyers—regardless of their own buying behavior and regardless of their communication style—prefer to work with salespeople who are composed, focused on the task, highly trustworthy, and "cooperative," a style that "is characterized by receptivity, precision, friendliness, and a lack of contentiousness." As you can see, these attributes are identical to the characteristics Carnegie advocated in *How to Win Friends and Influence People.* Comstock and Higgins add that the research shows that salespeople "should temper their focus on task [that is, on making the sale] by treating buyers with warmth and respect, without becoming too disclosive or informal." Salespeople will be most successful, according to the research, if they can balance immediacy (the quality of emotional "openness" or rapport) with credibility. "Low immediacy detracts from trust and approachability, while high immediacy detracts from credibility and task accomplishment. In simple terms, too little or too much immediacy may turn the buyer off."[4]

Other research studies have also illustrated the fundamental importance of the relationship established between the sales rep and the buyer. A study by Harald Biong and Fred Selnes in 1996 showed that a salesperson's attitude and behavior during the sales process—that is, the way the salesperson interacts with the customer—has a direct impact on the buyer's willingness to continue the relationship. What's more, a strong, positive relationship with the salesperson tends to increase the customer's perception of the supplier company's reliability and the perceived value of the supplier's services. From this study, it's clear that one of the sales professional's most important roles is that of relationship manager, which was exactly Carnegie's point.[5]

Another researcher analyzed how 124 retail buyers and 52 vendor representatives got along, and found that trust was the most important factor in establishing a long-term relationship.[6] Having a close working relationship was typically seen by the customer as a way to safeguard important projects and assets and as a way to hedge against uncertainty or unexpected complications. In situations in which a salesperson engages in repetitive business with a buyer—as Carnegie did when he represented Armour, for example—the vendor companies were able to charge somewhat higher prices when there was a strong "relational element" between the buyer and the salesperson—in other words, if they liked each other.[7]

The relationship model of selling that Carnegie advocated is the one that Saturn has adopted as a differentiator in the automobile industry, that Ritz Carlton uses to separate itself in the highly competitive hotel industry, and that Nordstrom follows in the retail industry. Obviously, the appeal to friendship—the fact that somebody likes you and you like that person back—is the basis for such in-home selling programs as Tupperware, Avon, Mary Kay, and Amway. For all of these companies, relationship selling has proven to be effective and profitable. At a more local level, thousands of retail salespeople, insurance agents, financial planners, community bankers, and other service providers have achieved prominence in their areas by following a consistent program of relationship selling.

Later, in Part 5, we'll look at the career of Joe Girard, a man who was by far the most successful car salesman in the world. In that section, we'll focus on an innovative idea that he developed for keeping his pipeline filled, but in terms of his selling methodology, he was a pure Carnegie man. All he ever claimed to do was to offer customers a fair price and someone they liked to buy from.

PLAYING THE ROLE

Since Carnegie's day, salespeople have learned some shortcuts to establishing rapport with prospects and customers. For example, numerous studies have shown that we will feel a more immediate rapport with people who dress the way we do. The entire "dress for success" movement that John Molloy launched in the 1980s was based on the notion that a salesperson who dresses like an executive is going to find it easier to connect with that executive.

Of course, Molloy didn't invent that idea out of whole cloth (no pun intended). Patterson laid down strict guidelines for his sales agents and the way they dressed; Thomas Watson did the same thing even more famously at IBM. In fact, Dale Carnegie himself indirectly endorsed the idea of dressing the part to achieve success. After the stock market crash of 1929, men began worrying about keeping their job—if they had one. They tried to dress in a way that would please the boss, that would make them look like the kind of employee the boss would want to hang on to. The Sears, Roebuck catalogue preyed on that anxiety in 1939 when it urged men to "Prepare for Leadership, Wear the Right Clothes." But what were the right clothes? For the aspiring salesperson, it was a suit offered by Sears called the Staunton. According to the catalogue copy, the Staunton, tailored to Dale

Carnegie's own specifications by Sears's master tailors, "wins more friends, influences more people."[8]

But dressing to match the way the customer dresses is only one step toward establishing a bond quickly. Having a similar background and interests also creates an immediate positive impression. Carnegie clearly recommended looking for those interests, but his disciple, Frank Bettger, raised the process to a fine art. Just after returning from a lecture tour he had undertaken with Dale Carnegie, Bettger went to meet the president of a huge dairy products company in Philadelphia. When he entered the man's office, he was greeted warmly.

> "Frank," he said, "tell me all about your trip."
> "All right, Jim," I replied, "but first, I'm anxious to hear about you. What have you been doing? How is Mary? And how is your business?"

Well, Bettger's client was more than willing to share what he had been up to. He went on at length about his business and his family, and he launched into a lengthy description of a poker party he and his wife had attended where they had played a game called "Red Dog." As Bettger admits, he had never heard of Red Dog and he had no interest in ever playing the game, but he listened "with eagerness" to the man's story.

> He seemed to have a grand time and when I started to leave he said: "Frank, we've been considering insuring the superintendent of the plant. What would $25,000 cost on his life?"
> I never *did* get a chance to talk about myself but I left there with a nice order which some other salesman sold, but probably talked himself out of.[9]

By forcing himself to be interested in the other man first, Bettger had established a level of rapport and trust that won him what was a big order in his day. Was he being a phony? No, but he *was* playing a role. He was the Relationship Manager, and in that role he was consciously feeding his customer's ego to maintain a high level of cooperation and trust.

CHAPTER 11

CARNEGIE'S HEIRS

Dale Carnegie continues to exert an influence on American selling practices. His books continue to sell. Dale Carnegie & Associates, the company he founded, continues to enroll thousands of people in sales-training courses that are based on his principles.

Those factors alone assure the continuing influence of his ideas in American business, particularly in the practice of selling.

In addition, there are other consultants and writers who are clearly working in the same vein of human relationships that he first mined. There are the people who preach about the importance of positive thinking and of maintaining an optimistic outlook. There are the ones who teach people generally about how to get their lives in order, how to straighten out their priorities, how to create more successful relationships with their families and friends. And, of course, there are sales consultants who strongly recommend the use of relationship-building techniques to increase sales.

THE GOSPEL OF OPTIMISM AND SELF-IMPROVEMENT

Carnegie wasn't the first American writer to talk about the importance of staying optimistic and thinking positive thoughts. There is a long tradition of that kind of writing, starting with Benjamin Franklin's *Autobiography* and *Poor Richard's Almanac*. Later, in the nineteenth century, Horatio Alger's dime novels told the stories of Ragged Dick or Tattered Tom, poor boys who rose from rags to riches by virtue of hard work, honesty, and an indomitable spirit. These inspiring tales became part of American folklore, mingled with true stories of triumph over poverty such as those of Andrew Carnegie, David Sarnoff, John H. Johnson, and others.

Inspirational authors from Franklin onward have consistently returned to the same two themes: First, that financial success is an outward sign of virtue and the approval of Providence, and second, that the mind has the power to control outcomes. Time after time, these messages appear in the writings of inspirational authors. One of the most successful of these authors, Napoleon Hill, was a near contemporary of Dale Carnegie's. In 1908, Hill was working as a reporter for a motivational magazine. While he was interviewing the great industrialist Andrew Carnegie as a living embodiment of rags-to-riches success, Carnegie supposedly gave the young man a challenge: Was he willing to undertake a scientific study of the true causes of success and failure by investigating successful people around the world? If he would do it, his work would be of tremendous value to humble but ambitious people everywhere, for it would enable them to follow the principles used by those who were already successful and thus make themselves prosperous as well. Carnegie took out his watch and told Hill that he had 60 seconds to answer. Before the second hand had reached the halfway point, Hill agreed. As a result of Carnegie's challenge, he interviewed more than 500 business and industry leaders, consolidating their insights and rules into a book called *Law of Success.* Then he took the material and wrote another volume, *Think and Grow Rich,* which was published at almost the same time as Carnegie's *How to Win Friends and Influence People* appeared and which sold almost as furiously. To date, *Think and Grow Rich* has sold over 30 million copies!

The essence of Hill's approach is that the successful individual is one who is open to the creative abundance of the universe. Meditation, prayer, visualization, affirmations: These are the tools of positive thinking, and Hill embraces them all.

There is the slightly awkward problem that nowhere in Andrew Carnegie's papers at the Library of Congress is there any mention of Napoleon Hill, of an interview with Hill, or of any subsequent correspondence with him. So maybe Hill made up the whole story.[1] There's also the problem that despite following the secrets he learned from Andrew Carnegie and other industrial giants, Hill himself had a lifelong history of failed businesses, failed marriages, and lost fortunes. On the other hand, he did sell 30 million books, so . . .

By far the most popular self-help writer of the second half of the twentieth century was Norman Vincent Peale, a preacher whose *The Power of Positive Thinking* gave people permission to stop worrying and to love themselves exactly the way they are: "If you can think in positive terms you will get positive results. That is the simple fact." That same kind of warm, reassuring message comes through in the preaching of Robert Schuller. In recent years, Stephen Covey has had phenomenal success, following in Carnegie's footsteps in offering general advice about how to live a happy life. A whole series of books based on his original best-seller, *The 7 Habits of Highly Successful People,* has spawned an industry producing everything from greeting cards to wall posters. Others who have followed in Carnegie's and Hill's footsteps include Tony Robbins, who preaches a philosophy of self-empowerment that he claims will unleash incredible power through positive thinking. Hot coals and bare feet are optional, though highly recommended. Even earlier, Maxwell Maltz taught people how to gain control of their lives in his *Psycho-Cybernetics,* a 1960 book that purported to show how to use the power of the subconscious mind.

Does positive thinking really work? Does Dale Carnegie's advice to act "as if" you were enthusiastic and optimistic produce positive results? Research in the field of social cognitive psychology suggests that it does work, but it must be tied to action. A positive attitude can be sustained if it is tied to effort that produces results, even small results. The salesperson who takes a positive attitude, applies some new skills to a couple of sales calls, and actually closes a deal will become even more optimistic and more self-confident. As one study puts it, "The truth embodied in the concept of self-efficacy [that is, the power of positive thinking] can encourage us to not resign ourselves to bad situations, to persist despite initial failures, to exert effort without being overly distracted by self-doubts."[2] Of course, this can go a bit too far, with the result that people who struggle are consistently blamed for their problems—if they just believed harder, if they just maintained a more positive attitude, they wouldn't fail. We know, however, that circumstances outside of an individual's control can sometimes overcome even the most resolute positive thinker. As a result, the most sensible and healthiest attitude "mixes ample positive thinking with enough realism to discriminate those things we can control from those we cannot."[3]

Today's self-improvement market is enormous. From diets to addictions, people want advice, guidelines, and rules that will make their lives better. Carnegie wasn't the first to write a self-improvement book, but he was one of the first to get rich from it. His success has inspired hundreds of others. For salespeople, who face tremendous pressures to be self-reliant and successful, and who are often alone on the firing line, facing repeated rejection by bored, cynical, distracted, or otherwise difficult clients, books filled with optimistic messages about the power of good intentions, positive thinking, and will power to produce successful outcomes have had a consistent appeal.

RELATIONSHIP SALES STRATEGIES

More to the point, perhaps, are the sales trainers who have focused their methods on developing a strong, personal relationship with the customer.

One of the most successful of these gurus was Harvey Mackay, whose book *Swim with the Sharks Without Being Eaten Alive* includes the "Mackay Envelope 66-Question Customer Profile." This is simply a form on which Mackay collects every scrap of information about the customer that he can lay his hands on. "It's critical to know about your customer," he says. "Armed with the right knowledge, we can outsell, outmanage, outmotivate, and outnegotiate our competitors." In spite of the unfortunate echoes of the *Survivor* TV show motto, Mackay's point is clear: Knowing the customer gives you a competitive advantage. He cites Lee Iacocca approvingly: "Anyone who doesn't get along with people doesn't belong in this business, because that's all we've got around here." And of all the people it's vital to get along with, the most important of all is the customer.

Buyers are naturally suspicious and skeptical, Mackay asserts. But we can transform ourselves from an adversary into a colleague by gathering and using information about the customer. "All of us gather data about other people—especially people we want to influence. The only question is how well we understand it and what we do with it." So what does Mackay want to know? He wants salespeople, marketing folks, even secretaries, to gather all kinds of personal information about clients. He wants to know their height and weight, their marital status, their religious and political affiliations, even their hobbies and what they like to eat. On and on it goes. There are, as you probably guessed, 66 different questions that Mackay wants answered.

I think it's interesting that it's not until question 63 that we record, "What are the key problems as the customer sees them?" The next question is, "What are the priorities of the customer's management?" And then, "Can you help with these problems?" It's safe to say that this approach would have brought John Henry Patterson out of his chair, screaming and kicking desks. While he wanted to get immediately to the bottom-line business issues—increasing profits, cutting down on theft, or eliminating losses caused by carelessness—Mackay seems to place those issues pretty far down the list in terms of importance.[4]

Of course, Mackay is selling a commodity. His company makes business envelopes. He's not so much selling a solution as selling an ongoing relationship. And that's one of the key differences between the process approach and relationship-driven selling. The process approach works beautifully if you have a product or service that solves a pressing business need, that can be differentiated in ways that add value to the customer's business, or that can be clearly linked to payback. It works well for complex sales of technical solutions. But if you are selling a true commodity—envelopes, or rock salt, or mulch—and you want to insulate your business a bit against the pressure to cut prices, you will need to develop a strong, personal relationship. Or if you are trying to influence opinion and indirectly influence behavior, as is often the case in pharmaceutical sales, for example, a relationship approach is your best choice.

You can find other versions of the relationship-oriented approach to sales in the books written by Anthony Parinello, starting with *Selling to VITO (the Very Important Top Officer)*. Parinello focuses on helping the salesperson understand the top executive's personality and priorities and learn how to talk to the top executive in a compelling way, how to write effective letters, how to leave voicemails that a top executive will return, and other tactical aspects of selling at the senior levels of the customer organization. He also echoes Carnegie in emphasizing the importance of taking a positive attitude ("unshakeable confidence," as he puts it), building rapport, and being enthusiastic and energetic.

The relationship approach has been very successful among consulting organizations and others whose primary deliverable is expertise. In *Clients for Life,* for example, Jagdish Sheth and Andrew Sobel discuss what is involved in becoming a "trusted adviser." Banking and financial services often refer to the salesperson or business development manager as a "trusted adviser," but Sheth and Sobel point out that this is not a title that you just can claim for yourself. You have to earn it. You achieve that status by demonstrating impartiality, integrity, empathy, dedication, and other such character traits. Your customers, in turn, will demonstrate that they trust you and see you as an adviser if they share confidential information with you, if they share their long-term plans with you, if they ask for your advice about business matters that are not related to your company's line of business or products, if they offer to be a demo site or to serve as a key reference site for you, and so on.

To learn how to develop a strong relationship with your customers or to improve the quality of the relationships you have, you might want to look at some of the research into personality types and their impact on selling styles. Based largely on the personality traits identified by the Myers-Briggs Personality Inventory, they result in definitions of certain kinds of buyers. There are people who are mainly motivated by facts, though they don't want too many, and who are quick to make decisions, particularly if they see a bottom-line impact. These people are called *pragmatics* or *drivers* or *commanders.* Others manifest buying behavior in which they require detailed presentations. These people demand accuracy and thoroughness, and they tend to take their time in reaching a decision. They hate to be pushed. Usually these people are called *analyticals,* although other names are sometimes used to describe them. *Expressives* or *visionaries* are customers who are quick to act, but who respond based on emotional insights. They tend to be big-picture people. They are less interested in your product than they are in whether it will help them achieve their own ideas. *Consensus seekers* or *amiables* tend to value close working relationships. They often get confused or intimidated by a lot of technical detail, but they do respond to the personal touch. Among the sales programs that show you how to adjust your selling style to match the personality of the buyer are courses put out by Wilson Learning Systems and Tony Alessandro.

Similarly, Geoffrey Moore's breakthrough book, *Crossing the Chasm*, talks about the different types of buyers you may encounter if you're trying to introduce a new product and how best to approach each of them. He distinguishes between *early adopters* and *laggards,* the people who are quick to try a new product or technology and those who resist introducing anything new for as long as possible. In between are the mainstream buyers, divided into the *early majority* and the *late majority.* The early adopters are people "who find it easy to imagine, understand, and appreciate the benefits of a new technology" and who are willing to rely on their own intuition and vision in making decisions.[5] The early majority, in contrast, understand and relate to technology, but they make decisions pragmatically. They want to see well-known references and proof that the technology works and delivers its promised benefits. The late majority, on the other hand, wait until a technical approach has become the industry standard before adopting it, and the laggards will fight its adoption right up to the last moment. Moore presents strategies for selling to each of these customer types, which is vital for anyone who is bringing an innovative product or service to market, since the number of early adopters is very small.

For example, Moore discusses the technique of defining target customers and how your product can be applied to each customer's environment to create positive impact. For each target customer, Moore recommends creating a personal profile and job description, to make our sense of that customer more tangible. (Abstract concepts of market segments just won't work, he claims. We need to be able to see the customer to whom we are selling as an individual human being.) We then think about the kinds of technology that this particular target customer currently uses, and the level of sophistication she is likely to have. Next, we create a brief narrative that describes what a typical day in the life of this target customer is like, and we identify the specific problem or dilemma that would motivate her to buy our product. We then go back and rethink the narrative of a typical workday, imagining how it will be different if the target customer has bought our product.

Clearly, this approach requires an intense awareness of customers' personalities, values, and attitudes. In addition, we need to have enough insight into the customer's role and responsibilities to accurately predict potential uses for our products. We must put ourselves in the customer's position, thinking the way the customer thinks. By definition, sales approaches that require us to spend a lot of time understanding the customer, defining the customer's behavior, or detecting patterns in that behavior and sales approaches that focus on techniques for managing the customer's attitudes and behavior are all descendants of Dale Carnegie's original relationship-oriented approach.

CHAPTER 12

MAKING IT WORK FOR YOU

We all want to have warm, friendly working relationships. You want to like your prospect, and you want your prospect to like you. Unfortunately, even for students of Dale Carnegie's ideas, that isn't always easy, particularly during a first call.

You want to be sincere, to be yourself. You also want your client to be relaxed and at ease with you, with no sense of pretense or discomfort.

So . . . how do we achieve this comfortable balance?

Here are some tips for establishing rapport and building conscious relationships with your prospects:

1. Be your professional self. Don't try to act like somebody other than who you are. If you do, it'll come across as insincere or false.

   You can listen with interest and enthusiasm as a prospect talks about his recent trip to watch a NASCAR event, even if auto racing is about as appealing to you as having your teeth drilled. Remember—it's his story. But don't try to pretend to be a "good old boy" and fake a personal interest in racing that you don't have.

2. Dress simply and professionally. Minimize jewelry, and wear a good watch and polished shoes. Keep the focus on the customer and away from your wardrobe.

3. Be forthright. Extend your hand, look the other person in the eye, and tell him how good it is to meet with him.

4. Take a second to scan her office. Do you see signs of a similar interest? Pictures of the family or a hobby? Awards she has won? Make a connection.

"I see you love golf. I've been working on my game lately and got fitted for new irons. It turned out that the ones I was using were an inch too short. No wonder I couldn't hit the ball! Where do you usually play?"

If you truly don't have the same interests and cannot see a personal connection, look for a professional connection.

"Bill, I've been in banking for 15 years, started in the trust department. How about you?"

5. Always set a time frame at the beginning of the meeting, whether it is on the telephone or in person.

    "Beth, I've planned an hour for our meeting; does that work for you? We'll wrap up by 2:00 pm."

6. At the start of a meeting, resist the temptation to show off all you have learned about the customer's business and industry from reading the company's 10-K and annual report. You'll make a bigger impression if you wait to display your knowledge by asking an incisive question later, after you've established rapport.

7. When the customer talks, listen. Look directly at him. Nod. Don't interrupt. If you like to take extensive notes, ask permission to do so. (People don't like to have someone writing down every word they say—it's too much like giving a deposition and too little like having a conversation.) When the other person has made his point, wait for three counts before you say anything back to him. Linger over what he's said. Give him a chance to take a breath. Show him that you are listening by stopping to absorb what he just said.

    One effective technique for remaining focused and interested, yet keeping your own ego in check and your emotions in the background, is to pretend that you are a journalist whose assignment is to interview this businessperson. What questions would you ask to encourage her to talk? What mannerisms and body language would you use to convincingly act the part of a professional interviewer? How do interviewers on television look at the person they are interviewing? How do they communicate interest nonverbally? You can use those techniques, too.

8. After listening, always feed back what you heard. This is the highest compliment you can pay someone. It is the most important sign of a truly conscious relationship. You listened, and you want to get it right.

"Let me make sure I have this right, Mary. As you said, you've been in banking for 20 years, and you've never seen banking fees so low. Your concern is finding alternative sources of revenue to make up for what's being lost from fee reductions. Is that right?"

You should always recap at the end of a meeting, but it's also a good idea to take these small validation steps every 10 minutes or so. One of the most important questions you can ask is, "Why?" after you've fed back what you heard.

"Mary, why do you suppose fees are so low now?"

"Sam, besides your point about the accounting system being difficult to learn, do you think there are other reasons why the group isn't using it effectively?"

9. Stay on the topic, but don't try to control the conversation too tightly. If the customer wants to talk about how the war is affecting the company's profit, listen; you may gain insights into business needs that you would never get by asking directly. As need statements emerge, be sure to write them down so that you can later match a solution and/or benefit to each need.

10. Treat your customers or prospects as your equals, as partners in having a successful meeting. Let them explain their problems and how their business and their decision processes work, and then carefully explain to them how your sales cycle usually progresses.

11. Never argue with the customer. Instead, if you disagree, take a few minutes to make sure you understand his position. Go back to tip 8 and feed back what you heard. Make sure you truly see the customer's point of view. You are not there to judge him, you are there to solve his problems and provide a benefit to him and his company. One of the best ways to resolve conflict is to ask, "Why?"

"Brad, why are you concerned that senior management won't support this initiative?"

"Sandra, why do you feel that computer-based training is not as effective as classroom training? Besides the concern you expressed about people not taking the training seriously, what else concerns you?"

12. When leaving, extend your hand and offer a firm handshake and a smile, look the customer in the eyes, and thank her for her hospitality. Remind her of your next agreed-upon step.

"Jane, now that we have a firm understanding of your needs, we'll be back on Friday, July 22, to present the system to your decision-making team. I'll e-mail you to discuss a list of the attendees."

The most important step in achieving rapport and a friendly relationship with your prospect or client is to seek a conscious relationship. What do I mean by that? The phrase is one that is used in a form of psychotherapy and counseling called Imago Therapy, developed by Harville Hendrix. Although he is working primarily with people whose family relationships—with their spouse, their parents, or their children—are uncomfortable or unsatisfying, the principles that he uses apply to work relationships, too. Hendrix has found that people often "zone out" during an interaction with another person, focusing on their own issues, fears, or agendas. Instead of listening closely to the other person and showing the most intense interest we can muster in what the other person is telling us, we don't listen at all. Instead, we just sit quietly, waiting to jump in so that we can make our points and deliver our message. The result is a superficial relationship and poor communication. Hendrix maintains that there are only two kinds of relationships in life: those that are unconscious and those that are conscious. In an unconscious relationship, the people involved don't consciously acknowledge their own goals or agenda, what they hope to get from the relationship, so they become locked in a power struggle, trying to get what they need through various forms of coercion—groveling, belligerence, withdrawal, complaining, withholding time or information, and so on. In a conscious relationship, both people understand that they are engaged in building trust, and they both understand that they have their own agendas and goals. Through open, honest communication, they collaborate with each other and *decide* to do what is necessary to help each other achieve their goals. Building a conscious relationship implies that you are acting with full awareness of what you are saying and doing and with good intentions toward the other person. Yes, you would like to close business, but not at the expense of pretending to be someone you are not.

The Dale Carnegie approach is fundamentally about improving our relationships with other people, not about selling them more stuff. The Carnegie approach is about getting what you want by helping someone else get what he or she wants. In that sense, it's very much about establishing a trusting relationship built on sincere acceptance of the other person's point of view, on honest communication, and on sharing an open agenda.

People often wonder what it takes to establish rapport quickly and build it into a strong working relationship. If they are looking for tricks or subtle, manipulative techniques, they'll be disappointed. I remember reading about a sales rep who happened to be huge—over six and a half feet tall and nearly three hundred pounds. His sheer size, he felt, intimidated people. So he made a habit of tripping or banging his shin on a piece of furniture when he first entered someone's office, to make himself look vulnerable. If it worked for him, great, but it struck me as a dishonest way to begin a meeting. Besides, how many times can you bang your shins? If he wasn't able to establish some kind of substantive connection with the customer that would carry over from one meeting to the next, what had he accomplished with his playacting? Obviously, you want to do your homework before you meet with a client, so that you can come to the meeting prepared with insights and information relevant to the client's business. That's a logical first step. But the most important thing you can do is to listen closely and attentively. People underestimate how powerful it is to have someone listen to us with sincere interest. Nothing builds trust and rapport faster than listening.

But Dale Carnegie already told us that, didn't he?

PART FOUR

ELMER WHEELER

THE MAGIC OF WORDS

1. Don't sell the steak—sell the sizzle
2. Don't write—telegraph
3. Say it with flowers
4. Don't ask if—ask which
5. Watch your bark

CHAPTER 13

MAKING YOUR SALES *SIZZLE*

O f the four key figures profiled in this book, Elmer Wheeler is probably the least known today. That's too bad, because Wheeler did some of the twentieth century's most innovative thinking about how to sell and came up with phrases that have shaped American culture.

For example, you may have heard the phrase, "Don't sell the steak, sell the sizzle." Most people have. It has achieved the status of a proverb or a bit of folk wisdom. But it was invented by Elmer Wheeler as a way of making the point that bland, factual details don't work. You have to show the customer what the benefits are.

Wheeler claimed to have learned the power of using the right words early in his career. His father owned a gas station near Rochester, New York. On weekends, Elmer helped his dad at the station, and one day a gasoline salesman from Standard Oil approached him. He asked Elmer, "What do you say to sell gasoline to a motorist?"

Elmer didn't have any particular way of asking, so he replied, "Sometimes I ask people if they want five or ten; other times I just say, 'How much today?'"

The salesman said, "The next motorist who comes in, say this to him: 'Shall I fill it up?'"[1]

Elmer used the sentence, and the motorist told him to fill the tank, which meant that Elmer sold fifteen gallons, instead of just five or ten. More importantly, he gained a vivid lesson in the power of asking the right question. As Wheeler later remarked, "What a sure-fire method of getting tanks filled up! The sentence worked, and has been working successfully now for twenty years."

It would probably still be working today if gasoline companies hadn't discovered that it was cheaper and easier to do away with service entirely and make the consumer do the work.

Similarly, during the late stages of the Great Depression, the management of the Statler Hotel wanted to increase sales of wine. Prohibition had been repealed, yet most men merely ordered a glass of beer, if they ordered anything at all. Then, as now, fine wines were high-margin items that added to the profitability of the restaurant. By now a recognized expert in using words effectively to increase sales, Wheeler was asked to develop a way to increase beer and wine sales. He noticed that in most restaurants, the waiter or waitress would simply ask the customer, "Can I take your drink orders now?" or "What would you like to drink?" Obviously, that wasn't going to help sell more wine. Having the staff ask, "Would you like any wine with your meal?" was only a tiny bit better. It was too easy for the customer to answer, "No."[2]

Wheeler's approach was to train the staff to ask diners a different question: "Would you prefer red or white wine with your meal tonight?" When the question was phrased that way, sales of wine shot up dramatically. As Wheeler found, it's more effective to ask customers *which* than to ask them *if.* When they are asked which type of a product they want, customers are more likely to choose one of the options you give them. In contrast, asking them if they want a product at all is more likely to produce a clear no.

This approach still works. In my own career, I found that it was tricky to sell customer support as an add-on to software. Customers wanted support for free, and they pushed back if we asked them if they wanted "maintenance" or "support." Then we got smart and began asking them *which* instead of *if.*

> "Which support package will work better for you? Do you want 24/7 coverage? Or do you want business-hours only?"

By asking customers which package they wanted instead of if they wanted support at all, we moved sales of customer support well above the 90 percent mark.

As these examples indicate, Elmer Wheeler's focus was on the importance of using language in the most effective way possible to stimulate sales. For nearly a quarter of a century, he was one of the best-known figures in sales training. He wrote more than 20 books, including a couple that sold hundreds of thousands of copies. He established the Wheeler Word Laboratories and the Wheeler Sales Institute, where he trained thousands of professional salespeople and worked with many of the largest companies in America. Wheeler claimed to have used 105,000 sentences on 36 million consumers, under the auspices of the various companies that were his clients, observing which specific combinations of words produced the best results.[3] What he was looking for was empirical evidence that one particular way of saying something was more effective than another. From all his tests, he eventually generalized a number of principles—"Wheelerpoints" he called them, none too modestly—that are still basically valid today. He was a friend of J. C. Penney, the founder of the Penney's retail chain; H. W. Hoover, founder of the Hoover vacuum cleaner company, wrote the introduction to one of his books. And now he's virtually forgotten.

I have to admit that I had never heard of Elmer Wheeler until Gerhard Gschwandtner, the publisher of *Selling Power* magazine, mentioned him to me. But the more I learned about him, the more interested I became. What Wheeler focused on was crucially important, and it's an aspect of selling that's more important now than ever.

ELMER WHO?

Wheeler came by his interest in language naturally—early in his career he sold display advertising for newspapers. He worked for the *Los Angeles Herald*, the *Rochester Journal*, the *Albany Times-Union*, and the *Baltimore News-Post*, selling ad space to a variety of local businesses. Apparently, Wheeler was pretty successful at the job, but he became frustrated because he wasn't able to establish a causal link between the ads a merchant placed in the paper and an increase in that merchant's business. Like any good advertising sales professional, Wheeler had all the statistics about circulation and exposure. The problem was that the store owners he called on were skeptical: Sure, the ads brought people into their stores, but that didn't necessarily correlate with increased sales. Instead, they got a lot of "lookers" and "browsers" and "tire kickers" who wandered through the store, but seldom reached into their wallets or purses to buy anything.

As Wheeler saw it, at least early in his career, he was doing his job. Wasn't the purpose of newspaper ads to get people into the stores? After that it was up to the store manager and various sales clerks to make things happen. But Wheeler was savvy enough to know that even if the ads he placed were unbelievably successful, the store manager would see them as a failure, a waste of money, if they didn't result in sales. Wheeler mulled the problem over for some years, and he eventually convinced his boss at the *Baltimore News-Post,* Erwin Huber, to fund a little research.

First, Wheeler evaluated the kinds of products that stores were offering. As far as he could tell, they appeared to have the right merchandise at the right price and at the right season.

Next, he looked at the ads themselves. In general, they seemed pretty effective. They delivered clear messages. They got customers to come into the stores.

So where was the problem? Wheeler began to look at the "moment of truth"—the interaction between customer and salesperson. Could it be that the sales clerks were so ineffective that their interactions with customers actually created obstacles that got in the way of people's buying the things they were interested in?

To find out, Wheeler gave 20 of the *Baltimore News-Post's* reporters five dollars each, telling them to go to the May Company and buy as many men's shirts as the five dollars would purchase and as the clerks would sell them. (Remember, this was back in the 1930s, and five bucks went a long way then. You could buy a quality men's shirt for less than a dollar.)

When the reporters returned from the store, 15 of them hadn't bought a single shirt, because, as they told Wheeler, the clerks had made no attempt to sell them one. They had been left to wander around the men's department on their own without being approached by a sales clerk at all. The five reporters who did buy shirts purchased only one each, explaining that the clerk did not suggest a second, third, or fourth shirt. Wheeler guessed that perhaps these salespeople figured that since a man can wear only one shirt at a time, he probably wants to buy only one at a time.

Wheeler showed the results to the head of the May department store chain, Wilbur May, who realized instantly that although he might have a million-dollar establishment, with a million dollars worth of merchandise on the shelves, the real control of his business was in the hands of his minimum-wage sales clerks. However, in one regard, Wheeler's little experiment back-fired. Rather than proving the value of newspaper advertising, what it proved to May was that he needed to train his sales clerks to sell more effectively.

And with that, Elmer Wheeler changed careers.

By 1937, he had published *Tested Sentences That Sell,* his first major book. In it, he presented five "Wheelerpoints," gave his readers examples of how they work, and even speculated about why they work. Over the next 20 years, *Tested Sentences That Sell* outsold all other books on selling ever written.[4] Wheeler became one of the best-known speakers in the country, delivering thousands of speeches to businesses, associations, and conferences. He established training programs that were taught, according to his own account, at 125 business schools and colleges around the world. He wrote more than 20 books besides *Tested Sentences That Sell* (1937), including the *Sizzle Book* (1938), *Word Magic* (1939), *Tested Public Speaking* (1939 and 1947), *Sizzlemanship* (1940), *How to Sell Yourself to Others* (1947), *How to Make Your Sales Sizzle in 17 Days* (1953), *Selling Dangerously* (1956), and *Tested Ways to Close the Sale* (1957), plus other books on retail sales, direct sales, overcoming shyness, losing weight, setting goals, and quitting cigarettes!

In 1938, the young Elmer Wheeler was profiled in an article in the *New*

Yorker, which identified him as the head of the Tested Selling Institute, located on Fifth Avenue. It gives examples of some of Wheeler's most successful sentences: "Is your oil at the proper level today?" for Texaco, a sentence for which Wheeler was paid $5,000—or $555.55 a word, as the profile's author points out.[5] (You could buy a fine large house in 1938 for just $3,000!) Presumably Texaco felt that this was money well spent, since the company was able to get under 250,000 hoods in one week by having its filling station attendants ask this question. Another successful sentence was "One or two eggs today?" for Abraham & Straus, which increased the store's profit on malted milks dramatically, inducing seven out of ten customers to take at least one egg. Both sentences are typical of what Wheeler produced. They're short, they're easy to say, and they're easy to remember.

The psychological insights that were the foundation of Wheeler's points were based on his own common sense and his observations—his "testing" of the various approaches embodied in specific words, phrases, and sentences. Today we would use different words to make the points and different examples to illustrate them, but that doesn't mean they don't still work. In fact, you'll see that a lot of his ideas are similar to those of popular contemporary writers, particularly Steven Covey.

At the beginning, Wheeler had five points about how to use language to make sales. These five points were the core of his training programs and were the foundation of his various sales books. Later he came up with some additional points, but let's start with the original five. Here they are, in the order in which he presented them:

Wheelerpoint 1: Don't sell the steak, sell the sizzle!
Wheelerpoint 2: Don't write—telegraph.
Wheelerpoint 3: Say it with flowers.
Wheelerpoint 4: Don't ask if—ask which!
Wheelerpoint 5: Watch your bark!

These principles are not exactly self-explanatory, as you can see. In fact, Wheeler himself said that he had taken a wisecrack ("Don't sell the steak— sell the sizzle!") and turned it into a business philosophy. Before we look at his principles in detail, though, I think it would be helpful to understand a little about the way language works and how Wheeler's principles match up to the fundamental structure of language.

CHAPTER 14

THINKING AND BUYING

To understand the genius of what Wheeler wrote and to see why it still has relevance, we need to take a little detour into a field that probably seems about as unrelated to sales as anything could be: linguistics. But hang in there. It won't take long, and when we emerge on the other side, you'll see how relevant it is for professional sales. In fact, I think you'll be surprised at how much insight it gives us into the best ways to use language to make a sale. (As a side note, Wheeler seems to have had a pretty clear intuition of all this. His first book, published in 1932, was titled *Tested Selling Sentences: The Language of the Brain*.)

BRAINS AND WORDS

For most people, the magic and mystery of language comes home to them most forcibly when they watch their children learn to talk. From the early stages of baby babble that begin during the first year of life, children rapidly gain command of thousands of words of vocabulary and complex, nuanced rules of grammar. How on earth can they do that when they're not capable of tying their own shoes or telling time yet?

That question began to intrigue psychologists and linguists during the twentieth century. Research into the origins of various languages had revealed that our everyday vocabulary often had roots going back thousands of years to words used by our Indo-European ancestors. For example, the words *father* in English and *Vater* in German can be traced back to the Latin *pater* and ultimately to a Sanskrit word, *pitar*, all of which refer to "dad."

Researchers then began to wonder: What about the rules that govern how a language operates? Are they similar at some level from one language to another? That question triggered a revolution in the way we think about language and what came to be known as its "deep structure," because researchers and philosophers concluded that at a deep level, all languages work the same way. Moreover, they concluded that the ability to understand that deep structure is innate within the human brain. Thus, a baby doesn't learn a language from nothing, contrary to John Locke's theory of the "blank slate," but rather has an already deep understanding of language awakened and filled in by exposure to the language of the surrounding environment. A baby born in Boston will grow up speaking English with a Boston accent, because mommy and daddy speak that way, but if the same baby were transplanted to Paris or Prague or Beijing, the child would speak French or Czech or Chinese. The actual language spoken is an accident of birth, but the ability to use language is an important part of what makes us human.

This discipline came to be known as *structural linguistics*, because it focused on the cognitive structures that control how languages work. Its insights created a revolution in other fields, too, including psychology and anthropology. One of the pioneers of the discipline was a genius named Roman Jakobson. In an extremely influential essay, Jakobson described the six elements that need to be present in order for any act of communication to occur.[1] The six elements and their relationship to one another can be explained via Figure 14-1.[2]

Let's start with the two most basic elements—the sender and the receiver. The *sender* is the person who is doing the speaking, writing, gesturing, or grimacing, or who otherwise engages in an act of communication. The *receiver* is the person or group of people who hear the sales pitch, read the e-mail or the proposal, or observe the body language. The receiver might be in close physical proximity to the sender or might be far away in both time and distance. (For example, we "receive" messages from William Shakespeare every time we attend a performance of one of his plays, even though he has been dead for more than four hundred years. At a Christian church service, the congregation receives messages from the apostles who followed Jesus every time they read one of the four gospels, although they are thousands of miles and a couple of thousand years removed from them.)

The relevance of this to a sales situation is obvious. The salesperson sends

Figure 14-1

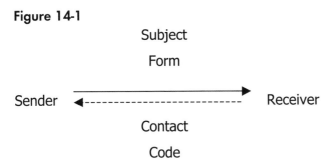

a particular message; the potential customer receives it. That's what the solid arrow indicates—the main direction in which communication flows. But notice that there's a dotted arrow heading back in the other direction. That represents feedback, something that customers who are directly present with us give us in the form of facial expressions, body language, gestures, and sometimes questions, objections, interruptions, or other verbal behavior.

The *subject* is the factual stuff we're actually communicating. If you describe to me the current limitations of my company's warehousing scheme and how those limitations are resulting in prolonged dwell times for merchandise before it reaches my stores, you are communicating information to me about my current transportation and logistics system. I may or may not agree with your interpretation of what those facts mean, but both of us are probably visualizing a map of transportation centers, rows of shelves inside the warehouses filled with merchandise, trucks backing into loading docks, and so on. Neither of us is visualizing puppy dogs playing or the upcoming city council elections, given the message that is being transmitted. (Unless one of us is psychotic, of course. One of the characteristics of schizophrenia is the inability to process language in predictable ways that match the way others around us are processing it.)

These three elements of communication (see Figure 14-2) have been recognized since the time of Aristotle. The *sender, receiver,* and *subject* form a basic triad, and paying close attention to each of them gives us some insights into its role in communication. But the other three elements of Jakobson's diagram represent a recent insight into how language works. And they give us valuable insights into how language works in a selling situation.

Figure 14-2

Subject

Sender   Receiver

For example, the factor that I call *form* (see Figure 14-3) covers the way in which a message is put together. Similar ideas are expressed by the terms *organization* and *structure.* Here are some examples.

During a class where I was helping national account salespeople from AT&T develop their presentation skills, a woman began her mock sales presentation with a joke. She said,

> "When I was a little girl I loved everything to do with Disneyland and all the Disney characters. One year, for my birthday, I asked my father to buy me a Mickey Mouse outfit. So he bought me ten shares of AT&T."

Figure 14-3

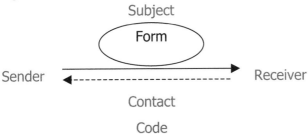

The first reaction from her audience was pained silence. Then there was a smattering of nervous laughter. Her audience's reaction made it clear to her that her joke was "wrong." From that point on, her whole presentation fell apart, because she knew she had already blown it.

But why was her little joke such a loser? Would it have worked if the audience had been made up of customers instead of colleagues?

It was wrong because it attacked the organization she worked for and was representing. It suggested that she didn't respect the company, that she was unhappy with it. Her joke undercut her role as a trusted adviser and a loyal employee. If she really felt that way about her company, why would she be there recommending to us that we use its products and services? No, that joke was wrong from every perspective. It would have failed just as brutally with customers as it did with her colleagues, and for the same reasons. A customer would wonder, "If you feel that negative about your company, why are you here recommending that we buy from it?" The openings in sales messages are particularly important, and this opening said all the wrong things. By starting her presentation with a joke that attacked her company, she chose a form that implied hostility or negativity.

Here's another example in which the *way* a message is delivered—its form—can undercut what it means. Suppose a salesperson is asked a question about her product and answers by saying, "To be perfectly honest with you . . ." That phrase, which appears rather meaningless in itself, may actually set off alarm bells in the customer's head. *Has the salesperson not been "perfectly honest" previously? Why does the salesperson think it's important to stress her honesty now?* The use of that phrase may be nothing more than a nervous tic, but it can call attention to the answer in ways that are likely to be unproductive and nonpersuasive.

Finally, here's something we've all seen in our careers. Suppose an engineer or technical expert is asked to contribute to a sales proposal by answering a complex question. Not having any training in persuasive writing, the engineer answers the question using the same format he uses to write a technical memo: detailed, factual, and informative, with careful consideration of all the pros and cons. That answer is probably well suited to communicating factual information to other engineers in a technical environment, but it's a disaster in a proposal. It's probably too long, too detailed, uses too much jargon, makes too many assumptions, and calls attention to issues or concerns that the customer doesn't need to know about at this point.

In summary, then, the way we "format" a particular message—the way we organize our thoughts into words—is extremely important in determining how effectively the message communicates.

The other two elements of communication also influence our success in a sales situation. When Jakobson talks about *contact* (see Figure 14-4), he is referring to the fact that we must establish a channel of communication and keep that channel open. Often we use ritualized forms of communication to attract the attention of our audience or to indicate that we wish to speak with them: *"Good morning." "How are you?" "Thank you for making room for me in your schedule."* Even when we are writing, we may lapse into rituals. For example, the salutation line in a letter (*Dear Mary Ann,*) is simply a way of saying, "The letter starts here." The word *dear* doesn't actually communicate our feelings about the recipient in a meaningful way.

But establishing and maintaining contact goes beyond the ritualized formulas of politeness. If we think about what Dale Carnegie taught, we can see that establishing rapport with the audience is an important aspect of opening a clear communication channel. Asking questions about the audience, expressing interest in their opinions, and engaging in the other behaviors that Carnegie argued would give us influence are all ways of establishing strong bonds of contact with our audience. After all, if people like us and respect us, they will be more eager to listen to us.

Figure 14-4

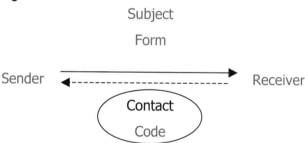

Last, there's the element that Jakobson called *code* (see Figure 14-5). What he means here is that we have to share the same language in order to communicate. That's pretty obvious if you've tried to do business in Latin America with a limited knowledge of Spanish, or if you've tried to sell prod-

Figure 14-5

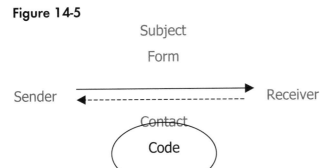

ucts in the Far East without good fluency in the customer's language. But even among people who speak the same language, there can be problems. One of the frustrations most people experience in dealing with lawyers is "legal language"—the jargon and specialized forms of expression that attorneys use to communicate with one another. An attorney once told me that the main purpose of legal language was to make work for other lawyers, but hopefully that's not true. Sometimes the use of professional jargon increases precision. That's often the case in medical writing. A physician might write something like this in a patient's file:

> Patient has a dark erythematous slightly raised rash over vertex area that barely crosses midline. No vesicles or open lesion. Head is normocephalic, atraumatic. Eyes: Conjuctiva clear, sclerae white.

Chances are that that language communicates a lot to another physician and virtually nothing to a lay person. We can recognize the use of specialized code when it's from a field other than our own, but sometimes people have difficulty recognizing their own jargon and acronyms. For example, here are a few terms that appeared in the executive summary of a proposal written by a company seeking to conduct clinical trials on behalf of a major pharmaceutical company. How many of these do you understand?

TQM	EMG	CMG
EMEA	ACCS	CNC
PIC	TEC	TMC
SC	CCS	BPI
PRIDE Team	CRP	ISRs
TMM	SSSS	IAACMP

More importantly, how many do you think the intended client was likely to understand? You might assume that because the customer is in the pharmaceutical industry, the people reading this probably recognized and understood these acronyms. However, you'd be wrong, because over half of them were internally used—and when I put them up on the screen, many of the firm's own employees actually disagreed about what they meant!

Many years ago I was working with a major telecommunications firm to develop a sales approach for a capability that could handle extremely large volumes of voice and data traffic. Unfortunately, the description of the service had been written by engineers, using acronyms and making technical leaps that the typical CEO or CFO was unlikely to follow. Apparently I made a nuisance of myself by demanding that the language be simplified and the jargon removed, because finally one of the telecom engineers said to me with undisguised exasperation: "Tom, look, if the customers don't understand this, they shouldn't be buying it!" To which I could only reply, "Don't worry. They won't." Unfortunately, the reality is that when customers are confused by the words we use, they seldom reach for their wallets.

DOMINATION TENDENCIES

So those are the six elements that need to be working in order for communication to occur—sender, receiver, message, form, contact, and code. We need somebody who is doing the talking or writing, somebody who is receiving it, a subject that the sender and receiver are discussing, a format for the message that's appropriate to its purpose, an open channel, and a shared code. All of these have to be there. If one of them is missing, communication breaks down.

But here's the other important point we need to know: In any given communication, one element will dominate over the others.

For example, a dictionary focuses on the *code* element—it uses language to explain language. So does a nomenclature table or a list of acronyms in a technical manual.

Contact is often the dominant element in purely social activities. Think about what happens at a networking event—people mill around, make small talk, and exchange business cards. There's not a lot of substantive information exchanged. Nobody is solving technical problems. Opportunities aren't being qualified. In fact, in most networking events, people aren't even offering many opinions. It's all about establishing a bit of rapport, a contact that you can follow up on later.

If the *form* of the communication is its most important element, we may be dealing with literature (the form of a sonnet or of a mystery novel helps determine the way we read it and how we react) or with a joke, where we know the structure of what's coming (a punch line, a limerick), although we probably don't know the actual words.

However, in a business setting, none of these elements is likely to dominate. Contact, code, and format are typically means to an end.

The dominant elements of communication in a business setting are the *subject matter*, the *sender*, and the *receiver*.

When we focus on the *subject matter*, we're attempting to communicate factual *information* as clearly and concisely as possible, so that someone else can understand that information and use it to do her job:

> *"Here are the three steps necessary to submit your expense report."*
> *"We have completed spectrographic analysis of the alloy samples, following thermal stress testing. Results indicate . . ."*
> *"We are pleased to announce that Pat Edwards has joined our staff as senior account manager. Pat will be responsible for Mettering Memorial Hospital as well as several large group practices."*

As Joe Friday said, it's just the facts, ma'am, and if we present them clearly enough, people can understand them quickly, determine whether they need them, and proceed accordingly.

If the dominant element in a business communication is the *sender*, we are dealing with an *evaluation*. Whenever we present facts and then offer our (presumably) informed opinion about what those facts mean, we are engaged in an act of evaluation. The focus is on us as the sender—as an expert, or at least as somebody who has done a bit of research and thinking. For example, if you're a sales manager, you might be asked by senior management to identify your top ten opportunities and indicate why you think they will or will not close this quarter. Management wants your opinion. You'll present some facts (size of the deal, feedback from the customer, relative weakness of the competition) to support your opinion, but it's still just your opinion. Likewise, if you have to conduct performance appraisals on your sales team, if you have to recommend a personalized training program for each rep, if you have to assess the success of a particular marketing campaign in generating qualified leads—you will refer to facts, but you'll end up offering an opinion. And that's all right.

Sometimes customers ask us for our opinion. They want to know what we think is the right course of action, what our strengths are compared to a competitor, what the important trends are in the industry. It's the same thing. We establish credibility by referring to the facts at our command, but unless we tell customers what we believe—what our opinion is—we're not really responding to their request. If we don't allow the communication process to focus on *us*—in the role of informed expert—we are failing to communicate effectively.

So what happens when the sixth element, the *audience*, dominates? Well, that, my friends, is the definition of *persuasion*. When we speak or write, using accurate facts and informed opinions, with the goal of influencing what people think, how they feel, or what they do, we are engaged in a form of communication in which the receiver is the most important component. We are *persuading*. Effective selling is all about speaking and writing in ways that affect the behavior of our customers, specifically, ways that lead them to make choices in our favor.

Over the years, I've come to believe that the worst mistakes in business communication have nothing to do with grammar or spelling or sentence structure. Instead, they stem from misunderstanding the purpose of our communication and using a format and focus that are not capable of achieving our goals. If we deliver informative, factual content, thinking that the facts will persuade our customer to buy, we have profoundly misunderstood the way communication works.

Wheeler's genius was in recognizing that the way you say something can make a huge difference in whether or not you convince the customer. He tried wording sales messages in different ways and tested them to find the wording that produced the best results. In both respects—focusing on the power of language to influence a customer and using empirical methods to find out what really works—he was way ahead of his time.

CHAPTER 15

WHEELER'S DEAL

In 1958, the popular TV show *To Tell the Truth* had as its featured guest the "famed sales authority Elmer Wheeler." Interestingly, the panel of celebrities, which consisted of Polly Bergen, Jackie Cooper, Kitty Carlisle, and Hy Gardner ("celebrities" who are nearly as lost to memory as poor Elmer), tried to guess which of three men was the real Elmer Wheeler.

Perhaps if they had listened carefully to the way he spoke, they would have gotten a clue or two. Wheeler was a rough but effective public speaker who had made LP albums teaching salespeople how to sell more effectively. But the panelists probably would have gotten even better hints from the way he put the words together than they could have gotten from the way he spoke them.

Elmer Wheeler was all about saying things in the most effective way. That's the focus of his "Wheelerpoints." If you want to produce the right results, you have to use the words in the right way. He wasn't claiming that certain words have "magic power" to motivate people. That's nonsense, and he knew it and said so. But he was saying that given the way people's brains work, some approaches will produce the right results and others won't. And when you use language effectively, it may seem like magic.

Let's take a look at each of his principles. And let's think about how we might use them in our digitized, twenty-first-century world.

DON'T SELL THE STEAK—SELL THE SIZZLE!

So what's a sizzle? And why should we focus on selling it instead of the actual product?

What Wheeler means by a "sizzle" is the primary appeal to customers— the aspect of our product or service that catches their attention and makes them think about what the product will do for them. It's the fact or detail that is most closely linked to the interests of the receiver. At one point, Wheeler said, "The sizzle has sold more steaks than the cow ever has, although the cow is, of course, mighty important."

Wheeler described "sizzles" as being the "best selling arguments" we can come up with, factors that have a real gut-level appeal to the buyer. To Wheeler, this appeal was spontaneous and irrational, and he used lots of food analogies to make his point—the sizzle of the steak, the bubbles in the wine, the tang of the cheese, the aroma of the coffee. (It probably won't surprise you to learn that Elmer Wheeler battled weight problems his entire life. In fact, his biggest-selling book of all time was *The Fat Boy's Book,* which recounted his personal "Battle of the Bulge" leading to a dramatic weight loss.[1])

All the same, his point is clear. People want to know, *what's in it for me?* And until they see that there is something in it for them, something that they want, they're not likely to listen to our sales pitch. If we can identify the "sizzles" in our sales message, we should mention them first to get the customer focused and excited.

Most of Wheeler's examples in *Tested Sentences That Sell* are drawn from retail sales—a clerk trying to sell perfume to a husband, a door-to-door salesman trying to convince a housewife to buy a vacuum cleaner. As a result, his book may seem dated and irrelevant to us, especially if we're selling business-to-business or selling high-tech solutions. But don't be fooled. His principle still applies.

For example, he describes the way a typical sales clerk trying to sell household appliances presents a canned sales pitch to a "little old woman," going through all the stove's features in order, including the durability of the enamel, the appliance's floor clearance, and other factors that the woman doesn't care about. He had one way of presenting the stove, and he would not be deterred. As a result, he missed the point and lost the sale.

Now you know that still happens today, and not just in retail.

For example, I was asked by sales and marketing executives at an enterprise software company to look at their sales proposals. The company was losing deals to a hated competitor, and they thought perhaps they could sharpen the message a little. This company had a very cool logo that consisted of its name written in curving script, similar to what you might see on a baseball uniform. When I started reading the executive summary in the first proposal, I was interested to see that they had chosen to start the executive summary by printing their logo to start the first sentence. And they started the second paragraph the same way. And the third. And the fourth. And the fifth, sixth, seventh, and so on for four solid pages! It was all about the company—not much sizzle in that. Even worse, it was all about the company's proprietary Web architecture and its unique data-handling methodology. Zero sizzle in that, either. When I picked up another proposal, I saw that it had the exact same executive summary as the first. In other words, the first and most important part of the sales message in the company's proposals was both canned and oriented toward factual content about the company itself.

Here's an example of somebody who understood the value of the sizzle: Al Lautenslager, who owns the Ink Well, a commercial printing and mailing company in Chicago, saw that Boeing was considering relocating its corporate headquarters to the Chicagoland area. Al immediately issued a press release to the *Tribune* and other local papers, announcing that he would print free business cards for Boeing employees if Boeing chose Chicago. He encouraged other local businesses to join him in offering free services. The story was picked up by a couple of papers. When Boeing did choose Chicago, Al then issued another press release, asking if Boeing chose Chicago because of the opportunity to get free business cards—not the millions of dollars worth of tax breaks that the city and state had offered. The follow-up piece generated five front-page articles! It was funny, it was harmless, and it generated a huge amount of positive attention for his business. What kind of coverage do you think he would have received if he had issued a boring, factual press release about the various services offered by his printing firm?

In *Crossing the Chasm*, Geoffrey Moore describes the structure of what he calls an "elevator speech"—the kind of quick-hitting, focused message that you dream of giving if you're riding up in an elevator with the CEO of the company you're trying to target. A good elevator speech, says Moore, identifies the kind of customers you serve, what their key needs are, and what kinds of benefits they're looking for. Why does it work? Because when you present the content in that order, it *sizzles*:

> For nonprofits that need to simplify the administration of their trusts, to maximize the return those trusts deliver, and to minimize their exposure to legal and financial risk . . .
>
> *Hmmm . . . that sounds like me!*
>
> Particularly if they are seeking to obtain a high ROI, reduce or eliminate administrative personnel, and operate in full compliance with their state's requirements . . .
>
> *Wait! I want those kinds of results!*
>
> Amalgamated Federal Savings Bank provides trustee investment management, administrative/record-keeping services, and unique tools to maximize returns.

Hey . . . maybe we need to talk.

Wheeler knew 75 years ago that going in with a canned sales message is a mistake. Assuming that "everyone" will be interested in a particular feature or a certain value proposition is insane. Failing to think about what the customer is interested in and then using that up front is a recipe for failure. Nothing has changed since Wheeler's day, and it never will, because that's the way human beings think. As a result, we have to get out of our own head and into the mindset of the customer—whether it's a "little old lady" buying a stove or a boardroom decision team mulling over the acquisition of multi-million-dollar enterprise software.

According to Wheeler, the rule to remember is this:

What is a "sizzle" to one person may be a "fizzle" or a whole bonfire to another person. Therefore, fit the "sizzle" to the prospect on hand!"[2]

Figure out the client's hot buttons and lead with that.

DON'T WRITE—TELEGRAPH!

Have you ever sent a telegram? They're pretty rare these days, but in Wheeler's time they were a common way to send urgent messages. They were extremely expensive, though, so people had to communicate as much as possible in as few words as possible. That's what Wheeler is getting at in this principle: You need to get the customer's **IMMEDIATE and FAVORABLE** attention in the fewest possible words."[3]

He had recognized the vital importance of starting a conversation, a phone call, a sales presentation, an e-mail, or any other kind of message in a way that grabs the audience's attention. We have to break through the "ho-hum factor." We have to sweep aside all the clutter of competing messages and data that constantly bombards our audience. "Your first ten words are more important than your next ten thousand," Wheeler wrote, "for you have only ten short seconds to catch the fleeting interest of the other person, and, if your first message doesn't 'click,' the prospect leaves you mentally—if not physically!"[4]

This principle is even more relevant today than it was in Wheeler's time. How long do you have to grab the reader's attention in an e-mail before she hits the delete key? How long do you have before the audience for your sales pitch begins to tune you out?

Leonard Zunin, a psychiatrist and educator, claimed that in our culture, we have about four minutes after we first meet a stranger to make a positive impression: "As a rule of social courtesy and congeniality . . . if neither party wishes to be rude, the two will converse for three to five minutes, or an average of four. This is the first courteous breaking-off point."[5] We often win or lose a potential relationship during that first four minutes, primarily, Zunin argued, because of the patterns of interaction we use. So clearly Wheeler was on to something. He suggested that we have about ten seconds. Maybe we have a bit more. But we can't expect much more than a couple of minutes before the other person's attention starts to wander or until he or she begins to form a negative opinion of us and our message.

What about a written document? How long does our audience pay attention to the document before forming an opinion about whether it's worth reading carefully? For e-mail, thanks to all the idiots who are flooding our inbox with spam, most of us are willing to spend less than 30 seconds glancing at a message before we kill it. In fact, many of us won't do any more than look at the subject line before we move on.

For longer, more complex documents that are delivered in a trusted format—for example, an actual letter or a formal proposal—the audience will give us a little more time. But not much. For example, research we did found that, on average, a person evaluating a formal proposal, one that may be 100 pages or more in length, will make up his or her mind in less than seven minutes—sometimes much less. What that means, by the way, is that readers decide whether to toss your proposal on the discard pile or shove it over to the keepers. Since their goal is to eliminate as many as possible as quickly as possible so that they can cut their work down to a manageable amount, you can see why it's important to "telegraph" a compelling message. Unfortunately, the most common way salespeople start their proposals is with an overview of the vendor company's history! More of a "snoozle" than a sizzle.

SAY IT WITH FLOWERS

What Wheeler means by this principle is that you must prove your claims. If you say to your spouse, "Happy anniversary," that's good, but if you also hold out a bouquet of flowers as you say it, that's better. As he says, "Give a quick customer benefit—but then prove it the next second."[6]

Wheeler seems to be suggesting that we use two different kinds of proof. On the one hand, we can substantiate our claims of benefits by offering a factual example or proof statement. On the other hand, we can provide emotional proof that we believe in our claims by demonstrating the kind of body language that communicates sincerity. "It's the little things you do," Wheeler tells us, "the movement of your hands—your head—your feet—that tells the prospect how sincere and honest you are."

The first kind of proof, where we support our claims, is particularly needed when salespeople start spouting marketing fluff:

> As an industry leader, we are committed to a partnership approach that
> incorporates best-of-breed products and innovative, proprietary solutions,

backed up by world-class service, all integrated to enhance the synergy of their unique architectures. As a result, customers find that our applications offer leading-edge performance in a user-friendly package.

About halfway through that spiel, the customer's built-in B.S. detector begins throbbing. Grandiose generalities, vague claims, and unsubstantiated assertions tend to do that to people.

Taking Wheeler's advice, we might say something like this:

Customers often worry about whether to buy technology or to build it themselves. Our customers find that we've completely eliminated that problem for them. How? First, we've identified the best products in the information storage field, including the three biggest sellers. Then we've created solutions that also include our own controls and reports. We've tested them thoroughly in our own labs, and we had them certified independently by the National Software Certification Board. The result is reliable solutions that are easy to install. In fact, most of our customers are up and running in less than 48 hours.

It's a little longer, but it's also a lot more convincing because of the supporting details.

The second kind of proof, the kind we communicate nonverbally, requires a level of self-awareness that few of us have. One of the best ways to see whether your expressions and movements express sincerity and honesty is to have yourself videotaped as you deliver a sales presentation. You might be shocked to discover that you have the habit of wringing your hands as you speak, or that you jingle the coins in your pocket, or twist your hair, or never look the customer directly in the eye. All of these unconscious actions can create an impression of nervousness, anxiety, perhaps even sneakiness. Most of the time they're just bad habits, but until you spot them, you won't be able to remove them. By the same token, speaking with enthusiasm and energy and acting like you are excited to be demonstrating your product or talking with the prospect are all part of saying it "with flowers."

Recent research on the psychology of persuasion confirms that Wheeler was right. Sometimes a decision maker is convinced by a logical approach that's based on facts. Sometimes what works is rooted in emotion. In your sales presentation, should you focus on building a strong argument? Or should you work on using peripheral cues, such as facial expressions, gestures, body language, and emotional appeals? Social psychologists who have conducted experiments in the field of persuasion have found that both approaches work. When a decision maker has the time to think carefully and systematically about his or her decision, a logical approach—what psychologists call a "central route"—works. However, when customers don't have much time, or when they are uninterested or distracted, they may focus instead on emotional elements that trigger a response without provoking conscious thought.[7] Quick TV and radio ads are more likely to use this indirect, emotional approach because they have so little time to make a point and because the audience is probably distracted. Using emotional language and value-laden imagery works better in that environment than providing facts. Think about the way a car is typically presented in an ad during prime time. The vehicle is shown being driven rapidly by beautiful people through gorgeous scenery. However, an ad for the same car that appears in a magazine for auto enthusiasts is likely to contain a lot more content, including engineering specifications and documented evidence for the car's superiority in some area of interest—handling, acceleration, gas mileage, or whatever. When applied to a sales call, the proper approach is to combine evidence with emotion, but it's wise to start with something that generates positive emotion. Starting a sales presentation, "I'm happy to tell you that we have identified a way to reduce your long distance charges by more than $3 million," will generate a quick, pleasurable reaction. You can then go on to prove it, explaining where the savings will come from and substantiating that your numbers are realistic and that the projected savings have been realized by some of your other clients.

I recently visited a new client, so one of the things I did to get ready was to visit their web site. It was not a good experience. The site was well designed, it had nice graphics, and it was easy to navigate. So what was the problem? The words. Everything they wrote about their services consisted of dull, worn-out clichés—"leading edge," "state of the art," "innovative," even that bloated loser "synergistic." Yuck! Their messages were vague and not the least bit persuasive. This kind of language—which I call "marketing fluff"—alienates readers because it makes grandiose claims without offering any proof.

Here are some more examples of marketing fluff. Anything look familiar?

+ Best of breed
+ World class
+ Quality focused
+ Uniquely qualified
+ High performance
+ Synergy
+ User friendly
+ Integrated
+ Partnership

+ Seamless
+ Robust

Customers are often faced with an overwhelming number of decisions to make, many of which take them out of their zone of expertise and familiarity. It's not surprising that in such a situation, they will make the decision impulsively and emotionally—that they will go with the biggest company, for example, or that they will choose to work again with the incumbent vendor. The decision heuristic is a simple one: "This company is known around the world, so it must be a safe choice." "I can trust the people I have worked with in the past." (This helps explain why incumbent vendors win over 90 percent of rebids in government contracts.) Overcoming the customer's tendency to make a snap, emotional decision may require you, during the sales process, to raise concerns that force the decision maker to slow down and think carefully. The concerns might be related to technology, contract terms, financial strength, follow-up procedures, costs, or any of a thousand other aspects of a contract. The goal is to get customers to focus on something that they think is important enough to slow down for, and to open themselves to a more logical, evidence-based persuasive message. As a result, when we "say it with flowers," as Wheeler recommends, we may need to choose flowers that have a few thorns—or that at least raise some thorny issues.

DON'T ASK IF—ASK WHICH!

This is one of Wheeler's best insights. As he explains in *Tested Sentences,* "We mean you should always frame your words (especially at the close) so that you give the prospect a choice between something and **SOMETHING**, never between something and **NOTHING**."[8] Most parents of toddlers have stumbled on the magic of this approach, but we may not see how the same psychology works with adults, too.

When asking for the order, when asking the customer to agree to move to the next stage of the sales process, when simply asking for an appointment—ask the customer in such a way that she or he must choose between two options, both of which you are happy with. You can ask which of a couple of options that customer wants to buy, when the product should be delivered, how many items should be in the initial order. But you don't ask *if* the customer wants to buy. This was the basis of Wheeler's sentence for the Abraham & Straus stores: "One egg or two?" If the counter clerk asked, "Do you want an egg in that?" the customer would have a choice between something and nothing, and a majority of them would choose nothing. As I mentioned earlier, Wheeler helped restaurants increase their wine sales by training the wait staff to ask, "Would you prefer red or white wine with dinner tonight?" And we increased our sales of maintenance contracts by asking, "Do you want maintenance coverage for business hours only, or do you want comprehensive, 24/7 coverage."

Obviously, the principle of *which, not if,* can apply to a written offer, too—giving a client a choice of two options and assuming that the client will take one of them is just as effective in your sales proposal as it is in a sales presentation.

For most businesses, the add-ons are lucrative, and research proves that the best time to ask customers to buy them is after they have just agreed to the main part of your offer. The momentum favors the client's saying yes again. Psychologists refer to this as the consistency principle—having made an initial decision in one direction, people tend to make other decisions the same way in order to be consistent with themselves. But it's even more likely that they will say yes if you ask the right way.

What Wheeler has framed in this principle is a form of the assumptive close. You simply act as though it's a given that the customer is going to buy. The only questions remaining are a few details—how many, what colors, what kind of delivery schedule, which customer service package. This approach works if you have accurately positioned your product or service with "sizzles" that customers care about, because they have already indicated that your offer addresses many of their key needs. Your confidence that they will go forward gives them the confidence to do it.

Wheeler also recognized that the art of asking leading questions, questions that couldn't be answered with a simple yes or no, was an important skill for salespeople. He compared it to an attorney examining a witness, asking leading questions, but always with a firm understanding of what the answer is going to be. And he strongly recommended using questions to revive the momentum in a sales presentation.

Asking "Why?" is particularly effective. If a customer objects that your price is too high, rather than arguing about the price, try asking, "Why do you think so?" The customer may have a ready answer—"Because your competitor is asking much less," or "Because it's twice as much as my budget," or "Because I don't think it's worth it." Now you have the opportunity to deal with the specific perceptions: The competitor's pricing is not complete, and its product has fewer features. The budget may not have been realistic to begin with, but by proceeding in a phased approach, you can help the customer stay within it and still get some benefits. The customer may have forgotten the value impact that solving the problem is likely to have on his or her organization. Wheeler's point, and it's still valid today, is that salespeople are afraid to ask "Why?" when they get objections, and they forget to ask "Which?" when it's time for the order.

WATCH YOUR BARK

Wheeler's final point means that you need to deliver your message effectively. It's not just using the right words, it's saying them the right way, that delivers results. In his own words: "The finest 'sizzle' that you 'telegraph' in ten seconds, with huge bouquets of 'flowers' and lots of 'which,' 'what,' 'where,' and 'how,' will flop if the voice is flat."[9]

In face-to-face selling, using a monotone or speaking in a whiny voice will undercut your message. Nervous gestures, like wringing your hands together or playing with your hair, will suggest that you are not confident of what you are saying. Communicating optimism, enthusiasm, and energy through your voice and gestures helps create those same feelings in the audience. This is a point that Dale Carnegie made, of course, and one that his disciple Frank Bettger repeated . . . enthusiastically.

Wheeler's point about being careful in the way we say something—the tone and nonverbal component of our message—has been validated extensively by a variety of researchers. Two psychologists found, for example, that 38 percent of all communication comes from the tone of voice and 55 percent comes from body language.[10]

People often worry that if they stumble while they are speaking, or if they use fillers like "uh" or "um," the audience will think they are incompetent. In reality, unless those behaviors occur so frequently that they become obtrusive, no one notices them. Perfect delivery is not a realistic goal. Effective delivery is. One of the best ways to improve your delivery skills, both in informal settings, such as a face-to-face conversation conducted over the client's desk, and in more formal venues, such as a product demo or an oral proposal before an evaluation team, is to videotape yourself. I have coached hundreds of salespeople and proposal teams in delivering oral presentations over the years, and without videotape the challenge of improving would be monumentally difficult. When people see themselves on tape, the experience is often uncomfortable. After all, most of us just aren't used to seeing ourselves on the TV screen. But the discomfort passes quickly, and then people begin to see clearly the strengths and weaknesses of their own delivery. In my experience, 99 professionals out of 100 can instantly spot their own weaknesses and identify what they need to do to improve. Oddly, they have a much more difficult time identifying their own strengths. I always require seminar participants to tell me first what they liked about their presentation. Often, they can't think of a thing. But they can immediately zero in on a handful of mistakes and bad habits that they want to eliminate.

One of the most frequent comments that I hear in these sessions is that the videotaped performance doesn't look as bad as the presenter thought it would. That's an important lesson. The audience can't see how you're feeling on the inside. People can only see what you're doing on the outside. If you can minimize the kind of external behavior that suggests you're nervous or worried, you'll project an attitude of confidence. You can be shaking on the inside, but if you look calm on the outside, the audience will conclude that you're calm and in control.

So how can you get this kind of feedback? The best way to do this is to take a course in presentation skills that videotapes student presentations and critiques them afterward. If there's no videotape, don't take the course. If you can't find a course, just get a camera, tape yourself, and watch it. Here are some things to look for:

1. *Did you look up from your notes?* Maintaining eye contact is a vital part of establishing and maintaining rapport. Don't try the trick of looking over the audience's heads, either—it gives you a glassy, Stepford-wife kind of look that will give your audience the creeps.

Never under any circumstances read your presentation. And that includes turning around to face the screen and reading the words on your slides. Face the audience and talk to them.

2. *Did you stand quietly? When you moved, did you move with a purpose— for example, to get closer to the audience to make an important point?* One of the most common behaviors for nervous speakers is to "dance"—to shift their weight back and forth from one foot to the other, or to pace forward and back as though learning to waltz, or to make a repetitive circuit, two steps left, then two steps forward, then two steps back.

Another habit that suggests nervousness is standing with your hands folded across your groin in a fig-leaf stance. Not quite as bad, but still unnatural, is standing with your hands clasped behind your back as though you were facing a firing squad. People worry about what to do with their hands. My advice? Don't do anything with them. You've been using them spontaneously for your whole life, so relax and you'll use them spontaneously as you speak.

3. *Did you speak at a normal, conversational pace?* Nervousness sometimes causes people to speak faster than normal. If you speak too fast, people will have a hard time understanding you.

4. *Did you smile occasionally?* Smiling works. It makes the other person feel comfortable, and it makes you look relaxed and self-confident.

5. *Did you gesture to reinforce important points? Were the gestures "generous"—that is, did they originate in your shoulder and involve broad movements, or were they little, cramped gestures from your wrists?* If you're in somebody's office and it's just the two of you, small gestures are appropriate. But if you're at the front of a room, presenting to a group, with PowerPoint slides projected on a screen, you need to be "larger than life," and making broad gestures will help keep the audience's focus on you and your message.

6. *Did you lapse into using your own jargon or acronyms? Or did you keep your language accessible?* Again, because of nerves, people sometimes lapse into using language that the customer doesn't understand. Because the presenter uses these terms around the office with colleagues, though, it feels "comfortable." It's not comfortable to the audience and may alienate them.

Your goal is to develop a presentation style that communicates confidence and openness. Relax. Remember that you have a good message, you understand your message better than anybody else in the room, and the customer is actually interested in hearing it. If the people in your audience ask questions or make objections, it's usually a wonderful sign that they are actively thinking about your recommendations and considering whether or not to buy from you.

So watch your bark, indeed. We communicate far more nonverbally than we do verbally, so gestures, posture, eye contact, and tone of voice can help you get your points across.

The same thing is true in writing. The tone of your written messages can come across as friendly and intelligent or stiff and bureaucratic. For example, long, convoluted sentences are likely to alienate the reader. In fact, when adults read a sequence of long sentences, their brains sometimes "shut down" and they stop comprehending the message. You've probably had this experience yourself—halfway through a paragraph from a contract or a technical manual or a white paper, you suddenly snap alert and realize that you haven't understood a word for several minutes, even though your eyes kept running over the lines of text. Typically, if we have to understand the material, we go back and start breaking it down into smaller units, essentially rewriting it as best we can into something we understand. To avoid making your readers' brains go blue screen and crash, keep your sentences to an average of 15 words or so. That's an easy length for people to decode. And when they find that something is easy to read, they tend to think that it makes sense otherwise. Clarity is the first element of persuasiveness.

The way you start sets the tone for how your reader reacts. A bad opening almost always guarantees a bad reaction.

> *"Thank you very much for allowing me to submit the enclosed proposal . . ."*
> *"Pursuant to your inquiry, please be advised . . ."*
> *"It is my pleasure to inform you that our company has released a new product that . . ."*

All of these openings are weak. The first one fails because of its tone. It sounds like you're groveling. The second one also has a bad tone, but in this case it sounds stuffy and old-fashioned. The third one is all right in terms of its tone, but it's focused on content that the reader probably doesn't care about.

Getting your message through is tricky. You need to sound friendly and natural. You also need to focus on something that will attract the reader's interest. Third, you need to be concise.

When you are writing, try to start with a brief statement that will be of interest to your reader. For example, if you are responding to a customer who has asked you for some information, the first thing you should say is: "Here's the information you asked for." If you are writing a factual memo or e-mail, tell the reader the most important fact right up front: "Lab tests conducted over the past seven weeks have established that the new disk alloy is 117 percent harder than the alloy you are currently using."

A common mistake that people make when they write factual memos and e-mails is that they present all the background information up front in a chronological narrative. Believe it or not, people almost never need to read that stuff first in order to understand your key point. Would it help you understand the point about the new alloy being harder if you first had a paragraph or two that covered all the lab tests you ran, why you ran them, and who authorized them? No, probably not. Writing chronologically almost always means presenting more information than the reader needs and doing it in a way that takes too long to get to the point.

Now, what if your letter or e-mail is persuasive? What if you're writing a sales proposal? In that case, you want to start by focusing on a key challenge or opportunity that the customer is facing. If you start by stating the problem that I'm worried about in a clear, succinct, nonjudgmental way, I'll go on reading in hopes of gaining insight or perhaps even seeing a solution.

For example, instead of starting our proposal by saying "Thank you for allowing me to submit . . . ," we could start it by saying:

> Based on the security analysis we conducted at ten of your retail locations, selected at random, we have found that you are highly susceptible to credit card fraud. Specifically, because of the verification systems in place at your registers, your retail sites are experiencing fraud rates approximately 20 percent higher than the national average. Translated into dollars and cents, you are losing about $7.5 million annually.

Can you see how an opening with that kind of specificity and precision would grab the reader's attention right away?

Get to the point—but make sure it's the point your customer wants to hear: *Here is the key fact. Here is the problem I'll help you solve.* Then the customer is more likely to keep reading.

There are other mistakes in writing that can give your message the wrong "bark." A sloppy e-mail full of misspelled words, drive-by punctuation, and fractured grammar will have the same effect on your audience that a hellacious case of bad breath would in person. Using the wrong client's name in your slides or your proposal will produce the same kind of reaction as if you murmured the wrong name during love making. And writing in a legalistic tone will suggest to your customers that you don't trust them, which will probably lead them to question whether they should trust you.

How often have you seen disclaimers in the cover letter of a proposal: "Nothing in this proposal should be construed as a binding promise to deliver nor a commitment to execute until such time as all contractual terms have been negotiated fully and . . . blah blah blah." In other words, read this proposal and agree to what we're saying, but just be aware that we're not going to stand by it until much later, after we have your signature on a few dozen documents. Hmmm . . . I don't think so. As my mother used to say, "Don't take that tone with me."

Tone is difficult to teach, yet we all recognize an inappropriate tone when we hear or read one. The tone you use in writing a sales letter, e-mail, or proposal will directly affect how the customer reacts to what you say.

Sales reps make another big mistake when they use passive-voice constructions in their e-mails and sales letters. Without going into the vagaries of English grammar, let it suffice to say that the *passive voice* is one of the three ways we can put a sentence together in English. Sometimes we use the *imperative voice*—the way of structuring commands or directions: "Close the window." "To restore a file after it has been deleted, follow these steps." Most of the time, though, we use the *active voice* when we speak—on average, about 90 percent of the time, in fact. In an active-voice sentence, the subject does the action expressed in the verb. For example, here's an active-voice sentence:

> We must decide which parts of the project to work on first in order to preserve resources and maintain the schedule.

Well, that's clear enough, isn't it? We need to establish our priorities before we start. Otherwise we may waste time and money. So what happens if we say the same thing in the passive voice?

> A decision must be made regarding which parts of the project to work on first in order to preserve resources and maintain the schedule.

Really? And who will make that decision? Now the subject of the sentence ("decision" in the passive-voice version) doesn't do anything at all. Something happens to the subject. The person or thing that actually does the action may be left out entirely. That's why passive-voice writing is often referred to as the language of nonresponsibility, and why it creates a sneaky tone. There's nothing grammatically or morally wrong with using the passive voice, but you do need to be aware of the effect it has on your tone. And if you use the passive voice in a really long sentence, you've cooked up a recipe for incomprehensibility.

Another of my pet peeves is the way people close their sales letters. The most common closing line is, "If you have any questions, please feel free to call." There are two fundamental problems with that language. First, it's a cliché, so it doesn't sound like you mean it. It sounds like you can't think for yourself, so you just repeat the standard business phrases that everybody else uses. Second, and far more serious, it presupposes that what you have just written is not clear and has raised questions or doubts in the customer's mind. I strongly recommend using a proactive close in your letters and e-mails to customers: "We are excited about these numbers, because they indicate you will achieve payback within six months." Or how about: "The next step is to present these specifications to the Finance Committee. I will call you on Tuesday to discuss setting up that meeting." Put your phone number under your name and title. If the customer has questions, she'll be smart enough to call you without your telling her it's okay.

One of the problems people have in writing e-mails, sales letters, marketing pieces, and related materials is to find the right level of formality. If they write the way they were taught to write in a college English class, they're probably too formal. The message won't sound like them. But if they lapse into slang and casual grammar, they may come across as unprofessional or even disrespectful. What to do?

One way to lighten your tone without going too far toward informality is to use contractions in your writing. We use contractions a lot more when we're speaking than we do when we're writing, but there's no reason to limit them just to speech. In fact, using contractions in your written messages will help to create a friendly, informal tone. If you're concerned that you're coming across as too informal, try reading the chunk of text you're worried about out loud. Your ears are usually much better at picking up the right tone than your eyes are. If it sounds okay when you read it out loud, go with it.

Another technique you can use to create an informal tone is to start sentences with coordinating conjunctions occasionally. The coordinating conjunctions are the little ones—*and, but, or, nor, yet, so,* and *for.* Time after time I have been asked in seminars whether it's "correct" to start a sentence with *and* or *but*—with the implicit assumption on the questioner's part that it is not. In reality, a coordinating conjunction's purpose is to link together two related things—words, phrases, clauses, or sentences. English writers have been starting sentences with these words since the days of Beowulf, so there's no reason you can't. However, as some salespeople have pointed out to me, what if the customer doesn't realize that it's okay? Will they think we are semiliterate? Careless? Poorly educated? It's possible, I suppose, although most people don't notice them unless they are used so frequently that they become obtrusive. Use your own judgment. But don't be afraid to start a sentence with a coordinating conjunction. And remember that they can make your writing sound a little friendlier, a little less formal.

The order in which you present your ideas or facts will affect the way the reader perceives them. Normally, the reader will assume that the first thing you discuss is what you consider most important. That's why it's so deadly to start off by talking or writing about your company's history or your product's features. The tone seems self-centered to the reader because putting this material first suggests that you think it is more important than anything to do with the reader. Your written and oral presentations will seem more customer-centric if you start off with information about the customer—the customer's key needs, key performance indicators, and objectives or plans.

Finally, watch your bark in terms of offensive language. You are better off using inclusive language whenever possible—*chair* instead of *chairman*, for example, or *salesperson* instead of *salesman*. This isn't just a matter of being politically correct, although *politically correct* is really just another way of saying *considerate*. It's also a matter of being smart. Using sexist language or making remarks that are based on stereotypes about race, ethnicity, age, sexual orientation, or disability will eventually undercut a salesperson's rapport and credibility with a customer, which means that that kind of language will eventually cost the salesperson a deal.

CHAPTER 16

THE LANGUAGE-BASED APPROACH TODAY

Long before Elmer Wheeler came on the scene, people had wondered whether certain words or patterns of words might produce specific effects in the brain. Belief in the power of magic words, spells, and incantations to affect reality predates recorded history. In more modern times, the work of Mesmer in the nineteenth century, which led to the development of hypnotism, made people wonder if there actually was something to the ancient notion of casting a "spell" on someone by saying certain potent words.

Psychologists in the early part of the twentieth century began to investigate brain function by measuring electrical stimulation. Ironically, Dale Carnegie was intrigued by the idea that words could produce a particular electrical signal in the brain. He wrote a magazine article about the research being done by a Dr. von David, who had developed an "attitude testing device." This machine used a voltmeter attached to the skull to measure a subject's response to words as they were projected on a screen. The experiment fascinated Carnegie. He thought it proved that words were powerful psychological forces that could instantly produce feelings of pleasure or depression.

Although Carnegie's stimulus/response notion of language's impact on the listener was about as primitive as Dr. von David's machine, he was on to something. Elmer Wheeler's later efforts to test reactions to complete sentences was a bit more useful, because the sentences embodied a complete thought—in most cases, a selling proposition or a call to action. But recent neuroscientific analyses of brain function have used CAT scans and similar tools to allow researchers to watch the brain's reactions noninvasively. And like the long-forgotten Dr. von David, researchers are trying to figure out what happens inside the brain when people think and feel, and to learn whether certain kinds of reactions are produced by certain kinds of stimuli—including words.

Although it is not specifically related to sales, some of the most interesting work on the way people speak and the way other people hear them has been done by Deborah Tannen. Her research into gender-based differences in the way people communicate in business settings provoked a great deal of debate when it first came out. Was she saying that men and women think differently? Is that why they use language in different ways? And were the differences somehow innate, twisted into the X or Y chromosome that determined gender in the first place? Or were they cultural in origin, the product of subtle reinforcements that teach boys how to communicate like men, and girls how to communicate like women?

In her best-selling book *You Just Don't Understand: Women and Men in Conversation*, Tannen proposed that women and men have difficulty communicating with one another because they understand messages in fundamentally different ways. A similar theme was developed by John Gray in *Men Are From Mars, Women Are From Venus*, a bit of pop psychology that became a best-seller. Tannen and Gray maintained that both styles are equally valid—that is, the masculine and the feminine styles of thinking, speaking, and interpreting messages both work—but they are so different that any communication between men and women represents a kind of cross-cultural communication. Gray and Tannen's books were based mainly on a broad theory supported by anecdotal evidence and observations of limited numbers of interactions, but they convinced a lot of people in academic settings and within the general population. Claims about the fundamental differences between women and men in their modes of communication, and the misunderstandings that these differences create, soon filled professional journals and college textbooks.

If Tannen's theory is true, her work might be taken to imply that women could not sell to men effectively, and vice versa. But that's the real question: *Is it true?*

With regard to fundamental gender differences, recent research has challenged the whole theory. As one comprehensive study put it,

> There appears to be virtually no relevant, credible evidence that supports the claim that men and women constitute different communication cultures or speech communities, especially with respect to supportive communication. The notion that men and women constitute different communication cultures appears to be little more than a myth—a myth that has outlived any useful purpose it may have once served.[1]

Intuition tells me that this debate is far from over. However, for now at least, we can go forward on the assumption that women can sell successfully to men, that men can sell successfully to women, and that the two sexes can, with a bit of effort, understand each other if they really want to.

NEUROLINGUISTIC PROGRAMMING

Another field that has drawn on theories of linguistics to justify a radical approach to communicating is neurolinguistic programming, or NLP. Originally developed by Richard Bandler and John Grinder, NLP drew in part on the linguistics theories of Noam Chomsky. In his original work on linguistic structures, Chomsky identified processes by which people single out aspects of experience on which to focus. These processes are *deletion, distortion,* and *generalization.*

We use deletion—the unconscious suppression of huge amounts of the data with which we are bombarded—to enable us to function. Research done by the psychologist George Miller found that people can handle only seven bits of information, plus or minus two, at any one time, so Chomskian deletion has been characterized as an unconscious means of ignoring all but the essential seven bits of sensory data that a person is currently trying to deal with.[2] Miller's essay has been subject to another of Chomsky's processes, distortion, since it was really about the ability of the brain to handle discrete and nonmeaningful bits of data, like tones or nonsense syllables, but regardless, it does point out that the brain has limitations and must create filters to prevent sensory and cognitive overload.

Distortion is the process of emphasizing or bringing to the foreground one aspect of an experience while minimizing another. Distortion can arise when we use imagination or when we use selective focus. Regardless, if you and I both attend a performance of *West Side Story* (or a soccer game) in which one of us has a child performing, you and I will have very different perceptions of both the event and the significance of that child's contribution. Although we both received the same set of data streaming into our sensory apparatus, we distorted what we received based on the particular interest one of us has in the role of little Madeline or Luke.

Generalization is the tendency for people to build broad conclusions on the basis of a couple of examples. We buy a supposed Persian rug from an Iranian rug merchant and then find out it was made in China. We generalize that all Iranian rug merchants are dishonest. On the face of it, that conclusion is illogical and unsupported, yet it's often the way our minds work. We use generalization to produce rules, guidelines, beliefs, and assumptions about what to expect, how to behave, and what to trust.

According to NLP, individuals create a map of the world by using these three filters in different ways. This is not an idea that originated with NLP, of course. The nineteenth-century psychologist William James, who is often cited by Dale Carnegie, argued that the process of transforming the booming, buzzing confusion of sensory stimuli that surrounds us when we are infants into a comprehensible understanding of the world is a process of creating mental maps of the relationships among bits of our experience. Where NLP introduces something new is in suggesting that by observing another person's outward behavior, we can figure out what kind of mental map that person is using, and that we can then use that information to control the other person's reactions.

Originally designed for use as a therapeutic technique, NLP quickly became a tool for salespeople and marketers. The assumption is that if we can understand how somebody else habitually processes information—the models of reality they use, or their "meta programs," to use NLP jargon—we can quickly change the way they think, what they do, even what they believe. There are other filters that people use to delete, distort, and generalize the data they receive, including values, belief systems, memories, and decisions we have made in the past.

A lot of this training deals with establishing rapport with the customer, but unlike the Carnegie approach, which was based on listening to the other person, showing some sincere appreciation, and showing interest in what the customer said, the NLP approach involves techniques called "mirroring" and "pacing."

Mirroring entails mimicking the other person's speech patterns, tone of voice, diction, body language, facial expressions, and other outward expressions of an individual's meta-style.

One important part of mirroring is a process called "matching the modality." (Yes, this is another bit of NLP jargon. If nothing else, the field of NLP has spawned a huge amount of jargon.) According to NLP theory, people have a dominant mode for handling information—they may be an auditory, a visual, or a kinesthetic. You pick up on the modality by listening to the metaphors customers use and by watching where their eyes go when they are thinking. Is the customer an *auditory*? You'll know that if their eyes roll off to the side and they say things like, "I hear you. That sounds good." Are they a *visual*? Then their eyes will go off at an angle and they will say, "I see your point. It's clear." The third type, the *kinesthetic,* manifests downward eye rolling and language that includes metaphors of touch. ("I feel that we need to get a handle on the new operating system ourselves before we push it into production.") A sales rep who is well trained in NLP techniques will be able to assess instantly which of these modes fits a given prospect and will adjust his or her own behavior to match the customer's. This includes actually copying the other person—trying to reproduce her posture, her expressions, her gestures, even her eye blinking. If she folds her arms and leans forward, you should do that. If she puts both hands palm down on the desk, you should put both of your hands palm down, too. If the customer leans forward, you lean forward. If the customer crosses her legs, you do, too. And so on. The notion is that the customer will unconsciously pick up the similarity and conclude that you are just like her.

Next, you try to match her voice. Is the customer speaking fast or slowly? Loud or soft? What are the key words and pet phrases she is using repeatedly? You should use them, too. You also try to match her breathing, inhaling when she does, holding it as long as she does, and exhaling when she does. Next, you focus on providing the customer with information that is packaged (in terms of amount and complexity of information) so that it matches what she usually deals with. Somebody who deals in abstractions and ideas is not going to respond to a highly detailed presentation of content. Finally, you try to match your experiences with the customer's—common interests, associations, beliefs, and values.

Once you have all this matching set up so that the two of you are humming along like a pair of synchronized swimmers, you can put the customer into what the NLP folks call a "state." As in "hypnotic state." Establishing rapport with somebody is not an end in itself because it's a good thing, it's a means for gaining control over the person's mind so that you can lead him to think the way you want him to think. The overt act of putting the customer into a state is triggered by asking him a question in the form, "Can you remember a time when you . . . ," and filling it in with whatever you want the person to visualize: *When you bought a product and were completely happy? When you changed textbooks and your students loved the new one?* The theory is that the customer will be totally relaxed because of all the mirroring, so he will turn inward and find a memory that matches the situation your question describes. He will then connect that happy previous experience with you and what you are selling.

As you can see, sales training based on NLP emphasizes the importance of asking questions about what the client values, needs, or wants, although these are not the kinds of questions that a Neil Rackham or a Mike Bosworth would probably feel comfortable asking. NLP also teaches the salesperson to pay attention to what the customer shares, then repeat it back with the information arranged so that what the client thinks is most important comes first, on down to the least important. In repeating this information, the salesperson should use the same words the customer used.

Another NLP sales technique is to ward off buyer's remorse by having the customer rehearse what critics might say about her buying decision. Yet another technique is to ask the customer to commit to providing referrals—a step that makes it more difficult for him to reverse the decision later.

People got real excited about this stuff for a while. Major corporations spent a lot of money to train their salespeople to recognize the "meta-styles" that customers display. Workshops included role-playing activities where a sales rep had to mirror an auditory or a kinesthetic. Other fields began to look at NLP, too, including the military and law enforcement, where it was thought that NLP could be a useful means for determining if a suspect were lying. An article in the FBI's *Law Enforcement Bulletin* even discussed how to use the principles of NLP to build rapport with witnesses.

But does it work? Do our brains really work this way? And if they do, can we figure out how someone else's brain is working, mirror and match that person, then put him in a "state" so that we can get him to do what we want?

At this point, nobody really knows. I have to confess that I'm skeptical for a number of reasons. However, there is some independent evidence that tends to substantiate some of the basic NLP concepts.

William Condon, a psychologist at Boston University Medical Center, has recorded high-speed films of ordinary interactions for more than 20 years, carefully analyzing at 24 frames per second how people's body language and speech are coordinated. He claims to have found that people typically coordinate their speech and movements in one-second pulses, and that when people are in harmony—for example, a family group or two people who are in love or a team that works in close collaboration—their "pulses" become synchronized, too. As Condon describes it, "Communication is thus like a dance, with everyone engaged in intricate and shared movements across many subtle dimensions." Biologist Timothy Perper has said that the sustained mirror synchrony that arises between two people who are closely engaged with each other is the "best indicator that exists of mutual involvement." It occurs during romantic courtship, between marriage partners, between parents and children, and between good friends.

What this research is describing is something far more subtle than simply scratching under your armpit when the customer scratches under hers. But it does suggest that mirroring may have some scientific validity.

But what about the broader claims about language use and "metaprograms" that determine how human beings filter information and respond to the world?

A careful review of evidence concluded that the connections between neurology and behavior that NLP's supporters claim to see probably don't really exist. Nor is there any evidence that NLP actually helps us read other people or control what other people hear and understand when we communicate with them. Instead, the effects that come from using NLP techniques—reading eye position and listening carefully for language patterns—probably arise just because people respond well when others give them focused, intense attention.[3]

My own hunch is that we don't have enough empirical data to be sure about some of this yet. It is awfully hard to incorporate into your sales methodology, however, so maybe we're better off focusing on some of the basic content issues—what is the customer's problem, what are the criteria that he or she will use to choose a vendor, stuff like that—and not worrying quite so much about hidden neurological cues.

STRUCTURES OF PERSUASION

Having knocked NLP, I have to admit, though, that in my own career I have found that using language effectively can have a huge impact on win ratios.

In *Persuasive Business Proposals,* I showed salespeople and proposal writers how to sequence the content in their executive summaries, case studies, résumés, solution descriptions, and RFP answers to produce the best possible results. These patterns of discourse are linked to some fundamental linguistic structures and to the inherent cognitive processes that human beings use when they are analyzing information and making decisions.

These processes work. That's not just my opinion. It's based on nearly 25 years of work with clients, using the patterns and testing the results. I won't claim to have run as many tests as Elmer Wheeler did, but we have seen clients in all sorts of industries increase their win rates by changing the way they present the message. One client went from a 17 percent win rate to over 65 percent—selling the same product at the same price point in the same markets. The only difference was the way in which the client delivered the sales message. In another instance, a centralized proposal team applied the structural patterns we recommend to all the proposals it worked on. Meanwhile, field sales teams, who were not required to use the services of the proposal team, continued to issue proposals using other patterns. At the end of a year, the field sales teams' proposals had won at an 18 percent clip. The proposals issued by the proposal center, meanwhile, won at a 33 percent clip. Again, same products, same pricing, same markets, same competitors. Overall, our clients have averaged an 18 percent increase in win rates.

Most of this success was based on a format that I called the Persuasive Paradigm. It's a pattern for presenting content that causes the decision maker to agree more readily than any other pattern. I discuss this pattern in detail in *Persuasive Business Proposals* and provide examples of how to use it in letters and executive summaries, but in a nutshell it involves presenting the following information in the following order:

1. Restate the customer's needs, problems, issues, or opportunities as you understand them in language that the customer will recognize and understand.
2. Indicate the positive impact that solving these problems or meeting these needs will have on the customer's organization.

3. Recommend a solution that ties back to both the customer's needs and the outcomes or results that the customer wants.
4. Provide evidence to prove that you can deliver the solution on time and on budget.

Most recently, I had the opportunity to work with one of the foremost providers of information technology integration services in the world. The company had found that when competing for major government contracts, it was not receiving the highest possible ratings for its past performance. Even though the company had done excellent work, the write-ups it provided and the comments of its customers were resulting in mediocre ratings. I worked with the company to redesign the sequence of information contained in these case studies. Some of the things we did included:

1. Identifying all of the tasks and decision criteria that the new RFP specified, then highlighting which of those were covered in the previous contract.
2. Identifying key value statements and win themes, then locating specific accomplishments that showed that the company could deliver on them.
3. Restructuring the narratives to eliminate chronological summaries of the projects. Instead, every past performance write-up was organized in three parts:
   a. The previous customer's problem or need.
   b. The specific work done by the company to solve the problem or meet the need, with an emphasis on those tasks or skills that the new RFP was calling for.
   c. Results—the impact of the company's work on the previous client's operation in terms of quantifiable performance indicators.
4. Conducting "interviews" with the contact person at the previous client's organization, to review what was accomplished and to identify key messages that we wanted the person to deliver if and when interviewed.

None of these steps changes the basic information. Either the prior work was good or it wasn't. But we did change the way that information was presented. The result? In the last two major bids (we're talking contracts worth more than $100 million), my client received the highest ratings for past performance and won either all or a major portion of both contract awards.

These are examples of using structural patterns in presenting information—a version of Wheeler's tested sentences, if you will—to produce the

best possible results. The examples I provided involve written documents, but they work just as well in oral presentations.

My approaches aren't the only ones that involve using language more effectively, of course. Linda Richardson describes similar results for sales presentations that are structured more as dialogues. In *Stop Telling, Start Selling,* she provides examples of salespeople who thought they were being consultative, but who were really just waiting for a cue from the customer to launch into a data dump. Similarly, Thomas Freese shows how to engage the customer by asking questions in *Secrets of Question-Based Selling.* He shows how questions, rather than statements, gain the customer's buy-in and arouse curiosity. It's an interesting approach, but basically, as Freese himself admits, it's a return to some fundamental concepts that we can trace back to Dale Carnegie—try to see things from the customer's point of view and start the conversation by asking about him first. In fact, it was Carnegie's friend and sales disciple Frank Bettger who found that the best sales technique he had was to simply ask the customer, "Why?" and then sit quietly and wait for an answer. "I don't need any life insurance!" "Oh. Why?" "I think that it costs way too much." "Do you? Why is that?"

Language, used effectively, is an enabling mechanism that allows two people to connect. But as Elmer Wheeler himself said, there are no magic words. There is only word magic—the skillful and insightful use of words to communicate a message clearly and persuasively.

CHAPTER 17

MAKING IT WORK FOR YOU

M ost of us have had the experience of seeing a master presenter deliver a message. Maybe it was a sales rep who left a roomful of customers mesmerized. Maybe it was a preacher who left an entire congregation slack jawed and emotionally drained. Maybe it was a teacher who somehow made the principles of double entry bookkeeping more fascinating than any TV show we've ever watched.

Is that the kind of skill we need to develop in order to use language effectively in our sales process? Fortunately, no. You don't need to be that good at presenting to be effective in selling. But applying some basic techniques, including Elmer Wheeler's points, will help you. And then, who knows—with practice and opportunity you may become one of those master presenters yourself.

Elmer's "Wheelerpoints" work, so why not start applying them in your sales calls and writing? Here are some additional tips for communicating effectively with your prospects.

ORAL COMMUNICATIONS

1. *Questions are more effective than statements in engaging a customer, particularly during the early stages of a sales process.* Think about the questions you need to ask in order to guide the customer's thinking and to obtain the right information.

    Remember Neil Rackham's research finding: The most successful salespeople prepare questions, not facts, before a sales call. Organize your questions to move from general to specific, from the current situation to the desired state of affairs. Most important, *listen to the answers*. Asking the questions is not an end in itself. The real goal is gaining information and insight that you can later connect to your recommendations.

2. *Create a printed agenda and share it with the customer.* Even informal, one-on-one meetings will benefit from having an agenda. An agenda provides an easy, nonconfrontational way of keeping your meeting on track. However, after you have shared your agenda at the outset of your meeting, ask the customer(s) if it meets their needs. If they want to rearrange it, do so. Having provided the agenda, don't give it too much control.

3. *Stay flexible and responsive to your audience's interests.* If your meeting goes off on a tangent, but you build rapport or gain insight into your client's concerns and values, it's still a successful meeting.

   This is particularly true in meetings that occur during the first half of a sales process. Later, when you're formalizing the details of a solution or negotiating contract points, sudden swerves away from the topic may indicate unresolved obstacles in the customer's mind.

4. *If you have a written proposal, a price quote, or other printed material, don't hand it out until the end of your presentation.* Otherwise, your audience will be distracted, reading the text while listening to your presentation and getting little from either source. An exception is providing your slides in handout format during a formal presentation so that the client can take notes.

5. *Welcome interruptions, objections, and questions from your audience.* They indicate interest and involvement. Total silence is the worst response. You may think you've kept the audience spellbound, but it's more likely that you've either bored them or failed to establish the relevance of your presentation.

   However, don't encourage disruptions on minor issues. Discussion that focuses on key points is useful; otherwise, respond concisely and move on to your next point. In general, allow someone to ask a question and one or possibly two follow-up questions. Then cut him off and suggest that you talk with him privately about the issue in the interests of time.

6. *Share responsibility for the outcome of your presentation with the audience.* That means giving up some of the control, being flexible, and articulating common objectives.

7. *Use visual aids in formal presentations and don't skimp on them.* It's better to have lots of charts and move through them quickly than to have only a few and spend a lot of time on each. However, there's nothing wrong with spending a long time on one chart if the audience finds it relevant.

8. *Practice important presentations using videotape to identify distracting*

mannerisms or habits. But practice in front of an audience, too—ideally someone who is similar to your client in personality and level of expertise. Get their candid feedback. What was clear? What was not? Was the message convincing? Should it be shorter or longer, more high-level or more detailed?

9. *Learn to control your nervousness.* There's nothing bad about being nervous unless your nervousness becomes so overwhelming that it interferes with your ability to perform. Great athletes are always nervous before a major competition, but they channel the nervousness into energy so that they perform better.

   Develop your own routine for calming yourself. I recommend that you adopt the following steps at a minimum:

   ◆ *Remind yourself.* You have a good message, you are the right person to deliver this message, and the customer wants to hear it.

   ◆ *Visualize success.* Picture yourself doing a great job and the customer showing signs of approval and agreement.

   ◆ *Right before you begin, breathe in to the count of six and out to the count of twelve.* Repeat four or five times.

10. *Use this pattern during initial meetings with the client to begin the probing and fact-finding process.*

    a. *Establish your purpose.*

       ◆ Greet the customer appropriately.

       ◆ Make a value statement to establish the relevance of your visit and relate it to the customer's business.

       ◆ Position your company as a credible resource, but keep this brief—no more than a mention of other clients in the same industry that this prospect is in.

       ◆ Share the agenda.

       ◆ Ask permission to pose a few questions.

    b. *Probe for needs and goals.*

       ◆ Use a process of "structured empathy" in posing your questions.

         Ask. Ask a combination of open and closed questions.

         Mirror. Repeat what you have heard and ask if you have it right.

         Validate. Acknowledge that the individual's ideas, observations, and feelings are reasonable.

       ◆ Probe for needs and goals in the following areas:

         Current processes or procedures

         "What media do you currently use to market your products and services?"

Competitive situation
"What are your key competitors doing?"
Gaps or inadequacies
"If you could change anything about the current marketing process, what would it be?"
Desirable outcomes
"What are the key measures for marketing success for you?"

- To identify key needs or requirements, ask, *"What do you want in X?"*
- To identify key goals, ask, *"What would it do for your operation to have X?"*

c. *Gain concurrence and close the call.*
- Review the agenda and summarize the call.
- Establish the next steps.
- Gain commitment for the next steps.

WRITTEN COMMUNICATIONS

1. *Check whether your sales proposals are client-centered or self-centered.* Count how many times your company's name appears in the cover letter and executive summary and how many times the client's name does. The client's name should appear two to three times more frequently than yours.

2. *Put the important stuff first.* People naturally assume that whatever comes first must be most important. So put your key points or information up front when you write. This rule goes for sentences, paragraphs, and the whole proposal.

3. *Send out the best work you're capable of producing.* Have someone you trust proofread and edit documents that you are sending to a client before you send them.

   The less the other person knows about the client and the deal and the more blunt he or she can be in giving you feedback, the better off you will be. We all make silly mistakes, like using the wrong client's name, but because we know what we meant to say, we don't notice the error until it's too late.

   For e-mails to clients, write them in your word processor first, edit them as if they were a letter, then cut and paste them into your e-mail system. You will avoid a lot of embarrassing typos and mistakes that way.

4. *Always* use your spelling and grammar checker. Always.

5. *Kill the marketing fluff.* Be ruthless about removing it from anything

you send to a client. Take a look at the list of fluff terms in Chapter 15 and look for them in your own writing.

Marketing fluff consists of grandiose claims that are unsubstantiated by any evidence. Remember Wheeler's point: Say it with flowers. Offer proof if you make a claim. Otherwise, delete it.

6. *Eliminate weasel words and booster words while you're at it. Booster words* are words that we throw into a sentence when we (unconsciously) suspect we're not making our point very well. They don't work, because adding an adverb or two doesn't make a sentence more emphatic or clearer. Booster words include:

very	obviously
really	somewhat
certainly	significant

Count the number of booster words you're using. If you find more than four or five booster words per page, your writing is probably boring. Take a look at sentence length, use of the passive voice, and whether or not you're putting the important point up front.

Weasel words start the reader's B.S. detector clanging like a fire bell. A weasel word tries to imply that we're saying one thing, when we're actually saying the exact opposite. They are very tricky and very destructive to trust and clear communications. Here are some examples:

help	"Helps you feel . . ." (In other words, it won't make things worse.)
like	"Works like a . . ." (So what do we mean by "like" anyway?)
virtually	"Virtually trouble-free . . ." (Virtual means "not real," and virtually trouble-free means that you should expect some trouble.)
can be	"Can be of value . . ." (Can be? Might be? But that doesn't necessarily mean it will be, right?)
up to	"Lasts up to eight hours . . ." (Yeah, somebody in Pittsburgh got it to last eight hours. The average among all users was 13 minutes.)

7. *Keep your documents as short as possible.* Research we did found that short proposals are usually read first and get higher evaluation scores.

Short documents are easier to understand and make a stronger impression.

Short sentences are better than long ones.

Bullet points help break things up, too, but remember the rule of "seven plus or minus two." Long strings of bullet points get skipped.

8. *Highlight your documents.* Most executives do not read every word of every document they receive. They can't. There isn't enough time. So they skim.

Make your document skimmable. Use headings and subheadings, boldface type, lists, tint blocks to set up a sidebar, bullet points, graphics, and other devices to make sure that the reader who skims still sees the key points.

9. *Use familiar, everyday language.* Avoid jargon and acronyms unless you're absolutely sure the reader understands them. *When in doubt, leave it out.*

Prefer short words over long ones; simple, direct words over unusual abstractions. (Maybe it does pay to increase your vocabulary, but that doesn't mean you have to abuse everybody with it.)

Instead of:	*Write:*
parameters	limits, variables
implement	do
viable	workable
interface	communicate with or connect
optimum	best
optimize	improve
to impact	to affect
finalize	finish, complete
utilize	use
endeavor	try
demonstrate	show
initiate	start
terminate	end, finish

PART FIVE

Joe Girard

PRIMING THE PUMP

CHAPTER 18

DOWN AND OUT IN DETROIT CITY

Joe Girard never knew why his father hated him. The explosions of rage, the beatings with fists and belts, the cursings—"You'll never amount to anything! You're no good! You'll end up in prison!"—it all seemed to come out of some inexplicable, black well of anger inside his father. All Joe knew from the time he was a toddler was that he was the one who got knocked around and screamed at. Not his older brother. Not his sisters. Just him.

Things were pretty grim anyway. Joe was born right at the start of the Great Depression. His father was a Sicilian immigrant with no trade, no skills, who seldom worked more than a few days at a time. Mainly the family survived on relief checks and handouts. The six of them lived in a tiny apartment in one of the worst neighborhoods in Detroit. To stay warm in the winter, Girard and his brother went across the street to the coal yard, scuttled under the fence, and stole loose pieces of coal that they stuffed in a burlap bag and dragged home. Sometimes there was virtually nothing to eat in the house. Girard started working when he was eight years old, squatting on the floor in filthy saloons, shining the shoes of the drunks who hung out there. Working late into the night, he brought home a few nickels—not bad in an age when a quart of milk was a nickel.

Later he took on another job, one that he could do in the mornings. Getting up at 6 a.m., he delivered the *Detroit Free Press* before heading off to school. And when the paper had a contest for signing up new subscribers, Girard rang every doorbell in every apartment house up and down the grimy streets, begging people to try the paper, just for a week. He sold enough new subscriptions to win the prize—a case of Pepsi, which he turned around and sold one bottle at a time for still more nickels.

Joe kept up this routine for the next five years. It meant that he wasn't getting much out of school, but he was helping to keep the family fed.

But still the beatings continued. His father would grab him, drag him down the stairs to the cellar, and tie him to the pipes coming out of the wall. Then he would take a big, thick leather strap, the kind they used to use to sharpen razors, and whip Joe over and over, screaming at him how he was rotten, he was no good, he was worthless.

Sometimes when his father exploded, Joe ran for it. He'd hightail it down to the train yard and sleep on the straw in an open boxcar. Or he'd hole up in a flophouse in the worst part of the slums. Or he'd go to the shelter where the winos and derelicts slept on cots in a big open room. Just a boy—10 or 11 years old—seeking shelter among the hobos and the alcoholics, because it was safer there than it was at home.

It's probably no surprise that Girard never finished high school—he got into fights and got expelled. It's probably no surprise that he got into trouble with the law: He and some friends stole a car, then robbed the till at a saloon. He spent a night in the juvenile detention center, which scared him witless, and then got one of the worst beatings ever from his father. A life of crime was not for him.

But what could he do? He had no skills, no education. No future.

And he had become a chronic stutterer, so it was hard for him to talk to people.

He drifted from one lousy job to another. Dishwasher, truck driver, assembler in a stove factory, in a Chrysler plant, at the Hudson car factory. Nothing lasted. He was constantly being fired or else he just quit. He joined the Army, but he got hurt during basic training and was discharged and sent home, to be greeted by his father's screams again. "I should have choked you to death when you were born!" he hollered. "You're no good. You're a disgrace to this family."

He finally caught a break when he went to work for a small-time home builder named Abe Saperstein. He started out working for Saperstein as a common laborer—mixing cement, hammering nails, driving a truck, whatever unskilled work needed to be done. Saperstein's construction business was strictly small-time, but it was profitable. He would buy an empty lot or two, put up a couple of houses for about $9,000, and sell them immediately for $12,000. This was the period right after World War II, when young G.I.s and their wives could get cheap home loans if they could find a house to buy. It was a good business, and Saperstein liked young Joe Girard. A few years later, when Saperstein passed away, he left the business to Girard. "That was not really as big as it sounded because all we had was an old truck, some tools, and a little cement mixer," Girard has written, "but I had learned how to put that and some experience together and run it on my own."[1] By now, Joe had a wife and two kids, so keeping the business going was his only focus.

The problem was that scrounging around to find an open lot here or there, then putting up a house or two was getting more and more difficult. The empty lots were becoming scarce, even as the demand for housing was skyrocketing. When Joe was approached by a real estate developer to buy a piece of property where he could put up a whole subdivision, it seemed like a "can't miss" opportunity.

Unfortunately, the developer had lied to him about one little detail. He told Girard that the city would be putting in sewer lines within the next few months. That was important, because the people in Detroit wouldn't buy a home that had a septic tank. They all wanted to be hooked up to the municipal sewer system. So Girard took out huge loans to buy the property on a land contract and buy the materials to build a spec home as a model, then waited for home buyers to come flooding in. What he didn't know was that the promise of sewer lines was a lie. There were no plans to put sewers in. This meant that it would be impossible to build and sell the homes in time to pay his debts.

Soon the notes were coming due. Creditors were banging on his door. They were terrorizing his wife on the phone. It got so bad that he had to park his car blocks away from where he lived and sneak down the alleyways, finally climbing the fence to get into his own backyard, because the bank was looking for the car to repossess it.

He hit bottom the night his wife asked him for some money to buy groceries. He told her, truthfully, that he didn't have any.

"Then what are the kids going to eat?" she asked.

Joe Girard sat up all night. He didn't know what he would do, but he had to do something. He would feed his kids. He would support his family. He would be a success.

Somehow he would prove his father wrong.

Flash forward. It's August 7, 2001. A distinguished-looking, grey-haired man in a beautifully tailored suit, wearing an expensive watch and first-quality shoes, mounts the podium to a standing ovation. He turns and beams a confident, friendly smile at the audience.

It's Joe Girard. And he has just been inducted into the Automobile Hall of Fame. He is the greatest car salesman in the world, and the only one ever honored with admission to the Hall of Fame.

In the course of a 14-year career in auto sales, stretching from 1963, when his wife told him there was no food in the house, until 1977, when he made over a quarter of a million dollars in commissions, Joe Girard sold more than 13,000 cars. And he sold them all at retail, one customer at a time. He sold more retail automobiles from his small office at Merollis Chevrolet in Eastpointe, Michigan, than anyone else anywhere in the world. He averaged selling six cars *a day*. On his best day, he sold 18 vehicles. In his best month, he sold 174. His best year totaled 1,425 cars sold. To put this in perspective, Joe Girard sold more cars by himself than 95 percent of all the *dealerships* in North America. In fact, he was so successful that Joe Girard is listed in the *Guinness Book of World Records* as "the world's greatest salesman." It'd be pretty hard to argue.

So how did he do it? And what big idea did this car salesman contribute?

Girard is basically a relationship salesperson. He's pretty explicit about it, in fact: "Make [the customer] a friend and he'll work for you." Even though Girard sold what anybody would call a commodity—Chevrolet cars and trucks—he actually saw himself as selling a relationship:

> A Chevrolet is a Chevrolet, you probably think. You can buy them in any town in the country. They're all alike. Right? Wrong! A Chevrolet sold by Joe Girard is not just a car. It is a whole relationship between me and that customer and his family and his friends and the people he works with.[2]

In describing his methods, he sounds a bit like a Carnegie kid. For example, he says that the only thing customers want is to have somebody listen to them and be friendly. You sell more cars by keeping your mouth shut and by being respectful, Girard says, than by giving a stranger who just walked into the showroom the old hard sell. As he stated in his book, *How to Sell Anything to Anybody*, "I believe one of the most important determining factors of a sale is, Does the prospect like, trust and believe me."[3]

To get the customer to like him, the salesperson has to stay conscious in the sense that we discussed it in our review of Carnegie's approach—sharing in the delights of the customer's recent trip to Vancouver, listening with rapt attention to the customer's fishing stories (even if the salesperson has never gone fishing), showing an interest in the customer's Aunt Ida in Rochester, who had to have gall bladder surgery, getting down on the floor to play with the customer's kids, giving the kids balloons, whatever. It's recognizing that the personal touch in a human interaction like sales is the only touch there can be. The customer won't be affected emotionally by the corporation that manufactured the car or by the finance company that provides the loan. It has to be the salesperson standing there in the showroom who makes the connection. Girard even admits that in an earlier, more naïve time, he kept all the popular brands of cigarettes in his office, along with a selection of liquors, the better to ply the customer with and build a bond. The bond is important, because selling one car is nice, but selling the customer every car he or she buys from then on is an annuity.[4]

Carnegie would have approved of Girard's idea that his first job is to listen to the customer, to learn "what the customer wants to do and what he ought to do and what he can afford to do."[5] You have to get the customer's name right away and use it frequently. You listen without contradicting or trying to show you're smarter. If the customer talks about catching a big fish, you don't say, "Well, that's nothing—I caught one *this* big last weekend." You pay the customer compliments—"You've kept your car in good shape!"—even if the trade-in is barely a notch above a junker. As Girard saw it, it was the customer's car, and it's possible that the customer loved it, no matter how much of a dog you might think it is. And since it's the customer's car, it's the customer's job to knock it. Otherwise, say something pleasant and complimentary. Yep, that's pure Dale Carnegie in action.

Girard understood that the goal in sales is to narrow the gap between you and the customer—to overcome the sense of "cognitive dissonance." Girard has a simple way to explain it:

> What it all comes down to is one word: *trust.* If a customer trusts me, he will buy from me. But I have to be sure that his trust lasts beyond the moment when he gets his car and pays for it.[6]

To narrow that gap, he recommends that you dress like your customers, talk like your customers, show interest in the things your customers enjoy. Since Girard was selling mainly to middle-class and lower-middle-class workers in the metro Detroit area, he never wore fancy suits and gold jewelry and the other signs of obvious wealth that some of his colleagues liked to wear. Rather, he'd come to the dealership in slacks and a sport shirt. He knew the location of all the bowling alleys around town, and he followed the local sports teams. He was a *mensch,* even though by then he was living in a mansion in Grosse Pointe. This was a sharp insight on Girard's part, since the initial impression that a person makes on a customer in the first four minutes—which means that appearance and body language are hugely important—will set the tone for the relationship going forward, and may even determine whether there *is* a relationship. NCR's emphasis on having its sales agents dress like business owners, a tradition carried forward in the IBM culture of white shirts and blue suits, were manifestations of the same principle—not that dressing upscale was a good idea, but a recognition that they were selling to successful executives and needed to match their appearance and expectations.

Elsewhere, Girard sounds like another edition of the "prince of pep," Carnegie's number one disciple, Frank Bettger, who made so much of the importance of having a work plan every day to stay focused. As Girard says, "The way to get the job done is to decide what it is—every day. I mean you must—I don't say should—take some time every morning and decide what you are going to do that day. And then you must do it. . . . I don't believe in hard work. I believe in good work. I believe in smart work. I believe in effective work—work that works."[7]

Also like Bettger, Girard warns about wasting time. Keep your enthusiasm up, stay positive, don't stand around in the bullpen with the rest of the sales team just waiting for your turn to be "up." Instead, stay busy, stay focused, make things happen. Use every minute to build your book of business, to create opportunities for yourself.

Like Wheeler, Girard recognized the importance of appealing to the customer's senses. He didn't sell the sizzle on that showroom floor, but he did sell the smell—the unmistakable, wonderful aroma of a brand new car. He liked his prospects to take test drives, long test drives, particularly around their own home neighborhoods, where their spouse and kids and neighbors could see them in a brand new Chevrolet. What Girard wanted was to fill their sinus cavities with the smell of that car and their eyeballs with the expressions of awe and delight when their friends and family saw them in it.

He even anticipated the NLP crowd in mirroring his customer's behavior. For example, he says, there are times when a prospect will come in to look at a new car and will actually get down on the floor to look underneath it. "So will I," Girard says. "It may sound crazy, but it is a very good opener. The man sees you just looking with him and maybe he laughs, and you are ready to start."[8]

And Girard echoes Patterson when he counsels that you should review every selling opportunity you have failed to close and ask yourself, "Why? What mistake did I make that prevented the customer from buying?" "One way to get over the dissatisfactions of a bad day is to review that day and try to understand why what happened to you happened. I do that at the end of every working day."[9] That kind of self-examination is tough for most people, but Girard, like Patterson 75 years earlier, claims that it's the only way to make consistent improvement in your methods and techniques.

In addition to all that, Girard has some ideas about follow-up and service after the sale, about asking questions to size up the customer's financial resources, and about staying motivated. But it's all pretty typical stuff.

So what makes Girard different? What idea did he develop that revolutionized selling?

It was the Law of 250.

CHAPTER 19

FINDING THE LAW OF 250 AT A FUNERAL

When Girard was first hired as a car salesman, he was desperate. There were no groceries in the house. There was no money in his pocket. Creditors were trying to take back his car and foreclose on his house. His wife's words, "What will I feed the children?" were ringing in his ears.

As a result, he did something foolish. After trying to get a friend who sold cars to get him a job, only to be turned down, Girard began going to car dealerships at random, begging for a job. Finally, one of the sales managers told him, "Look, the other sales guys don't want another pair of feet on the floor. That just cuts the pie into smaller pieces. Every salesperson I add diminishes the number of chances they have to sell to the people that walk into the showroom." So Girard impulsively said, "Fine. No problem. I won't sell to the people who walk in. I'll go find my own customers. I won't take any prospects who walk in from any of the other sales guys." On that basis, he got hired. Why not? He was on straight commission, so it wasn't costing the sales manager anything.

The first day he was on the job, however, he quickly realized that this was going to be much more difficult than he had imagined. Where would he find these people? How would he get them interested in buying a car from him? He started out by tearing two pages out of the metro Detroit phone book white pages, calling names on the list. Then the thought struck him that businesses buy trucks, so he tore two pages out of the Yellow Pages for good measure. He called all day long. Nothing.

Finally, late in the evening, long after the other salespeople had left for the day and Girard was the last person left in the dealership showroom, somebody walked in. Girard stared at him and saw opportunity. Nobody else was around, so he wasn't breaking his promise. And when he looked at that customer, Girard saw something that he needed desperately: a bag of groceries.

Girard made the sale. Using it as leverage, he borrowed $10 from the sales manager so that he could buy that bag of groceries. And he started his career.

But calling people at random, hoping to stumble across a prospect, was not an efficient way to work, and he knew it. He needed to figure out ways to drum up prospects. Although he had almost no experience in sales, he knew that he had to find an effective and efficient way of reaching potential customers. As he says in *How to Sell Anything to Anybody,* the "biggest advantage you can get is to come up with a better way of reaching and selling your customers."[1] Calling people randomly on the phone probably isn't it, though. (Even though Girard did develop some pretty clever ways of getting a stranger engaged on the phone and finding out if and when he might be in the market for a new car.)

Not long after he got a job selling cars, he went to a funeral home to pay his respects to the deceased mother of one of his friends. At Catholic funerals, it was standard practice to give out Mass cards with the name of the departed and the deceased's picture. Girard had seen them for years and never thought much about it. But this time he got to thinking. Printing all those Mass cards must be expensive. How could the funeral director know how many were needed? So he asked.

"It's just experience," the undertaker told him.

Over the years, he had looked in the visitors' book and counted the number of people who had signed. After a while he saw that the average number of people who come to a funeral was about 250.

It wasn't much later that he was selling a car to a man who ran a funeral home that catered primarily to Protestants. After closing the deal—one of his rules is not to let anything distract the customer from the deal—Girard asked this man how many people on average attended one of the funerals he conducted. "About 250," he was told.

One day Girard and his wife were attending a wedding, so he asked the person who owned the catering business what the average number of guests was at a wedding. "About 250 from the bride's side, and another 250 from the groom's," he was told.

Well, by now the light was blinking like a strobe in Joe Girard's head. There was a principle at work here, one that he could use to build business.

JOE GIRARD'S LAW OF 250

The principle is this: Most people have about 250 other people in their lives who are important enough to invite to a wedding or to a funeral.

Pretty simple, isn't it? But really powerful.

Of course, there are exceptions. Some people might know fewer than that. On the other hand, some people who are active in their communities or who have jobs that constantly bring them into contact with others— teachers, doctors, dentists, union bosses, politicians, preachers, barbers, hair stylists, yoga instructors—might know many times more than 250. Statistically, the mean was about 250, and that's the point.

Each person I do business with represents 250 other people. If I do a great job, 250 more people are likely to get a recommendation to buy from me. If I do a lousy job, I have just made 250 enemies. Consistently doing a good job—building strong relationships, treating people fairly, and giving them what they want—will make selling a lot easier in the long run.

That's obviously true for someone like Joe Girard, who is selling cars in the local community. It would make sense, too, for someone selling insurance or for a financial planner or for a banker. But what about the national account rep whose sales territory covers 12 states and who deals with senior executives in Fortune 500 companies?

Well, don't those executives also have 250 friends? Aren't some of those friends also executives in the same company or in related ones?

What Joe Girard noticed at that funeral home is one of those odd little details, one of those anomalies, that most people see and ignore their whole life long. An anomaly is a curious fact, an irregularity, something that deviates from the norm. And, as the authors of *Hardball: Are You Playing to Play or Playing to Win,* point out, an anomaly can be a signpost to a growth opportunity. In fact, as they demonstrate, there may be a chance to differentiate, to sell more effectively, lurking behind some oddball customer preference or seemingly aberrant employee behavior. Citing companies like Dell, Toyota, and Wal-Mart as "hardball" players, they list the principles by which they compete and win. Recognizing anomalies is one of them. One great example of an anomaly they cite that led to a huge competitive advantage: Girard's Law of 250.[2]

Given his sales record, it's pretty clear that Girard discovered something there that set him apart. What he had realized was that it made more sense to "prime the pump" by generating awareness and interest among prospects well before they ever needed a car.

DO THE MATH

Joe Girard never made it his goal to hit a home run with every pitch. Instead, he just wanted to have the most turns at bat. For him, it was simple arithmetic: If you normally close half of all the customers you see, and you see 100 customers a month, you will, on average, close 50 deals a month. If you increase the number of customers you see to 200, you will double your sales *even if you do nothing else different.* "For sure, you can get more people to come in to see you. And even if they only buy as often and as much as before, you will be on a permanent hot streak compared to your usual volume."[3]

Clearly, the principle holds true, whether we are engaged in complex selling at the highest levels with deals worth millions, or whether we are selling one at a time to customers in our local community.

But there's an even more important element to the principle. One satisfied customer can lead to referrals that can dramatically shorten the sales cycle and help fill the pipeline. Each customer has a circle of influence that potentially includes many people who might also become customers. Getting those customers to become recommenders meant that when new prospects arrived and asked for Joe Girard by name, they were already prequalified and warmed up.

But to turn happy customers into willing recommenders, Girard realized that he had to take action. He had to nurture the relationship and keep it alive.

For example, a few weeks after he sold a car to someone, he would call that person on the phone and ask how the car was running. "You would think that might be asking for trouble," he says, "but for me it is asking for future business and ensuring that I get it." Even if the person is having problems (in fact, particularly if he is having problems), Girard wants to know about it, so that he can do something to fix the situation.

In addition, each month every one of the people on Girard's list of customers would get a greeting card from him. In January, they would get a Happy New Year card. Inside it would say, "I like you," and he would sign his name. He also had a sticker or stamp that showed the name and address of the dealership where he worked. In February, the people on his list might get a Valentine's Day card. Again, on the inside was the same message: "I like you." Each card came in a different size and color of envelope, and each was hand-addressed and stamped. His goal was to get past the initial screen we all do on the mail we get, where we stand over a trash can and pitch the "junk" mail—all the ads, the credit card offers, the meaningless coupons, and similar trash—into the can. He wanted his customers to open the card, look at it, see his name, and smile. Month after month. Year after year. Because he knew that eventually they would need a new car. And when they did, he wanted only one name to pop into their heads as the man they should see: Joe Girard.

Before you conclude that this was a simple task, you need to know that Girard had over 9,000 names in his prospect file. Every month, he was sending out 9,000 cards. On average, he was mailing 400 to 500 cards *a day!* With first-class postage. Hand stamped.

Clearly, this took a lot of work. This was one of the ways he filled his open moments at the dealership, rather than standing around with the other salesmen shooting the breeze. Often he spent his evenings and weekends at home, addressing and signing cards. Eventually he even hired somebody to help him with the job. But he was convinced that it was worth it. And he was right. By the time he had been selling for a decade, nearly two-thirds of his sales were to repeat customers. It got to the point that customers had to call Giraard in advance and set an appointment to buy from him!

FREEZE OUT COLD CALLING

The system of generating leads and maintaining awareness among prospects that Joe Girard developed has been revived in recent years under new names. Seth Godin sold a lot of books with the concept of "permission marketing," which is basically a version of Girard's Law of 250 for the digital age. You get the exact sense of what he means by permission marketing in the subtitle of his book: *Turning Strangers Into Friends and Friends Into Customers.* That's as good a description of what Girard was doing with his cards and referral programs and networking as anything could be. The difference between what Girard recommended and what Godin tells us is basically that instead of sending out greeting cards, you send out e-mails. Godin even refers to Girard's process as a "super-low-tech way to use permission to sell cars"[4]— which seems a bit cheeky, since all he's done is give Girard's innovation a new name, then taken retroactive credit for the idea.

Others have called the technique *nurture marketing* or *relationship marketing.* Sales expert Gil Cargill used the term *closed loop marketing* to describe the technique, and he gives Girard full credit for being the first to develop it.

The idea of priming the pump with creative presales activities that generate leads and keep prospects aware of you has tremendous potential for improving sales force efficiency today. As Cargill points out, sales teams waste thousands of hours every year with cold calling. Even if they are calling from a better list than Girard started with—four pages ripped out of the phone book—the chances of finding somebody who's actually interested in buying your products or services from a cold call are abysmally low. Instead of using cold calling techniques, Cargill recommends adopting Girard's approach.

The first step is to create a profile of your best customers—or of what you assume your best customers would look like, if you don't currently have any. Looking at the kinds of customers who have bought from your company elsewhere or in the past, you can begin to identify likely "suspects"— companies and individuals who might buy in the future. Of course, as Girard knew, the very best set of prospects is previous customers who are happy.

You can buy lists, of course, but most people who have gone that route have found that the lists often aren't very accurate or very useful. They're usually better than a couple of pages ripped at random out of the phone book, but how much better depends on how targeted your prospect profile is and, often, on how much you pay for the list.

Anthony Parinello, well-known for his *Selling to VITO* sales approach, which updated the Carnegie method of relationship selling, also rejects cold calling. As an alternative, he recommends going to the library and doing old-fashioned research in newspapers, journals, business registries, and other resources to identify what your various existing customers have in common, then looking for other companies or organizations that also fit that profile.[5]

Once you know the profile of the kinds of customers who typically buy from you, and have either created or bought a list of potential prospects in your area, you can start your campaign.

For many salespeople, the trickiest step is to figure out how to approach the prospect. As the term *permission marketing* implies, you have to earn the right to communicate with these people who have never heard of you. Write a series of brief and focused messages—half a page is plenty—that will be of interest to your target customers. *Do not write about your products or services!* Girard didn't stick a brochure for the latest Chevy in each greeting card. He just sent his customers a message that he knew they'd like. That's all you should do, too. An anecdote, a new idea, a discovery, an item off the news-wires, a short book review, or a tip might work beautifully. A product spec sheet definitely won't.

Once you have your messages written (and I strongly urge you to write them all in advance—we're only talking about a dozen half-page messages here at most), start sending them. Jim Cecil, the "nurture marketing" guru, recommends mixing it up—send an e-mail, mail a letter, make a phone call and leave a voicemail message. Cargill's clients have found that combining the "warm" touch of a personal phone call with the slightly more impersonal contacts made via e-mail or a letter has produced even better results.

The important point is that this is the kind of activity you need to do every day. Just as Joe Girard used all of his empty schedule time at the dealership to sign cards and make calls, you need to make sure that you are doing something relevant to building up a base of interested prospects on a daily basis.

This approach takes time to develop. It won't start producing closed business the first month you use it. But over time, as Girard's career proves, this way of developing prospects will do away with the need for cold calling. And a series of relationship-oriented messages, particularly if they contain something of value, will separate you from your competitors, who probably aren't doing much more than sending out the occasional product slick.

If you understand who your best customers are and what interests them, you'll be able to craft messages that will appeal to them and to prospects who are similar to them. And you'll find that they welcome the messages just as much as those thousands of blue-collar workers in Detroit enjoyed getting a card from Joe Girard.

CHAPTER 20

FROM NETWORK TO NURTURE

Why does Girard's method work so well?

He was tapping into two principles that resulted in people knowing who he was and feeling positive about doing business with him. The first principle, the *recognition heuristic,* is the most fundamental step in decision making. The second principle, the concept of *obligation,* creates a psychological indebtedness in the customer's mind that he or she wants to discharge—by doing business with us.

THE RECOGNITION HEURISTIC

If you give customers a choice between a brand they have heard of and one they have not, they will overwhelmingly choose the one they've heard of. They'll do this even if the one they recognize is a little more expensive. The reason that we will choose things we've heard of and ignore or reject those we have not is that this method of decision making is hard-wired into our heads.

In *Persuasive Business Proposals,* I wrote about studies that had been conducted over many years and across a wide range of cultures, investigating how people make decisions. Contrary to common wisdom, people do not carefully amass all the information, sort it, and weigh it before coming to a decision. Instead, they make decisions very quickly, using the least amount of information possible. They do this because we have certain thought processes—called "heuristics" by the scientists who study them—that enable us to focus on a couple of salient facts and then stop the process by making a decision.[1] The first salient "fact" that we rely on isn't really a fact, and it isn't even conscious. It occurs in a primitive area of the brain that we share with dogs and cats and rats. It's recognition. It's just a binary reaction: *Yes. No.* That's it.

The basic principle is that if we recognize one of two things and we don't recognize the other, we assume that the one we recognize has more value. It's like throwing a switch—on/off. Yes, I recognize that person, or, no, I do not. We assume that the one we recognize is the better choice. End of story. End of decision process. When your dog picks up a scent or hears the sound of a human voice, his reaction is based on this principle. If it's the scent of a person in the family, his tail starts wagging. If not, he starts to growl. If it's a voice he recognizes, he starts to get excited and runs to the door. If it's a stranger's voice, he barks.

This is a very simple process. And it doesn't take a genius to see how it worked to the advantage of a guy like Joe Girard. There were hundreds of people selling cars in Detroit when he was active. But there was probably only one who had done enough self-promotion to make his name familiar to you. And if you were on Joe's prospect list, and you had been getting a nice card from him once a month, when you heard his name, your tail probably started wagging, too. Why would you choose to go to somebody else? The rest were total strangers.

Here's an example: Suppose your laptop computer suddenly dies. You go to your IT manager and tell her that you need a new one. She says, "Well, you're in luck, because I happen to have two brand new laptops with all the software installed. You can have either this IBM ThinkPad or this Kretzenheimer Millennial. Which one do you want?"

Chances are you'll take the IBM. Why? Because you've never heard of the other brand.

To test this principle, I have often distributed a "lunch menu" at the outset of training seminars. The so-called menu gives attendees two choices: a turkey club sandwich or baked gravlax with cremora sauce. As you might expect, over 90 percent of the participants will choose the turkey club sandwich. About three or four out of a hundred—a few adventurous souls who figure, "What the heck—we're in a Marriott, how risky can it be?"—will choose the gravlax. A few others will complain that there's no vegetarian option. But for everybody else, the only real choice was the one they had heard of. People usually are not willing to eat something that they've never heard of before.

By sending out his greeting cards each month, Girard was maintaining that recognition factor. And it was the repeated exposure that made the difference for him.

My friend Jim Cecil undertook a major study for Microsoft to determine what factors were most important in building the business of Microsoft's value-added resellers (VARs). Jim looked at lots of stores and interviewed dozens of owners and salespeople all over North America, and even in other countries. What he found was that the single most important factor that led to a steady increase in business was the consistent practice of contacting prospects and customers. It was the equivalent of Girard's monthly greeting card. In the case of the VARs, it was more likely to take the form of a phone call, an e-mail, a quick handwritten note attached to a clipping, a bit of intriguing information that the VAR passed along. But this process of regularly reaching out to "touch" prospects and existing customers, a process that Jim Cecil calls "nurturing" an account relationship, resulted in dramatic growth.

It didn't happen right away, however. Instead, the trend started to tick upward after half a dozen messages and really showed a jump after about a dozen. The steady repetition of a simple message—"We're out here, we care about you and your business, and we want to share something with you that has some value"—eventually permeated the customers' minds to the point that when they needed software or IT consulting or hardware or anything else of that nature, the VAR who had been communicating with them for the past months was the one they thought to call.

I used to think that corporate sponsorship of sports stadiums, golf tournaments, and so forth was a waste of corporate dollars. Naming rights seemed more like exercises in executive vanity than good investments of marketing dollars. However, as Joe Girard discovered, and as Jim Cecil's research proved, there is tremendous value in establishing instant, positive recognition. Advertising, marketing, and branding efforts will have significant value for our sales efforts downstream.

If you are a salesperson who represents a small company or a start-up, it's possible that your prospects have never heard of your company. You may have a difficult time making contact, getting an appointment, or having your proposal read when it's on a pile that contains much better-known names. In that situation, given the limited funds that most small or new companies have for marketing, you may have to take matters into your own hands to build recognition. That means taking the initiative to communicate with prospects and leads on a regular basis. E-mail is quick, and you can't beat the price. Why not send each prospect a link to an interesting article, or, better yet, cut and paste the article into your e-mail? Leave a voicemail congratulating her if you see her name in the paper. Send a note with a newspaper clipping attached. If you are selling at a higher level, how about locating a white paper or a book review that would be of interest to your prospective clients? When you send an e-mail message like this, even if you're sending it to 9,000 prospects the way Joe Girard did, you still have to follow his approach, of course. You have to do it in a way that makes it look personal to the individual client. We'll discuss later how you can do that.

THE POWER OF OBLIGATION

When someone feels obligated to you, he feels a subtle pressure to return the "favor" you have done him or to repay the "debt" he owes.

In *Influence: The Psychology of Persuasion,* Robert Cialdini tells an amusing story of a college professor who tried an experiment. He sent a batch of Christmas cards to total strangers. He thought he would get some sort of reaction, but what happened was startling. Responses came pouring in. He got holiday greetings from people he had never met, people who had no idea who the heck he was. They had simply reacted in robotic fashion, obeying what Cialdini calls the rule of reciprocation. Quoting the archaeologist Richard Leakey, Cialdini suggests that reciprocation may be deeply rooted in our very nature as human beings: "We are human because our ancestors learned to share their food and their skills in an honored network of obligation." The survival of the human race, not to mention our own survival as individuals, depended on our honoring that network of obligations.[2]

So when Joe Girard manages to remember your birthday and send you a card each year—something your own son didn't even do!—it does create a sense of obligation, doesn't it?

As Kurt Mortensen points out, "The Law of Obligation can be used to eliminate animosity or suspicion."[3] He summarizes a study conducted at Cornell in which two people were given the challenge of selling raffle tickets to coworkers. One person was instructed to be as nice as possible before selling the tickets. The other was instructed to be rude and obnoxious, but then to buy coworkers drinks just before trying to get them to buy the tickets. The results: The rude person sold twice as many tickets as the nice person! The workers apparently felt "indebted" for the free drink and had to reciprocate.

When someone does something for you, it generates good feelings. Irving Janis and his colleagues studied a group of students at Yale and found that they were more convinced by a persuasive message if they were given peanuts and a soft drink to enjoy while they read the message.[4] When the persuasive message is linked with good feelings, it becomes associated with those good feelings and becomes more acceptable. And Joe Girard certainly made stimulating good feelings his main objective when he sent out his cards. Every one of them had the same message inside: "I like you!"

He went even further when he was trying to close a deal. He would invite the customer into his office and ask, "What kind of cigarettes do you smoke?" (Remember, this was the 1960s—smoking was a lot more common, and nobody questioned smoking inside a place of business. Some things have changed for the better!) Whatever the customer said, Joe would have a carton—he kept all the popular brands in a cabinet. He would take out a pack and hand it to the customer. "Here—keep the pack!" He would even offer the customer a drink. "Well, sure, Joe, if you'll have one too." (Wow! Some things have really changed!) Anyway, Girard would pour the client a nice belt of scotch or bourbon or whatever and pour himself a drink of "vodka"—which was, of course, pure water. Leaning back in the chair in front of Girard's desk, with a cigarette in one hand and a glass of Jim Beam in the other, the customer was living large. "Sure! Let's do the deal! In fact, let's upgrade it. Let's add in the air conditioning!"

Was this manipulative? Yes, I suppose it was. Was it dishonest or unethical? No, I don't think so. Nobody made the customer take a free pack of cigarettes or a drink. And Girard still worked hard to provide the best possible deal for the man or woman to whom he was selling. He knew that if he didn't, long after they had forgotten the taste of Jameson whiskey, they'd remember that Joe Girard had screwed them royally. And they'd tell that story to 250 friends. So he kept the deal fair, gave them a good, competitive price, and worked hard to make sure they were happy after the sale was done.

He even let customers take a brand new car home with them with only a small amount of earnest money down, before they had their loan worked out. Foolish? It could have been, but he found that showing trust in the customer—and creating a major sense of obligation—resulted in closed deals nearly every time.

For many years I had the pleasure of working on a consulting basis with one of the greatest marketing machines in the world, Procter & Gamble. For more than a century the company had used this principle to introduce new products or to relaunch existing products with new features. How? By giving the product away. Sampling new products in a store or via the mail creates enough of an obligation in consumers that a large number of them will buy the product. Sampling is expensive. Trust me—if it didn't work, P&G never would have done it.

How can you as a salesperson use these principles? Obviously, you don't have to buy your customers popcorn and Pepsi to create good feelings. But you may have something that is far more valuable and much more difficult to obtain—information. Insight.

Sharing information that is relevant to your customer's business operation is an effective and ethical way to create an obligation. Sharing a little-known fact that most of your prospects didn't know is a way of creating pressure for reciprocation. For example, a friend of mine has been involved in the car business most of his working life. Recently he became convinced that there was a better way for people to buy a car—if they told him what they wanted, he would track the various automobile auctions around the state and buy the car they desired at auction, saving them thousands of dollars. But how could he find customers?

Because he had been active in various charitable and civic organizations around the county for years, he had plenty of contact names. He created a simple web site for his business that explained what he did and how it would help customers who had him buy for them—it would save money, save time, and give them the chance to grab exactly the car they wanted when it came through. And then we brainstormed a few things that his decades in the car business had taught him that most people didn't know. For example, most people didn't realize that there was no "lemon law" in his state. So we wrote up a brief message about that fact. Another brief message explained what factors were most important in determining resale value of a used car. And so on.

Once a month, out goes a brief message from him to each person on his list of contacts. He includes his contact information, including both his physical address (to be in compliance with the CAN SPAM law) and his Web address. And he invites people to pass his messages on to others.

He's establishing recognition. And he's creating a subtle form of obligation. Already, people are commenting to him about the e-mail they got from him, opening up opportunities for him to inquire if they need his help—or if perhaps a niece who's graduating from high school and needs a car for college, or an elderly parent who needs a reliable, safe car for tootling around town, might need it.

GUERRILLAS IN OUR MIDST

One of the most powerful movements in modern business has been the creation of "guerrilla marketing" by Jay Conrad Levinson. I can still remember the excitement I felt as a young man when I picked up a copy of Jay's first book and realized that it was all spelled out right there—everything I needed to know as a fledgling entrepreneur to get the word out about my business.

Apparently I wasn't the only one. In the years since *Guerrilla Marketing* first appeared, Jay Levinson has sold more than 14 million books. He's been translated into 41 different languages. And he's created both a franchise and a mindset that has had an enormous positive impact on business—especially for entrepreneurs, smaller businesses, and people who don't have access to big advertising budgets or high-priced advice. What he showed people was a more sophisticated version of Girard's Law of 250.

Levinson, who was formerly vice president and creative director at the J. Walter Thompson and Leo Burnett advertising agencies, offered small businesses creative answers to the basic challenge of gaining recognition. He showed how creativity was more important than money when it comes to getting attention. He demonstrated ways to generate free publicity that are more effective than throwing your business cards from the upper deck of a football stadium. And, most importantly, he argued that for a small business or an individual entrepreneur, marketing should target *individuals,* not demographic segments.

The ideas that Levinson and his coauthors have offered over the years remain some of the very best techniques for generating prospects. Other than a couple that may take more money than the typical sales rep has in her wallet, there aren't any guerrilla ideas that a salesperson can't use to build a solid prospect list.

For example, Levinson and his coauthor Mike McLaughlin have shown how consultants—who typically have to sell the service as well as deliver it—can use guerrilla marketing techniques to build steady business. Using e-mail and a web presence, publishing an e-zine, giving interviews and speeches, writing articles, even conducting surveys and publishing the results: These are just some of the low-cost or free methods that they illustrate. And all of them are methods that a salesperson—who is, after all, supposed to be "consultative" in his or her approach—can use to generate leads and establish recognition.

USING YOUR OWN TOOLBOX

Girard talked about his "toolbox"—his business cards, his list of prospects, the cards he sent out, and a few other things he used day in and day out to generate leads. What's in your toolbox? How do you generate recognition? How do you establish interest? Even create a bit of ethical obligation?

For us today, the task of staying in touch with customers is actually much easier than it was for Girard. For a couple of hundred dollars, we can install a reliable contact manager, like ACT! or GoldMine, on our laptop. Instead of having to copy names and addresses from file cards onto envelopes and lick stamps until we're ready to gag, we can simply select our clients from a drop list and fire off an e-mail. It's easy. And it's essentially free.

Of course the cretins who continue to flood everybody's in-box with offers to buy sex, drugs, or mortgage loans have fouled the waters somewhat. As a result, we have to be careful how we write our e-mail message so that it actually gets through the spam filters and reaches our prospects. And then we have to have something interesting and relevant to say so that our prospects actually glance at it.

But it wasn't any different for Joe Girard. He knew that the usual promotional mailings that dealerships and salespeople sent out all ended up in the trash. They looked like advertising, so they got pitched. They sounded generic, so they got tossed.

He couldn't afford to have that happen. So he made each month's message look as unique and personal as possible.

Joe Girard was also a master at networking. He built his contact list and gained exposure to hundreds of people he otherwise never would have met by using some pretty creative techniques. For example, he probably used his business card more effectively than any other salesperson before him. As he said, "I know a lot [of salespeople] who don't through a box of 500 in a year. I go through that many in a good week."[5] First, he made sure that his card was distinctive—in an era when everyone's business card was white with black lettering, his was in color with his picture on it. He would leave business cards along with a generous tip when he ate at a restaurant. He put a stack of them in the glove box of each car he sold, with an offer to pay $25 for a referral that led to a closed sale—just sign your name on the back of my card and tell your friend to hand it to me when he comes in. He even went so far as to throw them over the railing of the upper deck at Detroit Lions football games, letting them scatter down below on the "rich" seats like confetti. He figured that if just one card out of a hundred made it into somebody's hands, it was worth the effort.

Now that worked for Girard because he was selling a commodity, one that nearly anybody in that football stadium or waiting tables or attending a Kiwanis meeting might need to buy someday. But what about somebody who is selling business to business? There's no point in throwing cards over railings or leaving stacks of them at barber shops, is there?

No, of course not. But there are other things the professional salesperson can do to gain the same kind of exposure among the community of potential buyers for her products.

People complain that their involvement in networking activities—whether it's a monthly Chamber of Commerce meeting they attend, or a professional interest group focused on Macintosh computers, or maybe even giving a speech at a trade show—just doesn't generate any leads. If you feel that way, perhaps it's worth asking yourself four questions:

1. *Are you attending the right kinds of events?* If you provide outsourced IT services in the Santa Barbara area, attending meetings of the Central Coast SofTech Association might generate some leads and some recognition. But aren't you just one more goldfish in a crowded bowl at an event like that? What about attending the Business Marketing Association's monthly meeting—after all, marketing people don't know nearly as much about information technology as the people at the Software Association do, and they might be more interested in hiring you to help them.

2. *Are you an active or a passive participant?* Al Lautenslager, the entrepreneur who built 1-800-INKWELL into a leading provider of commercial printing in Chicago and who came up with the great P.R. stunt of offering free printing to Boeing, has some great advice for people who want to use meetings as networking opportunities: *Act like it's your meeting.*

Even though you're just another attendee, arrive early and help set up chairs. Greet people near the door. Help in any way you can. Acting as if you are responsible for the success of the meeting will give you the confidence to speak to other attendees and will certainly ingratiate you to the actual hosts.

Lautenslager also recommends going to each event with a specific goal in mind: Tonight I will meet ten new people, collect six business cards, and identify three people with whom I want to follow up. By setting yourself a target for participation at a networking event, you're more likely to get something out of it.

3. *Do you know how to make effective contact? How to maintain it?* One of the great moments of opportunity at any networking event is when a stranger asks you, "So, what do you do?" Why not have a clearly crafted answer to that question that focuses not so much on what you do, but on how customers benefit?

For example, think about the "elevator speech" we discussed in the previous section. If you have developed your own version, you can quickly explain to a stranger (1) the kind of customers you serve, (2) why they need you, (3) what you do, and (4) what separates you from other firms or individuals who do similar kinds of work.

But what if they don't ask? We know from Dale Carnegie that most people would rather talk about themselves than listen to you say anything at all. So why not give them that privilege? When you meet someone, ask her what she does for a living. Chances are that she won't be as prepared as you are with a focused elevator speech, but she'll be able to tell you that she provides mobile document shredding services or that she is the business reporter for the local newspaper or that she is a professor of finance at the local college. So shake that person's hand firmly, look her directly in the eye, and ask, "What is the biggest challenge for you in your role as . . . ?" Just watch her light up. As she begins to tell you about her challenges, maintain eye contact and use your best active listening skills.

When she runs out of steam, if she does, ask her, "What other factors are affecting the way you work these days?"

Once you've heard her describe the challenges she faces and the forces of change around her, you may have an idea if there's a fit. If there is, you can say, "You know, I've helped some other clients handle exactly that kind of problem recently." But if there isn't, you can just break off the conversation at this point, saying something polite like, "Alison, it's a pleasure to meet you. I don't personally have any answers for the kinds of challenges you're facing, but I'll keep my ears open tonight. If I meet somebody who does, I'll make sure they get in contact with you."

4. *Do you consistently follow up with the leads that you do generate?* If you made three contacts that are worth following up, you know what to do. Follow up! Quickly! Calling the next day is a good idea. And calling is better than e-mailing, because it gives you a chance to build more rapport, ask more questions, and engage in more of a true dialogue. Even if nothing happens at this point, add this person to your prospect list and start him on your program of regular contacts—e-mails, notes, clippings, occasional phone calls. Just because he's not ready or able to buy what you have today doesn't mean that he won't be in six months or a year.

It's all about marketing yourself. And it's about recognizing that, thanks to Joe Girard's Law of 250, for every impression you make on somebody, you potentially are making an impression on 250 other people as well.

CHAPTER 21

THE PROS AND CONS OF
PRIMING THE PUMP

It's hard to find too much fault with what Girard developed. Priming the pump makes good business sense. But there are a few risks to keep in mind.

THE CONS

It Can Seem Manipulative

Pretending to be someone's friend or to have her interests in mind when we're really just trying to get something out of her—well, it seems hypocritical, doesn't it? If Joe Girard is telling 10,000 people to have a "Happy Fourth of July!" this month, just how sincere is he?

At some point, we have to separate activities that we do because they are appropriate to our role in business from activities that we do because we have an intimate connection with someone. Both kinds of communication are appropriate. Sending a friendly message to a business prospect is, in my view, similar to starting out a business letter by calling the recipient "Dear David." As we discussed in the section on Elmer Wheeler and sales language, some uses of language are not referential. They are what Roman Jakobson called "phatic"—they're a form of language that we use to maintain good social relations or establish contact.

The messages we send to prospects to prime the pump fall into that category. They are no more manipulative or hypocritical than saying, when we first meet someone, "Hello. How are you? It's nice to meet you." The fact is, in a literal sense, we probably aren't interested in how they are, and meeting them isn't that big a deal. But as a way of being courteous, we say the appropriate thing. And the other person responds in like manner.

Keeping our roles separate and understanding what kind of message is appropriate and when is just part of being a responsible adult. If a salesperson loses track of that and uses this kind of system in a cynical, manipulative way, that person has much bigger problems in life than the way he is communicating with prospects.

The Messages Can Sound Canned

Not everybody is a good writer. Sometimes people lose their own voice when they write. Girard avoided the problem by sending everybody the same message—"I like you." Corny, perhaps, but pretty hard to mess up.

If you send out a regular message, you run the risk of sending something that sounds canned or fake. "I like you" is probably not enough today. We need something more substantive, and we probably need somebody to tell us how we sound when we write.

If you're worried that you're coming across as stiff or pompous or whatever, try this: Instead of writing the message, try *saying* it. Dictate the message into a tape recorder in your own words. Imagine that a prospect, just one, is sitting across from you and that you want to tell her about this cool fact you discovered. How would you say it in real life? Say it. Tape it. Transcribe it. Clean it up a bit for the sake of grammar and consistency, but not too much.

Sending Messages Can Become an End in Itself

This kind of work can become seductive. For some people, it's more fun, or at least safer, than actually selling anything. Working on your messages, addressing the envelopes, tweaking your contact management system—it's all cool. But it's not selling. And if it becomes an end in itself, it can be very destructive.

You need to allocate a certain minimum amount of time each week for working your list and communicating with some subset of your prospects. Ideally, this is something you do for a minimum amount of time every day. But you may also need to allocate a maximum amount of time to the activity, too. Otherwise you can blow five hours figuring out a cool new way to put a field in your ACT! customer record, which means that you weren't in front of actual human being–type customers at all.

You Can Lose Focus

These are intended to be customer-centered messages designed to build a personal relationship. That's all. But sometimes people forget that and start sending out product spec sheets or promotional material.

The other risk is allowing your brief little message to evolve into something bigger—a magazine or a journal. I've seen this happen with a couple of consulting firms over the past few years. They started out sending just a brief message, but gradually what they sent got more and more grandiose, more and more bloated, until it was far more than a touch point. They had turned their little monthly nurturing messages into full-blown "zines." Now they're in HTML with color graphics. Now there's a table of contents, and you have to click on the story you find interesting. Now it's . . . well, now it's more bother than it's worth.

Blogs, zines, newsletters. They're good. But they're *organizational* in nature. They aren't as effective in developing a focused, personal relationship between you as a salesperson and your prospect or customer as a simple, short, seemingly personal message. If we forget to make the message client-centered, the client will forget to read it.

THE PROS

There are lots of advantages to applying Girard's Law of 250 in your own sales practice.

There's No More Cold Calling

Would everybody who enjoys cold calling please raise their hands? A little higher, please. Higher—I'm not seeing any yet!

Hmm. Nobody?

Well, that's not surprising. On any list of sales-related tasks that salespeople hate, cold calling usually comes in first. A sales rep would rather try to collect payments from a deadbeat than "dial for dollars" the old-fashioned way.

One of the beauties of Girard's approach to priming the sales pump was that it eliminated the need for cold calling. Instead, he was soon able to count on buyers coming in from his prospect list or on referrals from people who were previous customers.

There are more productive ways for sales professionals to spend their days than dialing numbers at random and trying to engage whoever answers in a meaningful conversation.

It Establishes Your Expertise and Value

When you send a short, relevant message to a customer, something he finds useful or interesting, he sees you as an expert. He's glad he knows you because you add a bit of value to his life.

Trolling for the kind of information your customers will be glad to get isn't that hard, either. The Internet has become such a powerful tool for locating information, particularly if you set up interest groups to track topics you want to stay up on, that a lot of the grunt work has been eliminated.

The Cost Is Low

Girard paid for his greeting cards and postage himself. He thought it was worth it. And besides, as he pointed out, in his tax bracket, half of it was paid by the government anyway because it was a write-off.

Today, he'd be even happier. With digital media, you don't need to spend hundreds of dollars each month on postage. You just need to structure your e-mail to make it entertaining or interesting enough that it grabs attention before the customer hits the delete key.

If you have a simple contact management system, like Goldmine or ACT!, you can set up groups from your contact database so that the contact manager sends the messages to everybody in the group automatically. If your contact list is extremely large, you may find that it's easier and simpler to subcontract the actual distribution to one of the companies that handles that function. Even doing that, your costs per month will be less than what Girard spent for postage.

Of course, setting up your nurture campaign in the first place will take some time. And time is money. But this is an expenditure of time that can pay such huge dividends that it's hard to imagine why somebody wouldn't do it.

It Eliminates the Roller-Coaster Effect

One experience that every self-employed person has had is riding the business roller coaster. It's not much fun.

We scurry around and do all the marketing and networking things we know we should do in order to generate business. But then, in a few weeks, because these activities do eventually produce results, we get a contract or two. Because we're self-employed or have a very small staff, we then stop our marketing efforts to work on the billable activities we've landed. Money is coming in; life is good; we're doing the kind of work God put us here to do.

But then the job is completed. And we realize that there's nothing behind it. The money will quickly run out. So we career down into depression, worrying and fuming, until finally we kick ourselves out of the doldrums and go into a marketing frenzy again.

And so it goes. Up and down, around and around, like gerbils in a wheel; we're constantly running, but we're not getting ahead, and we're enjoying only a small portion of it.

Unfortunately, the same phenomenon happens to major account salespeople. They do all the activities necessary to generate interest from a big account. Once they secure that interest, they stop everything else to work on the deal. But then, when it closes, what happens? They're back at zero, and they have to start again.

Implementing the kind of nurture marketing program that Girard innovated will smooth out the highs and lows. By setting up a system to communicate with your entire database of prospects in a personal way on a monthly basis, you increase the chances that new contracts, new projects, will flow more regularly and consistently through your pipeline.

When Jim Cecil did his research for Microsoft on the practices of successful resellers, he found that resellers who consistently and systematically contacted customers and prospects grew their businesses at a dramatically faster rate than resellers who had no such program. The goal was to maintain top-of-mind awareness so that when a customer or a prospect needed the products and services the reseller had, that reseller's name was the first one to pop up. Just as the people in Detroit thought of Joe Girard as soon as they thought about buying a car, this kind of nurturing campaign prepares the customer to turn to you when she's ready to buy.

CHAPTER 22

MAKING IT WORK FOR YOU

We've already talked about a lot of the things you can do to make Girard's Law of 250 work for you so that it primes the pump of sales in your own business. Here are a few more suggestions on how you can make this idea work for you.

LEAD GENERATION

Before you go looking for leads, you need to be clear about a few things:

1. What you have to offer
2. What problems your product or service solves
3. Who your competitors are and what differentiates them
4. What differentiates you from your competition

Now, describe the 20 most profitable clients you currently have. What qualities and characteristics do they have in common? List these features. This becomes the profile of your target accounts and high-probability leads. The things you're looking to capture include the industry these clients are in, their size, who makes decisions, their buying patterns, and so forth. You might want to go back and review some of the questions that Harvey Mackay asked. They may give you some ideas of things to look for in your target audience. You want to find more people like them.

The next step is to map out your campaign. That means identifying your budget, in terms of both the money you can spend and the time you can invest. You also need to specifically list the activities you will perform and when you will do them.

Regarding your budget, ask yourself what you can afford to spend on campaigns. If the answer is nothing, that doesn't mean you can't mount a campaign, but it does mean you'll have to look to Jay Levinson for some of his no-cost guerrilla marketing ideas and then adapt them to your situation. Time is also an issue. How much time can you dedicate each week to lead generation? Girard spent hours every week doing his cards, but you may not want to spend that much time. Don't kid yourself, though, that you can accomplish anything meaningful without putting in an hour or two each week.

Where should you direct your efforts? As a rule of thumb, you should spend about 60 percent of your budget on your current clients, 30 percent on targeted audience lead generation, and 10 percent on name recognition marketing. Existing customers are your most likely source of new business, but everyone needs to keep fresh opportunities and new accounts moving into the pipeline. And as for name recognition, remember that the first heuristic of decision making is name recognition.

Once you know who you are and what kind of leads you want, you can focus on lead-generation tactics. Generating good leads means carrying out a plan, taking simple action steps to support the plan and completing them in a timely matter. Do something! And do it regularly! It's that simple. Here are some of the action steps you can take:

1. Create an easy-to-navigate, current, knowledge-based web site that encourages interaction with you. Don't forget to syndicate the headlines so that the Really Simple Syndication people can sweep your site and get the information to the search engines. Pay the annual fee to have your site listed on the major search engines. It's worth it. You'll be directing clients to your site for current information, white papers, and product or service information. Keep it simple and professional. If your company already has a web site, volunteer to sit on the committee that makes suggestions and improvements for the site. Even if you're part of a large corporation—in fact, especially if you are—look into creating a web site focused on you as a sales executive representing that company.

2. Create an e-mail newsletter that you send to your mailing list on a regular schedule. The newsletter should be informative, one page, easy to read, and accurate. This will touch your customers, target accounts, and general audience, keeping your name and expertise uppermost in their minds.

3. Another name-recognition tactic that costs very little is doing good works for the community or for your client's favorite charity. You can volunteer to work at a fund-raising event, participate in a charity walk, or do something else that brings you in contact with other community leaders and perhaps even with some of your customers, and at the same time makes a positive contribution to a worthy cause.

4. Publish articles in relevant trade magazines and put your picture, web site, and a brief biography at the top.

5. Even letters to local newspapers on topics of relevance to your business can be helpful. For example, if you sell restaurant equipment, you probably have an opinion about the pending changes to the standards used by the Board of Health.

6. Don't forget your local Chamber of Commerce, Women in Business, Kiwanis, Rotary, investment clubs, high-tech associations, and so on. They remain excellent sources of leads, particularly if you are a salesperson who covers a specific geographic territory. Volunteer to speak at these meetings about a relevant topic. At the meetings, make sure you collect business cards for your database. If you're a speaker, give away something meaningful at the end of your presentation.

7. Attend all relevant trade shows and try to secure a speaking engage-ment or sponsor a hospitality suite where you'll have one-on-one time with prospective buyers. If you have a booth at a trade show, keep it staffed at all times, and don't put a barrier (a wall, a counter, a row of chairs) between you and your client. (How many times have you approached a booth and found the salespeople sitting behind a table that is blocking the entrance to the booth and talking to one another?) Dress professionally, and make sure that everyone staffing the booth has a quick one-minute elevator speech ready. Make sure you get business cards for your database, perhaps by giving away something valuable, like a relevant book or an iPod.

8. Each quarter, update the media. Give them usable stories that include new products or services, successful clients, new processes or methods.

9. Advertise in the Yellow Pages. Give customers a discount if they men-tion the ad. Or give them a free gift if they call and mention the ad.

10. Use direct mail, but keep it personal and small so that you can measure the results easily. Create your own list—try not to use rented lists where you are unsure of the accuracy of the data. Address a specific business problem, direct it to the decision maker, say that you'll follow up, and then call on the day you said you would. Don't send gifts or tchotchkes.

11. If there are directories that list your type of services or products, make sure that you are in those directories and that the information is accu-rate.

12. If you have a successful story to tell, an innovative product, or an expertise that is unique, write a white paper, professionally publish it, and use it as a free market report for people who visit your site or respond to a direct-mail or e-mail campaign.

13. Send e-mails to current customers if you are offering an unusually good price or a new product or service and invite them to order early.

14. Get tickets to trade shows and local business events. Call and personally invite your prospects to attend.

15. Found a local organization that focuses on a specific industry. For example, if there isn't such an organization already, start a local Software Association.

16. Keep up with old friends, bosses, colleagues, and business associates. Once a month, take someone to lunch whom you haven't seen for a while, catch up, and talk about each other's business. You may have mutual leads to share.

17. Offer to do some pro bono work for the city or the business community.

18. Always follow up with anyone you meet at a trade show or conference, on a train or plane, or at a community meeting. A simple e-mail is enough.

19. Conduct quarterly lunch-and-learns. Provide a simple boxed lunch and have speakers on interesting topics.

20. Create links to other relevant web sites and place your links on those sites.

21. Send an e-mail and place a personal call to new presidents, vice presidents, and other people whose promotions have been announced in your local paper. Congratulate them on their promotion and wish them success. Don't forget to add them to your database.

22. Introduce yourself when you are at church, at a party, at a soccer game, at the neighborhood block party. Let people get to know you and your expertise.

23. Always offer a finder's fee to anyone who provides you with a lead. Offer one level of finder's fee for an unqualified lead and a higher amount for a closed lead.

24. Nurture relationships with companies that offer possible companion products or services. These alliances will generate leads for both you and them.

25. Always be respectful of your leads. Remember, they'll tell others, and those others will tell others. This was the whole premise of Girard's Law of 250. But that means that you have to do what you say you'll do on time. If someone wants to unsubscribe from your newsletter, do it immediately. If someone says that he is not interested, say "thank you" and quickly exit.

26. To advertise your product or service, donate a substantial gift to a local charity for a raffle or silent auction. Make sure your name and service are publicized. Ask if you can be the person who presents the gift to the lucky winner.

27. Call your current client base regularly to survey them about customer service. Are they happy? Are they getting what they need from you to continue using your products or services?

This list represents a whole basketful of ideas. Use the ones that you like and that you can afford. Adapt them so that they work for you. For example, if you don't have the budget to sponsor a "lunch and learn" seminar, don't do it. And if you can't afford to offer a finder's fee yourself, perhaps your company can offer something. Or maybe you just buy the person who provided the referral a nice box of candy.

If there's one thing that Joe Girard's career should teach us, it's the value of being creative. Use your imagination to gain exposure and to generate qualified leads. Do it every day. And maybe you'll end up in the *Guinness Book of World Records,* too.

PART SIX

CONCLUSION

CHAPTER 23

LOOKING BACK TO LOOK AHEAD

When I was about 12, my father was promoted from his senior sales job at Nabisco in Chicago to branch manager in Spokane. The branch he was taking over was in big trouble. They weren't holding their market share, they weren't hitting their numbers, and they were having problems in the warehouse.

Somehow I became aware that Dad had a sales rep in Pasco who wasn't doing well at all. He was going down to work with the man for a few days to try to get him on the right track. Otherwise, he would have to fire the man.

When Dad got back from his trip, I asked him, "Were you able to teach him how to do it?"

"How to do what?" he asked.

"How to sell."

Dad paused for a minute. "Well, actually, he already knows how to sell," he said. "He just needs to do it."

Sometimes the simplest answers are the hardest to put into action. *He just needs to do it.*

All of the sales methods we have looked at have one thing in common: They work. Some work better in certain circumstances than others, or one of them might work better with a certain kind of client than another one will. But when all the shouting is done, the fact remains: They work.

But they work only if you work them. They deliver results only if the salesperson shows up and puts in the effort.

In reading this book, you may have been interested in the history of selling and how it has evolved. If so, then I hope your needs were met.

But if you read the book to find answers, hoping to improve your own success in selling, then you know what I'm going to tell you next.

Choose one. Use one.

Do it every day.

Keep at it steadily, persistently, consistently.

You may choose to lay out a clear sales path based on an understanding of the process your customers will follow most easily. You might focus on developing stronger relationships and building trust with your customers. Maybe you will devote your attention to delivering the message in the most effective way, or you will develop a systematic way of generating leads to keep your pipeline full. Maybe, being the overachiever that you no doubt are, you will do all four.

But the bottom line is that you just need to do it.

◆ ◆ ◆

A century ago, before Patterson revolutionized sales methods, the focus of all sales presentations was on the product. In fact, the word "selling" was virtually synonymous with demoing. Companies did not enforce a systematic approach to selling, and there was no concern about delivering a consistent message. Salespeople were not trained. Sales management did not exist.

As we have seen, the situation changed because of the need for better methods and because of the pragmatic nature of the sales profession. Relationship-based methods grew from the traditional role of the commercial traveler and empowered the individual salesperson to make things happen as an individual. Focusing on the importance of building personal relationships with the customer or prospect, relationship-oriented methods placed greater importance on networking and communication skills. Meanwhile, the process-oriented models arose from the perceived need to standardize and professionalize the sales force. They focused on controlling the process and the people who carry it out. Emphasis is placed in these methods on identifying the steps or stages of the sales process and following them through in a logical, consistent way. Analytical skills and business acumen are necessary qualities for success in process-oriented sales methods.

If it's true that people buy from people they trust, we are wise to ask: *What is the source of trust?* The answer is that trust arises over time from a combination of rapport and credibility. How long it takes to develop trust depends on the customer's perception of risk. The more risk the customer perceives to be inherent in the relationship, the longer it will take to build trust. The relationship-oriented approaches to selling focus on maximizing the rapport component of trust. The process-oriented methods focus on establishing credibility.

So which approach is right for you? In general terms, relationship-oriented methods, the kind we have associated with Carnegie, are most effective at the two ends of the business spectrum. If you are engaged in transactional or commodity sales, or if you are engaged in enterprise or strategic sales, a relationship methodology may be most effective for you. In the case of purely transactional sales, the customer sees all the products, services, or solutions in a given category as being essentially the same and, therefore, as being interchangeable. The only potential differentiator is a good relationship with the salesperson. Efficiency in the sales process is one of the dominant values in transactional sales. Keeping things simple, reacting quickly, and providing cost transparency and flexibility are traits that the customer values. At the other end of the scale, where we are seeking a long-term, nonspecific contract to support an enterprise at a strategic level, top-level relationships set the agenda for the actual projects that will be funded. That's why a relationship approach is typically used by the "big five" consulting firms. And that's why so many senior administrators or top-level military leaders retire and go to work for government contractors. Relationships are one of the keys to success.

By contrast, process-oriented sales models work best when your business situation meets some of the following criteria:

1. The product or service you are selling can be differentiated.
2. The product or service can be or must be customized.
3. The customer doesn't automatically recognize how the product or service you are offering solves a problem or adds value in his or her organization.
4. Delivery, installation, or use of the product or service requires a coordinated effort.
5. The impact of the product or service is pervasive enough and margins are large enough that you can justify taking a longer, more costly sales approach.

As we have seen, the process-oriented methodologies began in "high tech," with the cash register, and were further developed by other high-tech firms, particularly IBM and Xerox. That doesn't mean that they are suitable only for high technology products or applications, but it does mean that the nature of a high-tech sale makes a process approach more effective.

The essential quality of the process models for sales that you must keep in mind is that they are based on a series of incremental agreements. They are not appropriate if you want to achieve a close on the first call. Instead, you must assume that you will be making several sales calls and presentations, that you will be presenting to multiple decision makers and influencers, and that you will need to document the various decisions and agreements reached along the way with letters, e-mails, or other forms of documentation. In essence, process-oriented sales methods apply project management skills to the sales process so that a complex task can be broken into its component parts and handled in an efficient, orderly way.

The methods developed by Wheeler and Girard support both approaches to handling the sales process. Whether you follow a relationship-oriented or a process-oriented model, your success will increase if you use language as effectively as possible, and your pipeline will stay full if you implement a program of nurturing leads and contacts.

So . . . which sales methodology is the best? I can't answer that, because the answer depends on you, on your typical customers, on what you are selling, and on the competitive environment in which you are working. However, there are six characteristics that you should look for in your current methods. If you find that your sales methodology is lacking in one of these, take steps to correct the deficiency.

1. *The sales method matches the customer's preferred mode of buying.* Forcing a customer who is looking for a close working relationship to follow you through a tightly controlled, logical sequence of steps will end up delaying success. By the same token, trying to build a warm, personal relationship with a committee that has laid out a detailed process for vendor selection may not yield the results you're after, either.

2. *The sales method is flexible enough to be self-correcting, incorporating lessons learned.* Blindly following a method, even when there is clear evidence right before you that it's not working, makes no sense. In fact, according to folk wisdom, doing the same thing over and over again and hoping for a different outcome is a definition of insanity. A sane approach to sales has to involve awareness. We need to stay conscious throughout the process. Otherwise, we lose opportunities to improve it.

3. *The sales process itself creates value, usually in the form of intellectual capital, for both the customer and the vendor.* If we invest all of the time and effort together that it requires to make a sale, we should both come out of it at the end with something more than a finalized contract. The contract may be the most important goal, but both of us should be able to point to specific information or insight we have gained from the promise that transcends the transaction itself. We have greater insight into operations or into the competitive landscape or into industry trends or something.

4. *The methodology we follow increases the efficiency of the sales process, making the sales cycle shorter or enabling the salesperson to handle a larger volume of accounts successfully.* The ultimate measure of success in choosing a sales methodology is the win ratio. If you are closing more

business by using a process-oriented or a relationship-based methodology, then by all means continue. But at the same time, keep an eye on the cost-of-sales factors. How long does it take to close a deal? How many salespeople does it take to handle a major opportunity? You may need to consider tradeoffs between a slightly higher win ratio and a significantly more complex or lengthy sales cycle.

5. *The methodology should be transferable across all skill levels.* Patterson struggled to get his experienced sales reps to use the Primer, and he didn't achieve the level of adoption that he sought until he instituted formal sales training. How easily can experienced salespeople adopt the methodology your company is implementing? What about sales reps who are brand new? Do they have enough experience to use it effectively? In a large organization, you will need to adopt a method that can be taught in stages, helping the new person acquire the basic skills as well as transitioning the veteran into a different approach without alienating him or her.

6. *The methodology is based on objectively measured events or tasks.* All four of the methods we have examined in this book have one thing in common: They are measurable. Patterson was a fiend for tracking results and measuring performance, and Wheeler based his credibility on testing thousands of sentences with millions of people. Girard kept careful track of his lead generation activities to make sure he was using those that worked and abandoning those that did not. Even Carnegie emphasized the importance of lists, goals, and measurements to make sure of forming new habits of interaction. Sales is no place for "gut feelings" or "hunches" or other subjective impressions of progress. We need to be able to focus on specific behaviors and the outcomes they produce to make intelligent choices about what's working and what isn't.

We started this book by ridiculing some of the overly optimistic predictions about how advertising or the web would eliminate the need for traditional sales. But if we step back and look at trends, we can see clearly that in the future professional sales will definitely involve the use of even more technology than it already does. Automation was a little late to arrive in sales, compared to manufacturing or finance or some other areas of the business. But we crossed that chasm a long time ago and sales is now fully dependent on digital technologies to save time and eliminate waste. The difference is that technology will be an enabling technology for sales people, not a replacement for them.

Where are we most likely to see new techniques for selling?

One area of potential impact is in the early stages of the sales cycle.

Instead of making several in-person sales calls, a sales rep in the future may connect with a prospect using a virtual meeting space.

Web conferencing is already one of the fastest growing applications in sales. Many companies find that it's more cost effective to have the salesperson conduct an initial conversation over the phone, where some basic qualification questions get answered. At that time it's usually possible to also probe into the customer's business to develop an understanding of her or his needs. If there appears to be interest and a good fit, the salesperson will then schedule a web conference where he or she can do a product demo without leaving the office. That demo can even be archived, so the customer can look at it again later or share it with colleagues who weren't able to attend the live broadcast. The cost savings to the salesperson are huge, in terms of eliminating travel expenses and the waste associated with going to the airport, waiting around, sitting on a plane, making a connection or two, getting a rental car, checking in to a hotel—well, if you do it for a living, you know full well how much of your time is spent in activities that add nothing of value to the sales process. There are cost savings for the customer, too, who can pursue information and gain insight into a potential solution without necessarily disrupting a huge portion of the day.

But at some point, the salesperson and the customer must come together in person. In complex sales with a high dollar value, in sales that change the way people do their work or that relocate control of valuable assets, such as money or information, or in sales that involve implementation and training—the salesperson and the customer must literally, physically come together. And the salesperson must understand how the decision process proceeds, what stage of the process the customer is at, and how to help move the process forward.

Another area where the salesperson will use even more technology is in researching the client's situation. For a publicly traded company, we can use the Internet to get a copy of the company's annual report and 10-K. These are invaluable in giving us insight into what the company thinks it needs to do to be successful, and where it sees potential problems or obstacles to success. Perusing the company's web site will quickly identify what they are using as key marketing messages, and looking at their main competitors' web sites will suggest where they may have weaknesses. If you subscribe to a service like Hoover's, you can get information about a potential client at greater depth, and if you use a service like FirstResearch you can get a detailed report on trends, performance measures, and key issues for the industry in which the potential client competes.

But after the salesperson has done the necessary research, he or she still needs to integrate it into a coherent message: *Here's what I understand you're trying to accomplish and some of the key challenges you face. Here are some ways in which achieving those goals and overcoming those obstacles will strengthen your business. And here's how we can help you succeed in that effort.*

Putting that message together still requires creativity and business insight, and delivering it effectively requires an ability to establish trust and credibility with an audience quickly.

The use of web technology to create a personalized experience based on mass customization and collaborative filtering will eventually move from the megasites like Amazon and become available at a local level. Even the individual salesperson will be able to create a web site where a customer can have an experience customized to his or her own interests and needs. And when a prospect visits that web site, the salesperson will be able to capture key information about the prospect unobtrusively, making it possible to follow up with a customized program of communications.

That program, furthermore, will run by itself for the most part. The salesperson will need to establish some key parameters and create some basic messages, but once it has been set up, the system will continue to contact each prospect or customer on a regular basis automatically. And yet to each recipient of a message, that message will feel unique and personal. That kind of technology isn't too far off.

But even when this type of system is as cheap and easy to use as a contact management system, the salesperson will still need to make personal contact periodically. High tech without any element of human touch will become less and less effective even as it becomes easier to implement. The very fact that it becomes easier and more common will undercut its effectiveness.

A lot of the tools and trappings of the sales profession will change in the coming decades. We'll see things happen that even the most visionary of us will not be able to predict.

But one thing that I don't believe we'll ever see is an end to the role of the professional salesperson. As the vital link between customer and company, as the energizing spark that helps the customer move along toward a decision, the salesperson remains the engine that drives the economy.

It's an important job. It's a tough one, too. And it's vitally important that we do it well.

CHAPTER 1

1. There are literally dozens of these books and articles. A lot of the articles appeared in journals that focused on the Internet economy—*Wired, Fast Company, Industry Standard.* Their bias is understandable, since they were halfway between business periodicals and special-interest publications. But similar articles appeared in *Fortune* and *BusinessWeek.* See, for example, Evan I. Swartz, "How Middlemen Can Come Out on Top: Nimble Businesses Can Change the Internet from a Threat into an Ally," *BusinessWeek,* February 9, 1998, where the author predicts that because of the power of the Web to change the rules of business, those firms that depend on selling products and services at the local level face a huge challenge. "For some," he writes, "extinction is almost certain." In particular, insurance agents, car dealerships, real estate brokers, financial service providers, and travel agents were largely doomed. As I write this, some seven years later, these predictions seem slightly cracked. Other experts wrote books, though, making the same basic points. There were literally dozens of these, but a couple that were widely read and quoted were Patricia Seybold, *Customers.com: How to Create a Profitable Business Strategy for the Internet and Beyond* (New York: Crown Business, 1998) and Frederick Newell, *Loyalty.com: Customer Relationship Management in the New Era of Internet Marketing* (New York: McGraw-Hill, 2002).

2. Quoted in Walter A. Friedman, *Birth of a Salesman: The Transformation of Selling in America* (Cambridge, Mass.: Harvard University Press, 2004), p. 255.

3. Scott's article, "The Psychology of Advertising," appeared in the *Atlantic Monthly,* vol. 93 (January 1904), pp. 29–36. Quoted in Timothy B. Spears, *100 Years on the Road: The Traveling Salesman in American Culture* (New Haven, Conn.: Yale University Press, 1995), p. 1.

4. Daniel Boorstin, *The Americans: The Democratic Experience* (New York: Random House, 1973), p. 135, quoted in Spears, p. xi.

5. College-level programs in professional sales are available at the University of Toledo and at Paterson University in New Jersey. The only comprehensive graduate-level program in strategic sales and sales management with which I am familiar is offered at Aurora University.

6. Arthur Miller, *Death of a Salesman: Certain Private Conversations in Two Acts and a Requiem* (New York: Viking, 1949), p. 138.

CHAPTER 3

1. Herbert N. Casson, *The History of the Telephone* (Chicago: A. C. McClurg, 1910), pp. 58–59.

2. Thomas C. Cochran, *200 Years of American Business* (New York: Basic Books, 1977), p. 79.

3. Ibid., p. 117.

4. Roy W. Johnson and Russell W. Lynch, *The Sales Strategy of John H. Patterson: Founder of the National Cash Register Company* (Chicago: Dartnell Corporation, 1932), p. 20.

5. Ibid, p. 145.

CHAPTER 4

1. Frederick W. Taylor, *The Principles of Scientific Management* (New York: Norton, 1967), p. 9.

2. Roy W. Johnson and Russell W. Lynch, *The Sales Strategy of John H. Patterson: Founder of the National Cash Register Company* (Chicago: Dartnell Corporation, 1932), p. 185.

3. Ibid., pp. 130–131.

4. Ibid., p. 132.

5. Ibid., p. 197.

6. Neil Rackham, *SPIN Selling* (New York: McGraw-Hill, 1988), p. 6.

7. K. W. Fischer, "A Theory of Cognitive Development: The Control and Construction of Hierarchies of Skills," *Psychological Review,* vol. 87 (1980), pp. 477–531.

8. See Mihaly Csikszentmihalyi, *FLOW: The Psychology of Optimal Experience* (New York: Harper & Row, 1990). The total immersion that he calls flow is, in the author's opinion, the source of joy and creativity in experience, and many of his examples are drawn from work.

9. For example, see David L. Watson and Roland G. Tharp, *Self-Directed Behav-*

ior: Self-Modification for Personal Adjustment (Belmont, Calif.: Wadsworth/ Thomson Learning, 2002); J. A. Adams, "Historical Review and Appraisal of Research on the Learning, Retention, and Transfer of Human Motor Skills," *Psychological Bulletin,* vol. 101 (1987), pp. 41–74.

10. Johnson and Lynch, *The Sales Strategy of John H. Patterson,* pp. 200–201.

11. Ibid, p. 170.

12. Ibid, p. 230.

CHAPTER 5

1. Roy W. Johnson and Russell W. Lynch, *The Sales Strategy of John H. Patterson: Founder of the National Cash Register Company* (Chicago: Dartnell Corporation, 1932), pp. 180–182.

2. Jeffrey Gitomer, *The Patterson Principles of Selling* (New York: John Wiley & Sons, 2004), p. 5.

3. John R. Schleppi, "'It Pays': John H. Patterson and Industrial Recreation at the National Cash Register Company," *Journal of Sport History,* vol. 6, no. 3 (Winter 1979), p. 22.

4. Johnson and Lynch, *The Sales Strategy of John H. Patterson,* p. 34.

5. Don Hammalian, personal correspondence and conversations.

6. Michael T. Bosworth, *Solution Selling: Creating Buyers in Difficult Selling Markets* (New York: McGraw-Hill, 1993).

7. Robert B. Miller and Stephen E. Heiman, *Strategic Selling: The Unique Sales System Proven Successful by America's Best Companies* (New York: Warner Books, 1986).

8. Neil Rackham, personal correspondence.

9. Neil Rackham and John R. DeVincentis, *Rethinking the Sales Force* (New York: McGraw-Hill, 1998), p. 7.

10. Neil Rackham, *SPIN Selling* (New York: McGraw-Hill, 1988), p. 3.

11. Miller and Heiman, *Strategic Selling,* p. 25.

12. Johnson and Lynch, *The Sales Strategy of John H. Patterson,* pp. 13–14.

CHAPTER 6

1. Walter A. Friedman, *Birth of a Salesman: The Transformation of Selling in America* (Cambridge, Mass.: Harvard University Press, 2004), pp. 127–128.

2. Target Account Selling was a method offered by a company called OnTarget Inc., based in Atlanta. In December 1999, Siebel Systems acquired the firm and now offers Target Account Selling courses through its Sales Methodology Experts group.

3. Roy W. Johnson and Russell W. Lynch, *The Sales Strategy of John H. Patterson: Founder of the National Cash Register Company* (Chicago: Dartnell Corporation, 1932), p. 205.

4. Holden is the founder of Holden Advisors (www.holdenadvisors.com), where you can obtain several white papers on pricing strategy. In addition, he is the coauthor with Thomas Nagle of *The Strategy and Tactics of Pricing: A Guide to Profitable Decision Making,* 3rd ed. (New York: Prentice-Hall, 2002).

CHAPTER 8

1. Giles Kemp and Edward Claflin, *Dale Carnegie: The Man Who Influenced Millions* (New York: St. Martin's Press, 1989), p. 7.

2. Ibid., p. 29.

3. Ibid., p. 31.

4. Ibid., p. 33.

CHAPTER 9

1. Dale Carnegie, *How to Stop Worrying and Start Living* (New York: Simon & Schuster, 1948), p. 97.

2. Irenäus Eibl-Eibesfeldt and Frank Kemp Salter, *Indoctrinability, Ideology, and Warfare: Evolutionary Perspectives* (New York: Berghahn Books, 1998).

3. Frank Bettger, *How I Raised Myself from Failure to Success in Selling* (New York: Simon & Schuster, 1986), p. 12.

4. Ibid., p. 13.

5. Quoted in Giles Kemp and Edward Claflin, *Dale Carnegie: The Man Who Influenced Millions* (New York: St. Martin's Press, 1989), p. 86.

6. Roz Paterson, "Living by the Book: Can Turning Over a New Leaf Really Help You Be a Success?" *Glasgow Daily Record,* January 11, 2001.

7. Dale Carnegie, *How to Win Friends and Influence People* (New York: Simon & Schuster, 1964), p. 30.

8. Ibid., p. 103.

9. Ibid., p. 58.

10. Leon Festinger, *A Theory of Cognitive Dissonance* (Palo Alto, Calif.: Stanford University Press, 1957), gives a complete review of the theory and supporting research. Of related interest is Festinger's research paper, "On Resistance to Persuasive Communications," *Journal of Abnormal and Social Psychology,* vol. 68 (1964), pp. 359–366.

11. Harry A. Overstreet, *Influencing Human Behavior,* (Whitefish, MT: Kessinger Publishing, 1925).

12. Carnegie, *How to Win Friends*, p. 41.

13. Ibid., p. 166.

CHAPTER 10

1. Giles Kemp and Edward Claflin, *Dale Carnegie: The Man Who Influenced Millions* (New York: St. Martin's Press, 1989), pp. 141–143. They cite an amusing story that shows that even after his fabulous success, Carnegie didn't take himself too seriously. He had married a French woman, Lolita Beaucaire, who called herself the "Countess." This mysterious woman was apparently pretty difficult to get along with, so much so that even Dale Carnegie couldn't handle it. After ten years of marriage, they were divorced—in an era when divorce was not easy to get. Shortly after his book hit the best-seller lists, he was invited to write a newspaper column by Charles McAdam of the McNaught Syndicate. McAdam came to dinner at Carnegie's house, and during the meal, he asked Carnegie, "Where is Mrs. Carnegie?" "Oh, hell," Carnegie replied, "we couldn't get along; we got divorced."

2. Robert B. Cialdini, *Influence: The Psychology of Persuasion* (New York: William Morrow, 1993), p. 167.

3. Jagdish Sheth and Andrew Sobel, *Clients for Life: How Great Professionals Develop Breakthrough Relationships* (New York: Simon & Schuster, 2000), p. 57.

4. Jamie Comstock and Gary Higgins, "Appropriate Relational Messages in Direct Selling Interaction: Should Salespeople Adapt to Buyers' Communicator Style?" *Journal of Business Communication*, vol. 34, no. 4 (1997), pp. 401ff.

5. H. Biong and F. Selnes. *The Strategic Role of the Salesperson in Established Buyer-Seller Relationships,* working paper, report nos. 96–118, Marketing Science Institute, Cambridge, Mass., 1996. Cited in Gerald J. Bauer, Mark S. Baunchalk, Thomas N. Ingram, and Raymond W. LaForge, *Emerging Trends in Sales Thought and Practice* (Westport, Conn.: Quorum Books, 1998), p. 16.

6. S. Ganesan, "Determinants of Long-Term Orientation in Buyer-Seller Relationships," *Journal of Marketing,* vol. 58 (April 1994), pp. 1–19.

7. T. G. Noordewier, G. John, and J. R. Nevin, "Performance Outcomes of Purchasing Arrangements in Industrial Buyer-Vendor Relationships," *Journal of Marketing,* vol. 54 (October 1990), pp. 80–93.

8. David L. Cohn, *The Good Old Days: A History of American Morals and Manners as Seen Through the Sears, Roebuck Catalogs 1905 to the Present* (New York: Simon & Schuster, 1940), p. 469.

9. Frank Bettger, *How I Raised Myself from Failure to Success in Selling* (New York: Simon & Schuster, 1986), pp. 76–77.

CHAPTER 11

1. Nicholas Lemann, "Is There a Science of Success?" *Atlantic Monthly*, vol 273, no. 2 (1994), p. 82.

2. David G. Myers, *Exploring Social Psychology* (New York: McGraw-Hill, 2004), p. 47.

3. Ibid., p. 49.

4. Harvey Mackay, *Swim With the Sharks Without Being Eaten Alive* (New York: Morrow, 1988), p. 43.

5. Geoffrey Moore, *Crossing the Chasm: Marketing and Selling High-Tech Products to Mainstream Customers* (New York: Harper Business, 1991), p. 13.

CHAPTER 13

1. Elmer Wheeler, *Tested Sentences That Sell* (New York: 1937), p. 70.

2. By the way, the next time you go into a nice restaurant, watch how the waiter or waitress handles this. My guess is that you'll find he just says something like, "Can I take your drink orders?" or maybe even, "Do you want anything to drink?"

3. The figure of 36 million is cited in the Foreword to *Tested Ways to Close the Sale* (New York: Harper & Brothers, 1957), p. vii. In earlier books, Wheeler claimed that his sentences had been tested, not merely used, on 19 million people.

4. Wheeler, "Foreword," *Tested Ways to Close the Sale,* p. viii.

5. John McNulty, "The Sizzle," *New Yorker,* April 16, 1938. McNulty's article, by the way, gives a completely different history for Wheeler from the one Wheeler himself gives in his books. In the profile, McNulty states—and we have to assume that he got this information from Wheeler—that Elmer was born in Rochester and began making money in high school by selling articles about school events to the local paper. Soon the events ran dry, so Wheeler started inventing them—sponsoring contests and creating fads that he then reported. He attended college for five years, split between the University of Rochester and the University of Syracuse, where he continued his combination of journalism and promotion. By 1923 he was a reporter, not an advertising sales rep, for a Rochester newspaper, then he moved to Greensboro, North Carolina, to become the publicity director for the local Chamber of Commerce. He returned to Rochester to become the local press agent for a chain of movie theaters, moved to Los Angeles, where he tried to sell real estate, then went to Baltimore, where, the profile claims, he became fed up with the routine ways of selling newspaper advertising and went to work in the May store himself. He began coining his selling sentences while working behind the counter, and stayed at the job for several months. His methods attracted attention from a

group of psychology professors at Johns Hopkins University, who had him give sales talks while members of the audience were hooked up to lie detector equipment. Publicity from these experiments at Johns Hopkins led to an offer from the Hecht Store in Washington, D.C., to help improve its sales. His success there led to his move to New York and the creation of the Wheeler Sales Institute.

So which story is true? After months of research, I have to admit that I have no idea. I have chosen to include Wheeler's own version of his background in the text because it is, after all, the one he chose to publish and repeat in several of his books. It might be a fabrication, however. There's definitely an air of the carnival and medicine wagon surrounding Elmer Wheeler, and the fact that his early career and the origins of his ideas should be shrouded in mystery is not that surprising.

CHAPTER 14

1. Roman Jakobson, "Concluding Statement: Linguistics and Poetics," in Thomas Sebeok, ed., *Style in Language* (Cambridge, Mass.: MIT Press, 1960), pp. 350–377.

2. Note that for clarity, I have modified Jakobson's terminology somewhat in my version of his diagram. He refers to the sender as the "addresser" and the receiver as the "addressee." The subject of a communication he calls the "context," and the form in which it is presented—an e-mail, a proposal, a sonnet—he calls the "message," which makes sense in linguistics but not quite as much in ordinary speech.

CHAPTER 15

1. Published in 1950, Wheeler's *The Fat Boy's Book: How Elmer Lost 40 Pounds in 80 Days* suddenly took off when the *Chicago Daily News* decided to serialize it. (Wheeler referred to himself as Fat Boy, perhaps an allusion to the character in Charles Dickens's *Pickwick Papers*.) When an offer of a slide rule to help count calories provoked 90,000 requests, the paper moved the serialization out of the Women's section and put it on the front page. Soon, more than 70 other papers were carrying his book, and sales soared into best-seller realms. Considering the quality of the advice, one wonders what people saw in the book. Losing 40 pounds in less than three months would be medically condemned today, but Wheeler's corny writing would be equally panned:

   + It isn't fate that puts on weight—it's food, food, food.
   + Put a halt to salt.
   + Women pout when their men get stout.
   + Nobody loves a fat man—but his mother.

◆ Women never get chatty with men who are fatty.

◆ A boiled dinner will make you thinner, but run and hide from one that's fried.

Corny or not, Wheeler eventually sold more than half a million copies of his diet book (including the special slide rule, of course). Within three months, 77 papers carried the serial. Many of them forced their heaviest reporter to start dieting, charting his progress in a sidebar next to Wheeler's book excerpts. Thanks to all the publicity, the book went on to sell more than half a million copies. Elmer Wheeler even wrote a song "The Fat Boy's Bounce," which was a modest hit, and in 1951 Parker Brothers brought out a board game, *Elmer Wheeler's The Fat Boy's Game*, in which players navigate their way through tough food choices, accumulating calories. Not exactly *Monopoly*, apparently, since it vanished even faster than his song. However, Wheeler did receive more than three million letters from newspaper readers who were concerned about their own weight problems. "It's no longer true that no one loves a fat man but his mother," Wheeler quipped. "All the editors do." Unfortunately, Wheeler had become so famous that he was invited on the speaker's circuit to talk about his success in battling weight. Like many other business travelers, he found it impossible to eat sensibly in hotels and restaurants and at banquets. Soon the weight was back on and he was busy writing his sequel, *The Fat Boy's Downfall—And How Elmer Learned to Keep It Off*. That book didn't do as well, needless to say. Nobody likes a fallen hero, even if his lapses consist of too much gravy and too many cream puffs. Much later, Wheeler gave the diet book game one more spin, writing *The Fat Boy Goes Poly-Unsaturated* in 1963. See Jesse Berrett, "Feeding the Organization Man: Diet and Masculinity in Postwar America," *Journal of Social History,* vol. 30, no. 4 (1997), pp. 805ff.

2. Elmer Wheeler, *Tested Sentences That Sell* (New York: 1937), p. 128.

3. Ibid.

4. Ibid.

5. Leonard Zunin, M.D., with Natalie Zunin, *Contact: The First Four Minutes* (New York: Ballantine Books, 1973), p. 17.

6. Wheeler, *Tested Sentences That Sell,* p. 129.

7. Richard Petty and John Cacioppo, *Communication and Persuasion: Central and Peripheral Routes to Attitude Change* (New York: Springer-Verlag, 1986). See also Alice Eagly and Sally Chaiken, *The Psychology of Attitudes* (San Diego: Harcourt Brace Jovanovich, 1993). One theory posits that the emotional and the logical modes are not two ways of approaching persuasion, but rather two aspects of one inseparable method. See Erik Thompson, Arie Kruglanski, and Scott Spiegel, "Attitudes as Knowledge Structures and Persuasion as a Specific Case of Subjective Knowledge Acquisition," in Gregory Maio and James M.

Olson (eds.): *Why We Evaluate: Function of Attitudes* (Mahwah, N.J.: Erlbaum Associates, 2000).

8. Wheeler, *Tested Sentences That Sell,* p. 130.

9. Ibid., p. 131.

10. A. Mehrabian and R. Ferris, "Inference of Attitudes from Non-Verbal Communication in Two Channels," *Journal of Counselling Psychology*, vol. 31 (1967), pp. 248–252.

CHAPTER 16

1. Bo Feng, Seth J. Gillihan, Angela R. Graves, and Erina L. Macgeorge, "The Myth of Gender Cultures: Similarities Outweigh Differences in Men's and Women's Provision of and Responses to Supportive Communication," *Sex Roles: A Journal of Research*, vol. 50, no. 3–4 (2004), pp. 143ff.

2. George A. Miller, "The Magical Number Seven, Plus or Minus Two: Some Limits on Our Capacity for Processing Information," *Psychological Review,* vol. 63 (1956), pp. 81–97.

3. Marjory Roberts, "Be All That You Can Be: In the Art of Self-Improvement, Some Offbeat Techniques Get the Scientific OK. Others Get KO'd," *Psychology Today*, vol. 22, no. 3 (March 1988), p. 28.

CHAPTER 18

1. Joe Girard, *How to Sell Anything to Anybody* (New York: Warner Books, 1970), p. 37.

2. Ibid., p. 202.

3. Ibid., p. 129.

4. Ibid., p. 142.

5. Ibid., p. 156.

6. Ibid., p. 179.

7. Ibid., p. 123.

8. Ibid., p. 147.

9. Ibid., p. 126.

CHAPTER 19

1. Joe Girard, *How to Sell Anything to Anybody* (New York: Warner Books, 1970), p. 225.

2. George Stalk and Rob Lachenauer, *Hardball: Are You Playing to Play or Playing to Win* (Cambridge, Mass.: Harvard Business School Press, 2004), pp. 39–40.

3. Girard, *How to Sell Anything to Anybody,* p. 122.

4. Seth Godin, *Permission Marketing: Turning Strangers Into Friends and Friends Into Customers* (New York: Simon & Schuster, 1999), p. 175.

5. Anthony Parinello, *Stop Cold Calling Forever: Confessions of a Reformed Serial Cold Caller* (New York: Entrepreneur Press, 2004).

CHAPTER 20

1. Gerd Gigerenzer, Peter M. Todd, and the ABC Research Group, *Simple Heuristics That Make Us Smart* (New York: Oxford University Press, 1999). Recognition is one of seven specific heuristics the authors discuss. It is covered in chapter 2, "The Recognition Heuristic: How Ignorance Makes Us Smart," by Daniel G. Goldstein and Gerd Gigerenzer, and in chapter 3, "Can Ignorance Beat the Stock Market?" by Bernhard Borges, Daniel G. Goldstein, Andreas Ortmann, and Gerd Gigerenzer.

2. Robert B. Cialdini, *Influence: The Psychology of Persuasion* (New York: William Morrow, 1993), p. 17.

3. Kurt W. Mortensen, *Maximum Influence: The 12 Universal Laws of Power Persuasion* (New York: AMACOM, 2004), p. 39.

4. J. M. Dabbs and I. L. Janis, "Why Does Eating While Reading Facilitate Opinion Change?" *Journal of Experimental Social Psychology,* vol. 1 (1965), pp. 133–144.

5. Joe Girard, *How to Sell Anything to Anybody* (New York: Warner Books, 1970), p. 88.